THE GREAT
WAGON ROAD

Other Dietz Press Books by Parke Rouse, Jr.

Below the James Lies Dixie: Smithfield and Southside Virgina, 1968

Cows on the Campus: Williamsburg in Bygone Days, 1973

When the Yankees Come: Civil War and Reconstruction on the Virginia Peninsula, 1977

A House for a President: 250 Years on the Campus of the College of William and Mary, 1981

The Good Old Days in Hampton and Newport News, 1986

Remembering Williamsburg: A Sentimental Journey Through Three Centuries, 1986

The James, Where A Nation Began, 1990

Along Virginia's Golden Shores, 1994

The Dietz Press
109 East Cary Street
Richmond, Virginia 23219

For Shep

Parke Rouse, Jr.

THE GREAT WAGON ROAD

from
Philadelphia
To the
South

Copyright © 1995 Parke Rouse, Jr.

All rights reserved. Printed in the United States of
America. No part of this publication may be reproduced,
stored in a retrieval system, or transmitted, in any form
or by any means, electronic, mechanical, photocopying,
recording, or otherwise, without the prior written permission of the publisher.

123456789BP BP79876543

Library of Congress Cataloging in Publication Data

Rouse, Parke, 1915–
    The Great Wagon Road: from Philadelphia to the
    South.
    (American trail series, v. 11)
    Bibliography: p. 271
1. United States—History—Colonial period.
2. United States—History—Revolution. 3. United
States—History—1783–1865. I. Title. II. Series:
American trail series (New York) v. 11.
E188.R85   973.2   72–8673
ISBN 0–07–054101–9

PROLOGUE

For nearly 150 years after North America was settled, it remained a green wilderness. Only a few trails cut through the vast forests which spread from New Hampshire to Georgia, for the Appalachian Mountains thrust a stern barrier between the Atlantic plateau and the unknown interior of the continent.

As settlers moved inland, they usually followed the paths over which Indians had hunted and traded. Many of these trails had been worn down in earlier ages by buffalo, which once had roamed the eastern uplands in search of grazing lands. These paths usually followed valleys and river shores.

Few trails in early America were more important than the Indian route which extended east of the Appalachians from Pennsylvania to Georgia. This ancient Warriors' Path was long used by Iroquois tribesmen of the north to come south and trade or make war in Virginia and the Carolinas. Then, by a series of treaties with the powerful Five Nations of the Iroquois, the English acquired the use of the Warriors' Path. After 1744, they took over the land itself.

The growth of the route after 1744 into the principal highway of the colonial back country is an important chapter in the development of a nation. Over this Great Philadelphia Wagon Road, vast numbers of English, Scotch-Irish, and Germanic settlers entered this continent and claimed lands.

The endless procession of new settlers, Indian traders, soldiers, and missionaries swelled as the Revolution approached. "In the last sixteen years of the colonial era," wrote the historian Carl Bridenbaugh, "southbound traffic along the Great Philadelphia Wagon Road was numbered in tens of thousands; it was the most heavily traveled road in all America and must have had more vehicles jolting along its rough and tortuous way than all other main roads put together."

As the principal highway of the eighteenth-century frontier southward from Pennsylvania, the Wagon Road also played an important part in the French and Indian wars and in the American Revolution. Daniel Boone and Davy Crockett traveled it as explorers. George Washington knew it as an Indian fighter. Countless soldiers— Andrew Jackson, Andrew Pickens, John Sevier, Andrew Lewis,

Francis Marion, Lighthorse Harry Lee, Daniel Morgan, and George Rogers Clark among them—fought over it.

When British forces captured Philadelphia early in the Revolution, the Continental Congress escaped and fled down the Great Wagon Road to York. Cornwallis and his troops traveled the Wagon Road in their attempt to neutralize the southern colonies. Many important battles were fought on or near the Road which became the War's western front: Kings Mountain, the Cowpens, Guilford Courthouse, Salisbury, and Camden were some of them.

From the Great Wagon Road, pioneers passed through Cumberland Gap and the Holston River settlements into the territories which became Kentucky and Tennessee. This route, which Daniel Boone opened in 1775, became an umbilical cord by which the first sizeable trans-Appalachian settlements were nurtured to statehood. Over this Wilderness Road went Henry Clay and the forebears of Abraham Lincoln, among countless others.

The chronicle of the Wagon Road is the chronicle of infant America, from 1607 until the age of the railway. It is the story of achievement against great odds. Breaking with the European traditions which they brought to America with them, the diverse settlers along the Wagon Road began to create the new American society which changed the nineteenth-century history of the world.

Parke Rouse, Jr.

Jamestown, Virginia

Contents

CONTENTS

·BOOK ONE·

The Appalachian
Warriors' Path
1607-1744

CHAPTER 1

The Search for Eldorado

The handful of brave Europeans who explored inland during the first hundred years of America's English settlement looked upon a wilderness which dazzled them with its beauty and richness.

Except for scattered Indian tribes, it was an untouched land of great trees and sparkling rivers. Flocks of wood pigeons, so endless that they darkened the sky, migrated with the seasons. Great flights of waterfowl—ducks, geese, and brant—flew south from their Canadian lair each fall, following the coastal rivers southward to nest in the marshes of Chesapeake basin. Woods buffalo and deer made trails through the dank forests.

But alas, much of this magic was lost on the early explorers in Virginia, Maryland, and Carolina. They could not rest until they had found their English Eldorado. Their hearts were set on finding rich veins of gold and silver, as the Spanish had found in South America.

Next to gold and silver, they sought a watercourse through North America to the "South Sea" or the "China Sea" (Pacific Ocean) and to the riches of the Orient. Time after time, Indian interpreters gave them cryptic and tantalizing reports of that nearby sea. And time after time, explorers found themselves balked by the steep mountains of the Appalachians.

The search had been started by John Smith when he reached Jamestown in 1607. One by one, he followed the Chesapeake Bay estuaries westward to their fall line, and each time he was halted. The ever hopeful Smith then sent a report to the Dutch explorer, Henry Hudson, urging him to continue the effort to find "a sea leading into the western ocean, by the north of the southern English colony," but Hudson had no greater success than Smith had enjoyed.

In 1646, ambitious young Abraham Wood, who had come to Virginia as an indentured servant and grown rich trading with the Indians, led an exploring party westward from the upper James River over the Occonneechee Traders' Path. He hoped to verify the Indian account that

within five days' journey to the westward and by south, there is a great high mountain, and at the foot thereof, great rivers that run

into a great sea; and that there are men that come thither in ships
. . . and have reed caps on their heads, and ride on beasts like horses,
but have much longer ears.[1]

The explorers did not find this, but the doughty Wood did not give
up. When he was an old man, he sent four experienced woodsmen
west again in 1671, headed by Thomas Batte, "for the finding out
the ebbing and flowing of the waters on the other side of the mountains in order to the discovery of the South Sea." After inching
through the Appalachians for sixteen days, the group was finally
forced back, after reaching a tributary of the Mississippi River. To
Wood they reported on their return: "We first proclaimed the King
in these words: 'Long live Charles the Second, by the grace of God,
King of England, Scotland, France, Ireland, and Virginia.'" Then
they had fired a salute and carved four trees with marks for Charles
II, Governor Berkeley of Virginia, Wood, and their Indian guide,
Perecute.

John Lederer, a German physician who had come to Virginia to
explore the west, was no more successful. Sent out by Governor
Berkeley three times in 1669–1670, he reached the top of the Blue
Ridge Mountains but mistook the haze of the valley beyond it for
an ocean's surface. "I had a beautiful prospect of the Atlantick
Ocean washing the Virginia-shore," he reported to Berkeley at
Jamestown, "but to the north and west, my sight was suddenly
bounded by mountains higher than that I stood upon."

Slowly, through countless disappointing probes, the coastal
settlers learned the immensity of the mountain range which paralleled the Atlantic Coast, several hundred miles inland, which the
Indians called the Appalachians. Extending southwesterly from
Canada to the Gulf Coast Plain in the South in a succession of
rocky ranges, they impeded the large-scale westward movement of
the English colonists until after the American Revolution.

Few passes cut through the Appalachians, and these were obscured by the dense growth of pines and hardwoods which covered
the face of colonial America. And though they were known to the
Indians, who found them by observing the course which eagles
followed across the mountains, the white men were slow to find
these gaps.

Just beyond the coastal plain, which Chesapeake settlers called
"Tidewater" and Carolinians called "the low country," a hilly mid-
land called "piedmont" (foot of the mountains) led upward to the

Appalachians. This was the fertile area which was destined to become the American frontier in the crucial years from 1761 to 1783, when the Appalachian settlers first fought the French and then the English. It was the piedmont which became the main artery of eighteenth-century settlement. To coastal settlers, this "upcountry" or "back country" had developed by the eighteenth century into a convenient buffer against threat of Indians and French invaders from the west.

The story of the Great Philadelphia Wagon Road is the story of the rise of this region, which became the first western frontier of the American nation created in 1789.

Like the Wagon Road itself, the eastern foothills of the Appalachians became a bridge by which poor but hopeful immigrants from Europe reached the Appalachians and the Deep South. In this picturesque region, which reminded some Germanic pioneers of the snowcapped terrain of Switzerland, are the mountain-stream headwaters of the rivers which flow eastward—Susquehanna, Potomac, James—foaming over rocks to the fall line to form estuaries of the Atlantic Ocean. Unlike the gentler undulations of the coastal plain, the land has a vigor which from its beginning encouraged individualism.

Of all the mountain ranges of Appalachia, the Blue Ridge is the oldest and most serene. Formed 200 million years ago, it has been weathered and softened by time. So gently does the piedmont ascend to it that it hardly seems to justify the heroic name "mountain." Beyond, in the blue haze to the west, lie newer and more rugged chains like the Alleghanies and the Cumberlands. Between these ranges—called "Old Appalachia" and "New Appalachia"—lies the Great Appalachian Valley, whose northern end is called the Shenandoah and whose southwestern end becomes the Tennessee. The green Eden thus encompassed is called the Valley of Virginia.

Not only did this upcountry of early America differ in its shape but in its climate and its plant and animal life. Longleaf pines dominate the low-country landscape, but as the land rises toward the Appalachians, these are intermixed with and finally replaced by hardwoods, spruce, and white pine. The flowing hillsides and mountains of the Appalachians produce a verdant growth of oak, maple, chestnut, and hickory, whose bright red leafage in fall have dazzled settlers from the time of Abraham Wood.

It was the chestnut which proved the upcountry's best wood.

Easily split into logs for cabins and rails for fences, it was sought for every settler's clearing along the western frontier. From its split timbers, shingles were rived with mallet and froe to cover houses and barns. From its bark, pioneers extracted tannic acid for tanning, dyeing, and for medicine. And from the chestnuts it produced in fall, the lean razorback hogs of the pioneers derived a fattening diet.

Almost equally valued was the hemlock, which grew in the damp glens of the mountains, surrounded by great mazes of pink rhododendron.

The shrubs and flowers of the Appalachians also differed from those of the lowlands farther east. The forest cover of the rocky mountaintops resembled the colder regions to the north, where spruce and white pine overlay a smaller growth of hardwoods. Many years later, the Appalachians were to be called "The Trail of the Lonesome Pine," for the slim, brave trees which thrust their trunks a hundred feet above the rocky heights of the mountain peaks.

The wilderness of the Appalachians abounded in animals and birds, whose night cries were as frightening as the Indians' and sometimes were imitated by them. Wolves rent the darkness with howls, and screech owls and hoot owls curdled it with terror. Panthers and wildcats preyed on poultry and small livestock, while rattlesnakes and copperheads offered a menace to both man and beast.

The most impressive of the Appalachians' animals was the woods buffalo, which had no counterpart in Europe. A peaceful "mammoth" which browsed among canebrakes and nibbled spruce and balsam buds, it was hunted to extinction in Virginia after 1794 and in Kentucky by 1810. Smaller than the plains buffalo of the western barrens, this shaggy mammoth roamed in groups of two or three— usually a cow and her calves. White settlers came to value its meat and hide as highly as the Indians did. Buffalo skins covered the roof beams of pioneer settlers' lean-tos and cabins.

Though primitive man had lived in eastern America for more than 10,000 years before Europeans settled in the Appalachians, evidences of Indian life were few there. The mountainous terrain which surrounded the Great Warriors' Path was a common hunting range for Siouan- and Algonquian-speaking tribes living to the east and Iroquois to the west.

The tribes which bounded the Great Warriors' Path were almost as diverse as the English farmers, French tradesmen, German protestants, and Scottish lowlanders who were to settle this portion of the New World. Each of the tribes belonged to one of four major language groups or "nations" which Europeans found living in the woodlands of eastern America in the early years of American colonization:

Iroquoian dependencies of the Five Nations spread over most of the territory which came to be Pennsylvania. Other Iroquoian tribes—chiefly the Cherokees and Tuscaroras—dominated the Warriors' Path area in western Virginia and the Carolinas.

Algonquians lived along the coast from Canada southward through the Carolinas, extending inland over the valley of the Potomac River into what later became West Virginia.

Siouans dominated the piedmont plateau southward from Maryland through South Carolina, wedged uncomfortably between the Algonquians of the Atlantic Coast and the Iroquoians of the Appalachian uplands.

Muskhogeans filled the Gulf coastal region from Georgia westward beyond the Mississippi River.

Among these tribesmen, it was the Cherokees of the Iroquoian group who chiefly controlled the upland region of the Great Warriors' Path. A large and widespread culture, the Cherokees lived in villages on the eastern and western slopes of the Appalachians, farming and hunting. Of all the southeastern Indian tribes, they were the most numerous and powerful, dominating the fur trade of the mountain South throughout the colonial years. As a result of effective English diplomacy among the Cherokee chiefs, the tribesmen were to fight with the English against the French in the 1760s and against the American colonists in the Revolution.

Next to the Cherokees, the Shawnees of the Ohio Valley—later Tennessee and Kentucky—were to offer the greatest resistance to colonization along the Great Warriors' Path. Belonging to the Algonquian language group, the Shawnees came east frequently to war against eastern tribes and later to devastate the western Virginia settlements. Living in numerous separated groups, they combed the Appalachian valleys in their wanderings. Many of the bloodiest massacres in colonial history were Shawnee reprisals against the westward movement of the English-speaking peoples.

The presence of the Indians in prehistoric America is one of the misty chapters of man's past. It is believed that they were products of the Ice Age emigration of small groups of Mongolian hunters, who crossed the Bering Straits as long as 50,000 years ago. Trekking southward and eastward through Alaska and Canada, successive generations of these hunters had followed herds of game onto the Atlantic shelf.

In the dim ages before Europeans discovered America, these nomads began to settle down and live as tribes. A thousand years or more before the birth of Christ, prehistoric Indian hunters were farming in small villages and building burial mounds in the region which the English settlers of 1607 had claimed as their own. Living in harmony with nature, these scattered tribes made but slight impact on the forests and streams of the region. Their wigwams and longhouses, covered with bark, hides, or reed mats and enclosed by stockades, were a rare interruption in the endless pine forests of the Appalachians and the undulating lands stretching eastward to the Atlantic.

The Indian's Stone Age civilization destroyed relatively little of the rich natural bounty of the land. True, they burned the vegetation from mountaintops and valleys, creating "balds" to attract game. However, except for buffalo and sturgeon, most species of animals, birds, and fish still abounded throughout the colonial years. In the Appalachians, from Pennsylvania southward to Georgia, bald and golden eagles nested in great numbers in the tall pines of the upland peaks. Wild turkeys were plentiful in forest deeps, and millions of beavers and martens were trapped for their fine furs.

Through years of living in nature, the Indans developed their senses of sight and smell and hearing to the keenness of animals. Watching the eagle soar over the mountains, they discovered passes through the rocks, like Swift Run Gap and Rockfish Gap. Following the buffaloes' trails, they had learned where lay the springs and salt licks. Unlike the white man, who later notched or "blazed" tree trunks to mark his route through the wilderness, the red man could easily follow a once used path.

In their wigwams and longhouses, the Indians lived on nature's uncertain bounty. In summer they cooked maize, squash, and beans, which they raised in scattered clearings outside their rustic palisade. They knew also the succulent roots and berries of woods and swamp. In October and November, shouting and shrilling, they routed the new-foaled buffalo from the forest and pursued it with arrows and spears into a burning clearing and its death. The best hunting came in fall, when animals were fat; after frost came, animal flesh too often tasted of spruce and balsam buds on which the hungry predators fed.

The Appalachian Indians' dress was as simple as their shelter. They made clothing from skins and decorated it with bits of shell and feathers. Men wore breechcloths and moccasins, to which they added shirts and leggings in winter. Women dressed in fur skirts or loose skin robes, ornamented with porcupine quills and bright bird wings. A mantle of turkey feathers denoted a chieftain's dignity. Wrote John Smith of the Indians of early Virginia:

> They are some time covered with the skinnes of wilde beasts, which in winter are dressed with the hayre, but in sommer without. The better sort use large mantels of deare skins, not much differing in fashion with the Irish mantels. Some imbrodered with white beads, some with copper, other painted after their manner. But the common sort have scarce to cover their nakednesse, but with grasse, the leaves of trees, or such like. We have seene some use mantels of Turky feathers, so prettily wrought and woven with threads that nothing could be discerned but the feathers. That was exceeding warm and very handsome. But the women are always covered about their middles with a skin, and very shamefast to be seene bare.[2]

Such was the upland empire of North America when Governor Alexander Spotswood led his Knights of the Golden Horseshoe to the peaks of the Blue Ridge Mountains in 1716 and anticipated England's colonization westward. It was a paradise which was to exceed even the expectations of the prophet Sir Walter Raleigh, whose vision of "a new English nation" had encouraged the settlement of Virginia in the first place.

Here, in the empire to the west, Alexander Spotswood believed that England had found her Eldorado.

CHAPTER 2

War among the Iroquois

By the year 1716, the mighty power of Great Britain was firmly planted in North America. From New Hampshire to South Carolina, twelve colonies were spread along the Atlantic seaboard, flying the Union Jack from courthouse flagstaffs and busily sending raw materials by sailing ships to England, 3,500 miles across the Atlantic.

Except for Pennsylvania, all the colonies hugged the shore. Lying along the coastal plain, most of their land was flat. Their largest towns—Boston, Annapolis, Williamsburg, and Charleston in South Carolina—had grown up close to the ocean, to serve as ports as well as capitals. Settlers looked eastward to the sea, which was the highway linking them to mother England. From London came most of the news to fill the columns of their weekly newssheets. London was Life: the source of new fashions, knowledge, and protection against the everlasting menace of France.

Toward the west, the colonies ran up against the Appalachian Mountain range, which slanted diagonally from New England toward the Gulf Coast. What lay behind it remained a dark mystery to the settlers for a hundred years. Beyond the Appalachians few Englishmen had ventured by 1715, for the peaks were high and awesome, covered by heavy growths of dense pine. Indians called the unknown territory "the dark and bloody land," and hinted that it was peopled by savage tribesmen, but few white men had seen it with their own eyes.

In Virginia, the oldest and largest of the colonies, a few talked of exploring and even settling in the mountains. For nearly a century, people had been content to stay below the fall line of Virginia's half-dozen major rivers, so that they could easily ship their tobacco by ocean-going ships to England. Once they had gone beyond the fall line, however, the taming of the mountains seemed only a matter of years. By 1715, a handful of hardy settlers already lived within clear sight of the easternmost range of the mountains.

Virginia's Governor, Colonel Alexander Spotswood, was not a man to ignore the challenge. A far-sighted man who shared Sir Walter

Raleigh's vision of "a new English nation" in North America, he proposed to the Virginia Council in 1716 that the colony send an exploring party to the peak of the easternmost Appalachians and discover what lay beyond. Accordingly, when the sixty-three horsemen rode out of Williamsburg two months later, the Governor himself rode at their head, determined that Virginia should claim the mountains in the name of King George I of England.

The mission of Spotswood and of his Knights of the Golden Horseshoe was more important for its assertion of Great Britain's claim to inland America than for any discovery. Struggling upward to the peak of the Blue Ridge range on September 5, the Governor and the Virginians for the first time looked upon the great Valley and to the Alleghanies beyond. It was indeed a breathtaking sight. To the east lay English America, descending to the sea. To the west, as far as they could see, lay the unsettled heart of North America, still a mystery to all except Indians and a few daring Europeans.

But Spotswood knew that other antagonists besides Indians lay beyond the Blue Ridge. France was moving settlers into the Mississippi region and laying claim to the interior. In the name of King Louis XIV, La Salle had reached the mouth of the Mississippi and had claimed all the land drained by that river and its tributaries. French traders and missionaries were busy in the area, and a military post had been established at Natchitoches, near the Gulf of Mexico. If England did not possess the west before French traders did, she might ultimately lose the race for empire.

For this reason, plus their hope of finding an inland lake which they believed to be the source of the James, Spotswood and his men had braved the heat and mosquitoes of Virginia's August.

Halting the caravan on the Blue Ridge, the lordly Governor called for a toast. Horsemen, soldiers, and servants all lifted their cups and, in the words of John Fontaine, one of their number, "drank King George's health, and the Royal Family's, at the very top of the . . . mountains." Then, remounting their new-shod horses, they descended into the Valley of Virginia for seven miles, until they reached the banks of a narrow river, named by Indians Shenandoah for the Daughter of the Stars. There Spotswood ceremoniously buried a bottle enclosing Virginia's claim to the land in the name of King George, who had ascended to the throne two years earlier. This, too, he said, was part of the new English nation.

That night—the night of September 5, 1716—was the climactic celebration of the journey.

> We had a good dinner [Ensign John Fontaine confided to his diary], and after it we got the men together, and loaded all their arms, and we drank the King's health in champagne, and fired a volley—the Princess's health in Burgundy, and fired a volley, and all the rest of the Royal Family in claret, and a volley. We drank the Governor's health and fired another volley. We had several sorts of liquors, viz., Virginia red wine and white wine, Irish usquebaugh, brandy, shrub, two sorts of rum, champagne, canary, cherry, punch, water, cider, &c.[1]

Having done what he set out to do, Alexander Spotswood next day turned homeward toward Williamsburg, taking most of his horsemen with him. However, he left a small group of rangers behind to explore the Great Valley.

Hacking their way through thick growths of mountain laurel, these rangers at length found themselves near the banks of a narrow river. Spotswood from afar had called it the "Euphrates," but Virginians would soon know it by its Indian name, Shenandoah. Close to the river were the signs of a trail, for trees had been notched with hatchet marks. This was the southern trading path of the powerful Great Lakes Indian tribes, the so-called Great Warriors' Path to Carolina.

Spotswood's handful of rangers, hacking their way through the summer leafage, were almost enveloped in forest gloom. High above them, eagles soared in the summer sky. In the huge trees, squirrels and woodpeckers kept up a din. The explorers kept a sharp lookout for rattlesnakes and copperheads underfoot.

Spotswood's rangers had been instructed to do no harm to the Indians. The Governor was anxious to revive Virginia's once productive fur trade and to bring peace between the powerful Iroquois tribes in Pennsylvania and New York and the Cherokees and Catawbas of His Majesty's colony of Carolina. He had urged the Virginia Assembly to recognize the Indians' continued right to travel unmolested over their Great Warriors' Path, but he also sought to discourage the Indians' coming east into the settled portions of Virginia.

Northward from Virginia, the Great Warriors' Path led across the Potomac River into western Maryland and thence through central Pennsylvania, through what later became Lancaster and Bethlehem, to the settlements of the Iroquois Confederacy around the Great Lakes. Southward, the path skirted the headwaters of the Roanoke River in Southern Virginia and led to the lands of the Cherokees and Catawbas in the Carolina uplands.

Warfare had flared along the Warriors' Path for years before English settlers began to colonize the Atlantic coastal region. Its intensity had increased around the year 1570, when the five major Iroquois tribes created the League of the Five Nations. Of all the tribesmen along the Atlantic headlands, the Five Nations were the most advanced. Numbering about 5,500 people, they lived in palisaded villages from the Hudson River north to the St. Lawrence. Before their combined might, the scattered Sioux and Algonquian tribes of the east fled in terror.

When the prophet Deganawidah and his disciple Hiawatha had founded the confederacy in 1570, they succeeded in ending cannibalism and warfare among five dominant tribes: Mohawks, Oneidas, Onondagas, Cayugas, and Senecas. Like the Romans of ancient Europe, these Iroquois tribesmen were the ablest warrior-statesmen of their time. By the year 1700, they had raised their strength by conquest to 16,000.

In their forays to the south, the Five Nations conquered and exacted tribute from many tribes, but they met savage resistance from two large Siouan groups: the Catawbas of South Carolina and the Cherokees, scattered throughout Carolina and the territory which became Georgia, Alabama, and Tennessee. Yet all of these tribesmen were friendly to the English, and Spotswood as Governor of Virginia looked for means to further befriend them and to encourage their peaceful use of the Warriors' Path as a buffer against the French.

As the Governor and his horsemen rode homeward from the mountains in the autumn of 1716, he realized more than ever the need for a concerted policy among the English colonies to ally the frontier Indians with the English and oppose French progress from the Mississippi toward the east.

The small and peaceful tribes living in eastern Virginia must be protected by the colony against threats from the larger tribes, but trade with the Five Nations using the Warriors' Path should be encouraged.

Warmed by the prospect of Britain's spread, Spotswood in Williamsburg dubbed his horsemen "Knights of the Golden Horseshoe" and gave each a golden emblem inscribed "Sic Juvat Transcendere Montes" (Behold, We Cross the Mountains). For the remaining years of his governorship, he devoted himself chiefly to allying the Indians with the English colonists and strengthening the Appalachian frontier against the French.

To achieve these ends, the imperious Spotswood in 1722 met with the Five Nations and the governors of New York and Pennsylvania at Albany, near the Iroquois settlements. The object was to brighten the covenant chain which the Iroquois had made with the colonies at Albany in 1685.

"Sachems and warriors of the Five Nations," Spotswood began, "you often say that your covenant chain with Virginia is grown rusty and have urged of late years that some commissioners from that colony should be sent to this place to brighten the same."[2]

After many courtesies, each translated while the chiefs nodded and smiled, Spotswood accused the Iroquois of coming south over the Warriors' Path and molesting Virginians and Carolinians. Describing these bloody attacks on southern Indians and frontiersmen, the Governor offered to renew the treaty. Holding up two gift belts of wampum, he was greeted with approving cries of "O-ha! O-ha!"

Then Assaragoa, as the Iroquois called Virginia's Governor, proposed a new treaty: Virginia would permit their continued use of the Warriors' Path if they would sign a treaty not to come east of the Blue Ridge or south of the Potomac.

Without awaiting a decision from the chiefs, Spotswood then relinquished the platform to Governor Sir William Keith of Pennsylvania and Governor William Burnet of New York, who made further proposals. Thus for nineteen days the negotiators met, the governors paving each step with compliments and gifts for "our brothers," the Five Nations.

At length the wily English brought forth the long-awaited casks of rum and brandy. With gurgles of sheer joy, the chiefs downed the welcome liquor. The stiff formality of the conference table was forgotten amid the camaraderie of the bottle.

When the conference resumed, it was the Indians' turn to speak. The Indian spokesman began by describing the arrival of the first white men in New York 109 years earlier. In those carefree days, he

said, his ancestors had carried off the ship's anchor to show the
Indians' welcome. The covenant of friendship which they made then
had been lengthened to a chain of friendship with Pennsylvania and
Virginia as the years passed.

To Assaragoa the spokesmen promised his tribesmen would con-
fine their southern journeys to the Great Warriors' Path, staying
west of the Blue Ridge and north of the Potomac. They would also
end their warfare with the Virginia tribes—mostly Sioux and Algonquins—who lived among the white men. To commemorate this
agreement, the Indians gave Spotswood a belt of wampum for himself and another for the Virginia Indians. Then the Indians shouted
in unison: "O-ha! O-ha! O-ha! O-ha! O-ha! O-ha!"—for the Five
Nations and their fellow Iroquois, the Tuscaroras, who had come
northward from Virginia to live with them.

Spotswood smiled and thanked them. Then he repeated the terms
of the treaty, warning that any who violated it would be put to
death or enslaved. To dramatize his act, he had his equerry lay
down ten guns, each representing a tributary tribe of Virginia. To
their great pleasure, he handed the guns to the chiefs.

The Governor also offered a reward to any Indian who returned
Negro slaves escaped from their masters and fled to the frontier.
(Having lost field hands from his own plantation, Spotswood spoke
feelingly):

> Now I make a general proposition to you on account of runaways
> and slaves belonging to Virginia, viz., that if any such Negro or
> slave shall hereafter fall in your hands, you shall straightway con-
> duct them to Col. George Mason's house on Potomac River, and I
> do . . . engage that you shall there receive immediately upon de-
> livery . . . one good gun and two blankets, or the value thereof, and
> in token of this proposition and engagement I lay down five guns
> and five hundred flints.[3]

The Governor admonished them finally never to let the chain
rust again, for Assaragoa would not come again. As they kept no
written records, he would imprint the treaty on their minds with
gifts so that every Iroquois would remember it. They agreed, ad-
mitting to "a great many bad actions" and producing a bundle of
furs and deerskins to recompense settler Robert Hix for his robbed
packhorse train.

One by one, the nineteen sachems made their mark on the Virginia treaty and its map denoting the Warriors' Path. Each mark was the symbol of a tribe: a turtle, stag, beaver, salmon, elk, and other animals. Spotswood in return gave them a golden horseshoe from his lapel to serve as a passport for any Iroquois who in emergency needed to come eastward over the Blue Ridge. Thus the treaty ended.

Happily, the governors and their staffs turned homeward. Soon they had boarded Spotswood's ship, H.M.S. *Enterprise,* and were on their way down the Hudson.

Spotswood, thinking of England's strengthened alliance with the Five Nations, was exultant. He had accomplished his Assembly's object: to "lay a lasting foundation for the peace and tranquility" of the frontier. For the moment, he was right. Peace reigned for many years thereafter along the Appalachian Warriors' Path, allowing young America a fortunate opportunity to grow strong. Increasingly after 1722, white men began to use the Warriors' Path.

·BOOK TWO·

The Philadelphia Wagon Road

1744-1774

CHAPTER 3

Germans in Pennsylvania

When Louis XIV revoked the Edict of Nantes in 1685, he caused an outpouring of Protestants from France which was felt in the faraway English colonies of North America for fifty years to come.

Many Alsatians fled across the French borders into the German Palatinate, lying along the Rhine River, and received shelter from the Great Elector, Frederick William. Angered, the Sun King sent General François Michel Louvois with 100,000 soldiers in 1689 to destroy the Palatinate. French soldiers laid waste to farms and destroyed towns and villages. In the War of the Spanish Succession which followed in 1702–1713, many more families living along the Rhine lost lives or property.

Then, in 1708 or 1709, an agent of William Penn visited the Palatines and encouraged them to emigrate, describing the religious freedom offered by William Penn's colony in the New World. By June 1709, the first shiploads of emigrants had succeeded in reaching England, seeking religious freedom. By October 1709, nearly 14,000 had come.

Queen Anne's Protestant government provided food and temporary housing for the homeless Germans. By order of the Queen, 1,000 tents from the Tower of London were erected in an open field. Other emigrants were housed in barns and warehouses.

A Germanic colony had already been established at Germantown, Pennsylvania, under Francis Daniel Pastorius in 1683. Now, after 1709, many other Germans and Swiss came. By 1717, so many had arrived that Pennsylvania's Governor, Sir William Keith, recommended that shipmasters bringing in foreign passengers should furnish the colony with their names. Within the next fifty-six years, a total of 68,872 had come in.

But the mass of ill-clothed Germans soon felt the hostility of the English and Welsh Quakers who had earlier sought religious freedom in Penn's Woods. Secretary James Logan on March 25, 1727, wrote William Penn's son in England to complain:

> We have many thousands of foreigners, most Palatines, so-called, already in ye Countrey, of whom near 1500 came in this last sum-

mer; many of them are a surly people, divers Papists amongst them, and ye men generally well arm'd.[1]

About the same time, many former Scottish families who had moved from their homeland earlier to establish the linen trade in Ireland, now found themselves forced from their new homeland by English taxes and also joined in the exodus to Pennsylvania and other colonies. "We have from the North of Ireland great numbers yearly," Secretary Logan wrote John Penn in 1727:

8 or 9 Ships this last fall discharged at Newcastle. Both of these sorts [Germans and Scotsmen] sitt frequently down on any spott of vacant Land they can find, without asking questions; the last Palatines say there will be twice the number next year, & ye Irish say ye same of their People.[2]

Even the tolerant Benjamin Franklin was disturbed by the newcomers. "Why should the Palatine boors be suffered to swarm into our settlement," he wrote in 1751:

and, by herding together, establish their language and manners, to the exclusion of ours? Why should Pennsylvania, founded by the English, become a colony of aliens, who will shortly be so numerous as to Germanize us, instead of our Anglicifying them, and will never adopt our language or customs any more than they can acquire our complexion?[3]

(Franklin later explained rather lamely that by "boor" he meant "farmer.")

Settling at first around Philadelphia, the German and Scotch-Irish slowly spread west and south. Soon many spread westward to the villages of Lancaster, which was laid out in 1721, and Conestoga and York, settled a few years later.

Resentment against the newcomers grew, and they increasingly chose to go southward from Lancaster along the Great Warriors' Path, which led into Maryland and Virginia.

Pennsylvania increasingly discouraged the newcomers and urged them to move southward, beyond their boundaries. The Philadelphian, Casper Wistar, painted this dismal picture to prospective settlers of Pennsylvania in 1732:

Some years ago this was a very fruitful country, and, like all new countries, but sparsely inhabited. Since the wilderness required much labor, and the inhabitants were few, ships that arrived with German emigrants were cordially welcomed. They were immediately discharged, and by their labor very easily earned enough to buy some land. Pennsylvania is but a small part of America, and has been open now for some years, so that not only many thousand Germans, but English and Irish have settled there, and filled all parts of the country; so that all who now seek land must go far into the wilderness, and purchase it at a higher price. . . . In view of these circumstances, and the tedious, expensive and perilous voyage, you should not advise any one for whom you wish well to come hither. All I can say is that those who think of coming should weigh well what has been above stated, and should count the cost, and, above all, should go to God for counsel and inquire whether it be His will, lest they may undertake that whereof they will afterward repent.[4]

Learning of cheaper lands southward in Maryland, Virginia, and Carolina, the Germans and Scotch-Irish began venturing down the Great Warriors' Path. Led by a few explorers and land speculators, the Germanic and Scotch-Irish migrations were to continue for nearly a century.

Having seen the rapid growth of Germanic and Scottish settlement in Pennsylvania, Maryland's proprietor, Lord Baltimore, in 1732, sent a proclamation northward to lure others south. His colony, "being Desireous to Increase the Number of Honest people" in Maryland, offered any family 200 acres free between the Potomac and Susquehanna, to be exempt from the payment of quit rents for three years after settlement and then at a rate of only four shillings sterling per hundred acres. Single persons were offered a hundred acres on the same terms.

His Lordship assured settlers that "they shall be as well Secured in their Liberty & property in Maryland as any of his Majesty's Subjects in any part of the British Plantations in America without Exception . . ." Many Germans and Scots were thus lured southward into Maryland, and a strong rivalry developed between the two proprietary colonies.

In 1733, Maryland had a population of only 31,470 males above the age of fifteen, but by 1756 the population had grown to 130,000. About the same time, Virginia began to receive the first of the Germans and Scotch-Irish. Jacob Stover led the first Germanic settlers down the Warriors' Path into Virginia in 1726. Many more came in 1732 when Joist Hite, an Alsatian who had first settled in

Pennsylvania, led a group of Alsatians to settle on 40,000 acres in upland Virginia which the Governor had granted to John and Isaac Van Meter, also of Pennsylvania.

Fear of attack by the Iroquois to the north also forced many Germans south. A number of Germanic settlers in the Colebrook Valley in 1728 petitioned the Governor for better protection against the savages. The accusation was made—to be heard often in colonial times—that English who had settled along the Atlantic coastal plain were using the Germans and Scotch-Irish as buffers against the frontier Indians.

Cheaper lands in Maryland and in the Valley of Virginia increasingly attracted Scots and Germans. In the stony uplands of the Valley of Virginia, land could be had for ten to twenty shillings an acre, so widespread was Virginia's frontier.

Before descending into Anglican Virginia, however, the Scotch-Irish assured themselves that they could worship there as they pleased, free of Church of England control. The Presbyterian Synod of Philadelphia wrote Virginia's Governor William Gooch in May 1738 to inquire about the "civil and religious liberties" in the colony. To this, Gooch replied that he had

> always been inclined to favour the people who have lately removed from other provinces, to settle on the western side of our great mountains . . . no interruption shall be given to any minister of your profession [denomination] who shall come among them, so long as they conform themselves to the rules prescribed by the act of toleration in England, by taking the oaths enjoined thereby, and registering the places of their meeting, and behave themselves peaceably towards the government . . .[5]

Most of the Germans chose fertile farmlands, clustering close together to help each other with their sowing and reaping, their house-raisings, and their hog-killing. Reared as farmers, they quickly converted their small holdings into verdant fields of grain, tobacco, and truck crops. From the Palatinate, they brought with them a practical knowledge of the use of manure in fertilizing new or worn-out fields. They thriftily used the limestone and fieldstone which they cleared from their acres to build their houses and fences.

One prominent Marylander, Daniel Dulany, wrote Governor Samuel Ogle in 1745 to report the transformation which the Germanic settlers were making in western Maryland. "You would be surprised to see how much the country is improved beyond the mountains," he wrote, "especially by the Germans, who are the best people that can be to settle a wilderness; and the fertility of the soil makes them ample amends for their industry."

A later governor, Charles Eden, sent a similarly enthusiastic report home to England. "They are generally an industrious laborious people," he wrote Britain's colonial secretary.

> Many of them have acquired a considerable share of property. Their improvement of a Wilderness into well-stocked plantations, the example and beneficent Effects of their extraordinary industry have raised in no small degree a spirit of emulation among the other inhabitants. That they are a most useful people and merit the public regard is acknowledged by all who are acquainted with them.[6]

Some Germanic settlers were skilled craftsmen, settling in Philadelphia, Lancaster, or further south along the Warriors' Path. Some were descendants of skilled French artisans who had emigrated to the Palatinate to escape persecution of Louis XIV. Among them were mechanics, gunsmiths, shoemakers, papermakers, butchers, watchmakers, blacksmiths, and ironworkers. They were soon supplying the neighboring English and Scotch-Irish with articles formerly imported from England and Scotland.

Germanic settlers formed much of the early population of Lancaster and York in Pennsylvania and Gettyburg and Hagerstown (originally Hagers Town), which slowly developed farther south on the Warriors' Path. Another German stronghold was Frederick Town, which developed near the Path in central Maryland. Within a few years of the Germanic influx it had become the third largest town in Maryland, next to Baltimore and Annapolis.

> The richness of the soil, and the salubriety of the air, operated [explained William Eddis] very powerfully to promote population; but what chiefly tended to the advancement of settlements in this remote district, was the arrival of many emigrants from the palatinate, and other Germanic states. . . . Provisions are cheap and plentiful, and excellent. In a word, here are to be found all conveniences, and many superfluities.[7]

The early Scots and Germans built rough-hewn log or wooden houses at first, sometimes replaced later by more permanent ones of stone or brick. Where limestone abounded, it was a favored

[25]

material. A house-raising was an occasion for fun as well as hard work, the men gathering early in the morning worked day after day until the building had been covered over. Meanwhile, the owner spurred on his neighbors with hearty meals, washed down with ale or stronger spirits.

The kitchen was the most important room, and often it was the largest. At one end a large open fireplace was built up with stone and mortar. German farmers often attached a stable and a cow barn to the house, for farm animals were valued and well cared for. A basement dug from the earth and sometimes entered by a trap door provided food storage and emergency escape in case of Indian attack. Sometimes a dairy house was dug deeply into the earth, to keep milk and butter cool throughout the summer. Hams, shoulders, and bacon cut from hogs killed each winter were cured over a constant hickory-wood fire in a smokehouse, built of stone over a brick and earthen floor.

The earliest frontier settlers traveled on foot or packhorse, for in many places the Warriors' Path was a clearing no more than three or four feet wide in the deep forest. From Europe they brought only a mere handful of possessions, and only the bare essentials of life could be carried on packhorses over this narrow defile. The settler and his wife had to make their own furniture, farm implements, and clothing. Crude iron utensils were traded or purchased from the nearest blacksmith. In broad fireplaces, often with a Dutch oven built into the brick or mortar, the frontier dweller cooked in iron pots and pans, resting on three-legged iron "spiders" or suspended by chains from a beam or iron bar built into the chimney.

The German emigrant built his tables from a split slab of wood, the top surface smoothed with an adz and four rounded legs set in auger holes. For lack of chairs he made three-legged stools or backless benches. Wooden pins driven into the inner walls of the house served as coat racks or shelf supports. Tallow candles or a fat-lamp produced light. Bear grease and hog fat were saved for this purpose, filling the house with the strong odor of burning lard as the light flickered. Platters were often of wood and plates and spoons usually of pewter.

The Germans brought from the Old World skill in making sausage, scrapple, and other smoked or pickled meats. Their pigs ran loose in the woods, eating acorns and roots, and in nine months were big enough to be slaughtered. Hog-killing day in December's first cold spell brought German neighbors together, working with sharp knives to kill, clean, and butcher their porkers for the winter ahead.

Hams and shoulders were immersed in brine before being hung in the smokehouse. From the hogs' entrails, casings were cleaned for yards of smoked sausage. Other meat was cut up with liver and kidneys and cooked into leberwurst or liver pudding. Water in which meat had been boiled was mixed with cornmeal to make *phannhase* or "pan-rabbit," a mush that was hardened in the pan and then sliced and fried.

Cattle, being slower growing and larger than pigs, were not as popular for meat. Venison, bear, and pork remained the preferred meats. William Byrd II declared "pork and pone"—a type of corn-bread—to be the favorite fare of the Virginia and North Carolina frontier.

On Shrove Tuesday, the German housewife cooked *fastnachts-kuchen,* made of dough and fried in fat. Germanic families also had such favorites as *sauerkraut und speck, schnitz und knopf,* noodles, dumplings, and other hearty fare.

Clothes were made by the German housewife. Sitting at night over her spinning wheel, she spun wool or flax and then wove it into homespun. A mixture of flax and wool known as linsey-woolsey was popular for clothes because of its warmth. Hunting shirts, worn with breeches, stockings, and moccasins, were usually made of it and fringed with brightly colored cloth of raveled edges.

The crafts of the Germans soon became evident. In Philadelphia and along the route of the Warriors' Path, German artisans began to acquire a good trade. They flourished especially as cabinetmak-ers, and Philadelphia by the 1740s had become the site of many small furniture makers. Besides using native pine and maple and walnut, they imported mahogany and followed the fashions of Europeans, like Thomas Chippendale and George Hepplewhite.

The Germans were also expert wagon makers, and at Conestoga and elsewhere in Pennsylvania built and sold sturdy vehicles to families migrated from the seacoast to the frontier. The first Germanic wagons were crude affairs, their wheels being disks sawed from buttonwood or gum trees. As ironsmiths and wheelwrights increased, better wagons were built. German tanners were esteemed

[27]

for their leather, and many a colonist sported a German-made saddle.

A German tanner named Matthias Nead posted this lament on the wall of his tannery near Clear Spring, Maryland:

Ye shoemakers, Cobblers, and others attend,
Just look at this Notice, it is from your friend;
My Purse is so empty, tis light as a feather,
You have worn out your Shoes, and not paid for the Leather.
Now take my Advice and pay off the old score,
Before you get trusted for any skins more;
I have Sheep Skins, & Calf Skins, & Upper, and Soal,
I have all kinds of Leather, from an Ox, to a Foal;
I have leather that's green, and leather that's dry,
But pay down the Rhino if any you'd buy;
A hint to the wise is sufficient tis said,
Pay! and take a Receipt from your good old Friend
Nead.[8]

Much as the Germans contributed to the frontier's growth, however, many other settlers continued to resent them. William Penn's sons wrote to Secretary James Logan in Pennsylvania in 1729, recommending that the Pennsylvania Assembly pass a law prohibiting further immigration by the Palatines. They promised to have King George II uphold it. However, the Germanic people had become too enmeshed in the growing fabric of colonial life to be halted. Throughout the 1730s, transplanted Swiss and Germans continued to pour into Philadelphia, spreading thence along the growing Appalachian frontier.

CHAPTER 4

Enter the Scotch-Irish

Close behind the wave of Germanic people which began to sweep over the Warriors' Path came the bold, adventurous Scotch-Irish. From the port of Belfast, in northern Ireland, many a shipload of hopeful Scottish Protestants sailed after 1725 for the Great Opportunity which beckoned from Philadelphia.

Like the Germans who emigrated from the Palatinate, the Scots who poured into America from Ulster were hardy middle-class farmers and craftsmen who suffered in the Old World from their industriousness and their religious beliefs. They came from the poor, rural countries of northern Ireland—Antrim, Armagh, Cavan, Donegal, Down, Firmanagh, Londonderry, and Tyrone, where English rule had grown increasingly severe.

The Scottish emigrants were offspring of lowland Presbyterians who had moved out of their ancient homeland after 1607, in response to English inducement to colonize Ireland and grab up cheap farmlands.

For nearly a hundred years before 1700, Scotsmen had emigrated from their country to Ireland, building up profitable linen and woolen manufactures there. Then, in 1698, English wool producers persuaded Parliament to suppress the exportation of Irish woolens. The subservient Irish Parliament agreed, and Scotch-Irish wool growers were forbidden to sell their product to any buyers except the English.

Besides this, Church of England bishops who sat in the Irish Parliament persuaded the government in 1692 to require all Irish officeholders to partake of the Lord's Supper three times a year in the Established Church. Penalties were imposed on any Scottish Presbyterian minister who preached against the rule by bishops.

Outvoted by Irish landholders, who generally upheld the Church of England, the Ulster Scots were persecuted both in politics and business. Not even the tolerant King William and Queen Mary, who had achieved official toleration of England's dissenters on their accession in 1689, were able to moderate the militant zeal of Ireland's Anglican conformists. In countless ways, they made life difficult for the followers of John Knox.

[29]

Discouraged by the treatment they received from the English and Irish, the younger sons and daughters of transplanted Ulster Scots began to move in small numbers to America. The exodus began about 1718. Ten years later, a bishop of the Church of England noticed that "above 4200 men, women, and children have been shipped off from hence for the West Indies, within three years." By this time, many of the 200,000 Presbyterians in the Synod of Ulster were on their way to America. So were many of their 130 ministers.

When famine struck Ulster in 1740, the stream of emigrants reached 12,000 yearly. "Thus was Ulster drained of the young, the enterprising, and the most energetic and desirable classes of its population," moaned a Scottish chronicler. "They left the land which had been saved to England by the swords of their fathers, and crossed the sea to escape from the galling tyranny of the bishops whom England had made rulers of that land."

Touring Ireland in these same years, Arthur Young painted a gloomy picture:

> The spirit of emigrating in Ireland appeared to be confined to two circumstances, the Presbyterian religion and the linen manufacture. I heard of very few emigrants except among manufacturers of that persuasion. The Catholics never went; they seem not only tied to the country, but almost to the parish in which their ancestors lived. As to emigrating in the North, it was in error in England to suppose it a novelty, which arose with the increase in rents. The contrary was the fact; it had subsisted perhaps forty years, insomuch that at the ports of Belfast, Derry, etc. the passage trade, as they called it, had long been a regular branch of commerce, which employed several ships, and consisted in carrying people to America. The increasing population of the country made it an increasing trade; but when the linen trade was low, the passenger trade was always high...[1]

Boarding ship at Belfast or Derry, the Ulster families brought with them to America only the few clothes, tools, kitchen implements, and books which they could pack in their wooden sea chests. Huddled below deck in the dark and stinking ship's hold, they endured a rough voyage which lasted eight weeks and often more.

> Last year one of the ships was driven about the ocean for twenty-four weeks [noted a Pennsylvanian in 1732], and of its one hundred

[30]

and fifty passengers, more than one hundred starved to death. To satisfy their hunger, they caught mice, and rats; and a mouse brought half a gulden. When the survivors at last reached land, their sufferings were aggravated by their arrest, and the exaction from them of the entire fare for both living and dead.[2]

Few vessels in these early years were of more than 150 tons, and passenger space was limited. The Ulstermen huddled below deck on straw mattresses or hammocks at night, avoiding the rheumy night air. By day they were permitted abovedeck, crowding the rails to watch the gray seas while the square-rigger beat her way at eight or ten knots across the 3,000 miles of sea which separated Ireland from the American coast.

Many emigrant vessels were stormbound or lost at sea, even though they avoided the tempestuous equinoctial storm months. A Philadelphian in 1732 described this ordeal:

> One of the vessels was seventeen weeks on the way and about sixty of its passengers died at sea. All the survivors are sick and feeble, and what is worst, poor and without means; hence, in a community like this where money is scarce, they are a burden, and every day there are deaths among them... When one is without the money, his only resource is to sell himself for a term from three to eight years or more, and to serve as a slave. Nothing but a poor suit of clothes is received when his time has expired. Families endure a great trial when they see the father purchased by one master, the mother by another, and each of the children by another. All this for the money only that they owe the Captain.
>
> And yet they are only too glad, when after waiting long, they at last find some one willing to buy them; for the money of the country is well nigh exhausted. ... If ready to hazard their lives and to endure patiently all the trials of the voyage, they must further think whether over and above the cost they will have enough to purchase cattle, and to provide for other necessities ...
>
> Young and able-bodied persons, who can do efficient work, can, nevertheless, always find some one who will purchase them for two, three or four years; but they must be unmarried. For young married persons, particularly when the wife is with child, no one cares to have. Of mechanics there are a considerable number already here; but a good mechanic who can bring with him sufficient capital to avoid beginning with debt, may do well, although of almost all classes and occupations, there are already more than too many ...[3]

[31]

The mad rush of Scotsmen to leave Ulster at length disturbed the Irish landowners, and they introduced a bill in the Irish Parliament in 1735 to restrict emigration. As a result, hundreds of families rushed to board ships the next spring before the threatened cutoff occurred. A thousand migrant families crowded into dockside Belfast early in 1736, pleading for passage to America.

When the landlords learned this, they tried to intimidate ship-masters into canceling their advertised voyages. A Dublin ship captain, John Stewart, wrote a letter of complaint to Thomas Penn, son of Pennsylvania's founder, whom he addressed as "Knight Pro-prietor of Pensilvania, now in London." Stewart reported on May 3, 1736, that ten ships lay at anchor in Belfast harbor because Irish landlords had issued warrants against any captain who attempted to load and sail.

Stewart appealed to Penn's cupidity with a postscript, pointing out the financial benefit of this emigration to Pennsylvania's pro-prietors:

> Of those ten Ships there is eight bound for Dalour [Delaware] & verry counciderable with them . . . there will be in a vessall that I bought last year in Margos Hucke [Marcus Hook] near Chister in or about seven hund. pounds Sterl. mostly in Speece [specie], if this [Irish action] does not prevent them from getting over alltogether.[4]

Fortunately, Ireland's courts denied to permit landlords to halt their tenants' emigration, and the Great Exodus continued.

Because of Pennsylvania's reputation for religious toleration, most of the Ulster Scots made their way to ports along the Delaware River. Besides Philadelphia, these were principally Lewes and New-Castle, which stood on the western bank of the Delaware in the southern part of Pennsylvania which later became Delaware. All three towns had Presbyterian congregations, and they received the emigrants with open arms, offering them help and a friendly roof until they could begin their trek westward.

Philadelphia in these years shone as a beacon of hope to many of the 200,000 Scotch-Irish—a third of all the Scotsmen then in Ire-land—who came to the American colonies before the American Revolution. Along the wharfs at Market Street docked an endless procession of merchant vessels, bringing settlers from Europe. There the emigrant Benjamin Franklin had arrived from Boston on a

Sunday morning in 1723, while most of the town was at church. There the produce boats brought crates of fruit and vegetables from the Jersey farms across the river, and there the fishermen sold their catch, on a hill between the wharf and the present Water Street.

So many emigrants entered the American colonies at this point that Market Street has been called "the most historic highway in America." From it, the Great Philadelphia Wagon Road eventually led southward into the American heartland. By the time of the Scotch-Irish emigration, Philadelphia had become a town of some 20,000 people, the largest in the American colonies. Gabriel Thomas had lauded it in a 1698 account as "This Magnificent City" and noted that:

> It hath in it Three Fairs every Year, and Two Markets every Week. They kill about Twenty Fat Bullocks every Week, in the hottest time in Summer, for their present spending in that City, besides many Sheep, Calves, and Hogs.[5]

Laid out in orderly squares, unlike earlier Jamestown in Virginia or Boston in Massachusetts, Philadelphia was well on its way to becoming the "green country town" to which William Penn had aspired when he designed it. Early frame houses were being replaced by handsomer brick ones, "all Inhabitated," Gabriel Thomas observed, "and most of the Stately . . . after the Mode in London." Not far away to the northeast stood William Penn's ambitious country house, largely abandoned since the great Quaker had returned to England in 1701 and died there in 1718. This "Great and Stately Pile," as Gabriel Thomas termed it, "he [William Penn] call'd Pennsbury-House."

Emigrants coming off their ships at Philadelphia found a cluster of inns and ordinaries near the dockside, ready to refresh any who had money enough to afford it. These rough-hewn structures were proclaimed by colorful hanging-signs: Blue Anchor, Crooked Billet, Pewter Platter, and Penny-Pot. Built a little later and more tidily were Seven Stars, Cross Keys, Hornet and Peacock, and others of brief or longer span.

Once ashore, the Scottish emigrant faced bewildering choices: Whom could he turn to? Where must he settle? Who had the best and cheapest land? For help, they turned to those who had come before. Presbyterian congregations in the favored regions to the west and south were helpful. In the growing Philadelphia hinterland, a healthy single man or woman had no trouble finding work with a household or a craftsman. A family that had a little money in the purse would probably do best to buy a packhorse to haul their few household goods and start westward toward cheaper lands.

Typical of the Scots was the family of Andrew Pickens, who came into Philadelphia before 1720 from Ulster. Encouraged by fellow emigrants, they first went westward to Paxton Township, near the later town of Harrisburg. There was born the second Andrew Pickens, one of several members of the family to become famous, who was to command South Carolina forces in the Revolution. Like many emigrants, however, they continued to be attracted by lands to the south, which were farther removed from the ominous threat of the Iroquois tribesmen north of Pennsylvania.

Accordingly, the family pulled up stakes in the 1730s, loaded their horses with the family goods, and started south over the Warriors' Path toward the cheaper lands in Virginia. Crossing the Potomac River by Williams' or Watkins' Ferry, near the later site of Williamsport, they followed the narrow footpath along the Shenandoah River. Past occasional clearings in the forest of the Valley of Virginia, they came after many days' journey to a gap in an earlier trail, named Buffalo Gap. There, seventeen miles southwest of the valley way station which grew into the town of Staunton, the Pickens family cleared land and farmed for nearly twenty years.

When the colony of Virginia introduced government in the Valley in 1745 and created Augusta County, the elder Andrew Pickens became the first justice of the peace. But the lure of the wilderness still called these and other pioneers. About 1750 Andrew Pickens led his family southward again, following the Warriors' Path into the land of the Waxhaw Indians, in western South Carolina. Ten years later they moved to Abbeville, where the younger Andrew grew to fame.

The story of the Great Philadelphia Wagon Road is the story of German and Scotch-Irish settlement in America. By 1720, the Scotch-Irish had spread their settlements westward to the mouth of the Susquehanna River. They had formed Presbyterian churches at Octarora, Nottingham, and Head of Elk.

The feisty Scotch-Irish continued to excite Quaker indignation, even though Pennsylvanians recognized them as a comfortable buffer against the western Indians. Secretary James Logan, himself a Scotsman, fumed in 1724 against these "bold and indigent strangers, saying as their excuse, when challenged for [land] titles, that we had solicited for colonists and they had come accordingly." He complained that they had settled uninvited on the 15,000-acre Conestoga Manor in an "audacious and disorderly manner," claiming prime farm lands which the Penn family had reserved for themselves. Their defense was that "it was against the law of God and nature that so much land should be idle while so many Christians wanted it to labor on and to raise their bread."

For a brief time in 1729, Logan and other anti-Ulsterites believed that the British Parliament would adopt measures to retard Scotch-Irish emigration. He wrote:

> It looks as if Ireland is to send all its inhabitants hither, for last week not less than six ships arrived, and every day, two or three arrive also. The common fear is that if they thus continue to come they will make themselves proprietors of the Province. It is strange that they thus crowd where they are not wanted.[6]

Logan, who was himself acquiring a fortune in land in these years, objected to the Scotsmen's forwardness in claiming the best farmlands.

> I must own [he fumed] from my experience in the land-office, that the settlement of five families from Ireland gives me more trouble than fifty of any other people. Before we were broke in upon, ancient Friends and first settlers lived happily; but now the case is quite altered.[7]

Pennsylvania's growth drove up land prices and this, too, prompted many newcomers to move south. A Pennsylvania Quaker, Robert Parke, described the boom to his sister in Ireland in 1725:

> Land is of all Prices Even from ten Pounds, to one hundred Pounds a hundred, according to the goodness or else the situation thereof, & Grows dearer every year by Reason of Vast Quantities of People that come here yearly from Several Parts of the world, therefore thee & thy family or any that I wish well I wod desire to make what Speed you can to come here the Sooner the better. We have traveled over a Pretty deal of this country to seek the Land, & [though] we met with many fine Tracts of Land here & there in the country, yet my father being curious & somewhat hard to Please Did not buy any land until the Second day of 10th mo.

[35]

This country yieldes Extraordinary Increase of all sorts of Grain Likewise—for nicholas hooper had of 3 Acres of Land & at mos 3 bushels of Seed above 80 bushels Increase so that it is as Plentifull a Country as any Can be if people will be Industrious. Wheat is 4 Shills. a bushel, Rye 2s 9d., oats 2.3 pence, barley 3 Shills., Indian Corn 2 Shills., all Strike measure. Beef is 2½ pence a pound; Sometimes more Sometimes less, mutton 2½, pork 2½ pound. Turnips 12 pence a bushell heap'd measure & so Plenty that an acre Produceth 20 bushells. All sorts of Provisions are Extraordinarily Plenty in Philadelphia market where Country people bring in their commodities. Their markets are on 4th day and 7th day.

This country abounds in fruit, Scarce an house but has an Apple, Peach & cherry orchard. As for chestnuts, Wallnuts, & hazel nuts, Strawberries, Billberys & Mulberrys they grow wild in the woods and fields in Vast Quantities . . .

There is 2 fairs, yearly & 2 markets weekly in Philadelphia also 2 fairs yearly in Chester & Likewise in new castle, but they sell no Cattle nor horses, no living Creatures, but altogether Merchants's Goods, as hatts, Linnen & woolen Cloth, handkerchiefs, knives, Scizars, tapes & treds buckels, Ribonds & all Sorts of necessarys fit for our wooden Country & here all young men and women that want wives or husbands may be Supplyed . . .

Thus the Great Exodus from Ireland and Germany continued through many decades of the eighteenth century. Turning their backs on the ancient tribal and religious hatreds of Europe, thousands crossed the Atlantic in search of the opportunity that the Old World had denied them.

CHAPTER 5

A Moravian Journey
to Carolina

The Germans who flooded into Pennsylvania in the 1700s wore the somber clothes of Protestant pilgrims: Amishmen, Mennonites (often called "Mennonists" in early documents), Lutherans, and Anabaptists.

None of these sects played a more active role than the followers of John Hüss, who called themselves the *Fratres Unitas,* but who were known to the world as Moravians. Though the denomination later declined in numbers and in influence, its kindly and hardworking adherents exemplified Christian humility perhaps more than did any other frontier sect. They sought to retain some of the values of monastic life while living in a familial society.

Originating in 1457 near Kunwald, in Bohemia, after Hüss had been martyred for his religious beliefs, the *Fratres* soon broke with the powerful Church of Rome. Hounded out of their homeland, they went into hiding. By 1722, most descendants of these pilgrims had perished, but those who kept the faith gathered on the estate of Count Nikolaus von Zinzendorf, in Saxony, where they built a town named Herrnhut. There in 1727 they began to spread their peculiar faith by missions to the West Indies, North and South America, Africa, and Asia.

In 1735, the Moravians entered North America through Philadelphia. Within the next five years, they had industriously planted small colonies at Bethlehem, Nazareth, and Lititz, Pennsylvania. From these settlements, they sent out missionaries to the Indians.

In November 1743, two Moravians began a journey down the Great Warriors' Path which brought them five months later to Georgia. They were Leonhard Schnell, a German, and Robert Hussey, an English convert. Schnell's diary gives a faithful picture of the difficulties of traversing the Path.

Leaving Bethlehem on November 6, they journeyed together to Philadelphia "in love and in the strength of the lamb." Two days after leaving Philadelphia they arrived at Lancaster, sixty-six miles away, and two days thereafter reached York, "where all the inhabitants are High Germans." At York an innkeeper asked Schnell to preach a sermon, which he soon did to an assemblage of villagers, rounded up by the innkeeper. Schnell preached on the text "The Son of Man is come to seek and to save that which is lost," and was urged to come again often.

Leaving York, the two pilgrims crossed the Conewago River in Adams County, Pennsylvania, and then descended into Maryland and forded in succession three shallow rivers. Schnell had to carry his companion across the third, the Monocacy, because the two men had walked forty miles since sunup and were very tired. In the vicinity of Frederick, Maryland, they found many Lutherans and Reformed members, who insisted on a sermon. "I felt very happy among them," Schnell wrote. "They are very plain people."

Between Frederick and the Potomac River, the travelers encountered only two houses. In this twenty-mile stretch they could get nothing to eat because the householders themselves had no bread. After crossing the river near the later Harper's Ferry, Schnell and Hussey spent the night in an English tavern, where the local people complained about their minister. "On account of his disorderly life, he had no influence among the people," Schnell reported. "At this place I handed to the landlady the Swedish catechism, which Bro. Bryzelius of Philadelphia gave me for his countrymen, who live three miles from here."

In upland Virginia, near the village of Winchester, the two men came to the inn of Joist Hite, a pioneer Germanic settler who encouraged countless others to come south from Philadelphia into upper Virginia. "He was very courteous when he heard that I was a minister," Schnell wrote.

> I asked him for the way to Carolina. He told me of one, which runs for 150 miles through Irish settlements, the district being known as the Irish tract. [An area of the Valley of Virginia which later became Rockingham, Augusta, Rockbridge, and Botetourt counties.] I had no desire to take this way, and as no one could tell me the right way, I felt somewhat depressed. I asked the Lord to show me the right way, but slept little that night.[1]

Arising next day, Schnell learned from a settler of another route which would avoid the dreaded Scotch-Irish settlements. "His name is Stephan Schmidt, a Catholic, but anxious to hear the word of the cross," Schnell recorded. "Many spiritually hungry people, of German nationality, live there, who have no minister."

Reaching the Shenandoah River, Schnell and Hussey found the ferryman unwilling to take them across until he learned that they had the fare. Reluctant to venture further because the next house was twenty-four miles away, they spent the night with an English family, who gave them shelter, after much urging.

> At first they said they could neither give us a meal nor a bed [but] we might sleep at the fire. But after a while they changed their minds and gave us something to eat and a good bed. We paid, and left the following day.[2]

The Moravian minister used an Indian hatchet to clear the pathway, which was often overgrown. Once he felled a tree across Goose Creek to serve as a footbridge.

While detouring around the Scotch-Irish, Schnell and Hussey encountered a German family near Warrenton, Virginia. One man told him that on his voyage to America, 150 passengers were drowned. "This gave me an opportunity to remind them how necessary it is to be ready at all times to leave this world," Pastor Schnell noted. "They at once took me to be a minister, and, as a result, showed us much love. They asked us to stay with them and preach for them on Sunday, as they had a church, but had not heard a sermon for six months . . ."

So moved were Schnell's listeners that they invited him to remain as their pastor, but he declined. They told him of the settlement of Moravian missionaries in Georgia in 1735, later abandoned when the group came up the Warriors' Path and joined another Moravian colony at Zinzendorf, in Pennsylvania. Without betraying his knowledge, Schnell asked what they had thought of the Reverend August Gottlieb Spangenberg, their pastor. One listener admired him because he had not tried to proselyte other believers. "He preached the word pure and undefiled to all who wanted to hear," he said of the Moravian.

In the November rains, the two Moravians started southward again. They found creeks swollen with muddy rainwater. When they reached the Rappahannock, they crossed in a canoe and stopped at an inn kept by a German emigrant named Christopher Kuefer. For several days they plodded through Virginia's highlands in the rain. Near Orange County Courthouse they were stopped by an English settler who demanded to see their passport. When Schnell demurred, several farmers conducted him with rifles to a justice of the peace of Orange County. But the German produced his passport there, and he and Hussey were permitted to proceed.

On December 2, the two pilgrims reached the Roanoke River, on the boundary between Virginia and Carolina. Here they found the rich farmlands which Colonel William Byrd II had purchased twenty years earlier and promoted to European emigrants as his New-found Eden. Schnell may have seen a copy of Byrd's *Neu-Gefundnes Eden in Virginia,* which had been printed (by Wilhelm Vogel, or William Byrd), in Switzerland in 1738 to induce Swiss and German immigrants to come south into Virginia and North Carolina.

In Craven County, North Carolina, the two Moravians met Jacob Schuetz, an elder of the German Reformed settlers living near the Trent River. "He and the people living in that district were very glad to see a German preacher and were eager to hear a sermon, as they had not heard a German sermon for several years," Schnell recorded. On December 8, "all the Germans assembled, about forty of them. The Saviour gave me grace to speak to their hearts and blessed my words visibly..." After the next day's sermon, one German, Abraham Bossert,

> made a great feast to all the persons present, at which many blessed discourses were held.... They also related to me that three days ago two men from Philadelphia had ... told them that there was again a new religion in Pennsylvania, in which the people were given a certain potion to drink, after which they would adhere to them [the denominationalists]. Not long ago a ship-load of people from Switzerland had arrived, who had been rich and respectable people, but as soon as they had taken this potion, they had gone over with all their possessions to the new religion.[3]

Packing food given them by Bossert, Schnell and Hussey set out again on their long walk. At night they heard the howls of wolves and other wild animals.

Winter had now fallen, and in mid-December a white pall enveloped the uplands. "During the night and the whole of the next day, so much snow fell that none in Carolina could remember the like," Schnell noted. "It compelled us to remain in doors all day."

Abandoning the back country, the Moravians turned eastward and at last reached Charles Town, South Carolina, on Christmas eve. Their host, a Huguenot named Brunet, told them of the "pitiable circumstances" of the Germanic ministers and people there and of evil reports which had been circulated of Count Zinzendorf and the Moravians. Schnell attributed this to a book by the Presbyterian minister, Gilbert Tennent, who had preached three sermons in New York the year before on "The Necessity of Holding Fast the Truth ... Relating to Errors lately vented by some Moravians in those parts."

Schnell was also distressed to learn that some German settlers in South Carolina had been turned against the Moravians by a letter which the Reverend Henry Melchior Muhlenberg, an early Lutheran in Pennsylvania, had written to South Carolina. Schnell was indignant. "In it many lies were told about our Brethren and many wicked things were falsely reported about them," he wrote. "This has stirred up the people against us."

At the village of Purysburg on the bank of the Savannah River, twenty miles from Savannah, Pastor Schnell on January 21 called on a German Reformed minister, the Reverend Henry Chiffelle, who had also been ordained by the Church of England to minister to the English colonies. Chiffelle greeted Schnell and showed him his garden and plantation, but he balked at letting Schnell preach in his church. "He said, personally he had no objection," Schnell wrote, "but explicit orders had been received from Charlestown according to which none should have permission to preach, except he had been ordained or licensed by the Bishop of London."

Chiffelle also expressed his opposition to Moravian doctrine, which accepted the Scriptures as a literal rule of faith and behavior. The Moravians' concept of themselves as a "congregation of saints," emphasizing conduct rather than doctrine as the road to salvation, was unacceptable to him as an Anglican. Chiffelle also told Schnell he had not been able to convert many German emigrants "because their hearts were very hard," but he wished Schnell more success with them.

Having concluded their missionary tour, extending more than 500 miles from Pennsylvania to Savannah, the two Moravians prepared to return to their mission. On January 15, they bade farewell to their South Carolina friends and boarded the sloop *John Penrose,* docked in Savannah's harbor. Soon they were at sea, bound for Pennsylvania by way of New York. They arrived at Bethlehem at last on April 10, 1744.

The Moravian mission was typical of many which that sect undertook during the years of the German settlements of the eighteenth century. Soon they would plant new settlements at Bethabara, Bethania, and Salem in North Carolina, traveling regularly from Pennsylvania to the southern colonies and back again.

To them and to other newcomers from the Old World, the Warriors' Path became a familiar and well-worn path. Of them and other unsung early pioneers, William Rose Benét wrote an appropriate epitaph:

> Little of brilliance did they write or say.
> They bore the battle of living and were gay.
> Little of wealth or fame they left behind.
> They were merely honorable, brave, and kind.[4]

CHAPTER 6

Along the Way South

When Alexander Spotswood led his Knights to the Virginia mountaintop in 1716 and foresaw the resistance which France would pose to the colonies' westward growth, he proved himself a farsighted statesman. Though Louis XIV had lost the Hudson Bay region to England, the French still held strong outposts beyond the Appalachians.

By 1744, the two great nations were at war again. France had erected fortresses along the St. Lawrence River, the Great Lakes, and the Mississippi. Increasingly, her trappers ventured eastward to trade with the Ohio Valley Indians. Along the eastern uplands, frontier settlers heard again the dreadful war cries of the Iroquois and the southern chieftains.

The Five Nations blamed the Catawbas. After the Treaty of Albany had been signed by the Five Nations with New York, Pennsylvania, and Virginia in 1722, they said they had asked the southern tribesmen to confirm it.

"The Catawbas refused to come," the Iroquois complained to the English signatories, "and sent us word that we were but women. That they were men, and double men, for they had two penises. That they would make women of us and would always be at war with us," Chief Gachradadow of the Cayugas told the Virginians. "They are a deceitful people. Our Brother Assaragoa is deceived by them."[1]

The Iroquois knew the meaning of the Catawbas' weird boast, for Indian warriors often kept a group of submissive males to perform domestic chores while the warriors fought and hunted. These pitiful male concubines, whom Europeans described as "transvestites," were forced by the tribesmen into sodomistic acts. Such was the fate with which the Catawbas had threatened the Iroquois.

As war again threatened between France and England, the governors of the middle colonies saw need again to meet with the warring tribesmen and brighten the chain of friendship. This was a part of the struggle between the two powers for Indian allies, finally to be fought out in the French and Indian Wars. After long

[43]

negotiations, the governors of Pennsylvania, Maryland, and Virginia traveled over the Warriors' Path in the spring of 1744 to meet once more with the Iroquois.

They chose as their meeting place the village of Lancaster, seat of one of Pennsylvania's eastern counties, thirty miles west of Philadelphia. Here, amid the tobacco and wheatfields of the Pennsylvania Dutch (as the Germanic settlers were called), gathered the chieftains of the Iroquois. Now known as the Six Nations since the Oneida had adopted the remnants of North Carolina's Tuscarora tribesmen about 1722, they came down from New York and encamped near the Conestoga River.

The proceedings followed the pattern which the Iroquois had laid down at Albany in 1685 and again in 1722. From Maryland came Governor Edmund Jenings and Philip Thomas, while Virginia was represented by councilors Thomas Lee of Westmoreland County and William Beverley of Essex County, who held the vast Beverley Manor tract in western Virginia. The handsome and ambitious Lee came as spokesman for Virginia's Governor, Colonel William Gooch, who had been wounded three years earlier in the British attack on Cartagena, on the coast of South America.

But the two principal figures in the Lancaster Treaty conference were Pennsylvanian: the experienced and trusted interpreter, Conrad Weiser, and the polished Governor, George Thomas. Thomas dominated the Lancaster conference just as Virginia's Governor Spotswood had guided the Albany treaty twenty-two years before. Adhering faithfully to William Penn's Quaker policy of treating the Indians peaceably and fairly, Governor Thomas insisted that Pennsylvanians buy lands from the natives instead of seizing them by conquest. Aided by the veteran German trader, Conrad Weiser, who was the colony's Indian interpreter, Governor Thomas preserved the peace between white man and Indian.

As one Virginia councilor conceded of Pennsylvania's policy:

> They have observed exact justice with all the natives that border upon them; they have purchased all their Lands from the Indians; and tho they paid but a trifle for them, it has procured them the credit of being more righteous than their neighbors. They have likewise had the produce to treat them kindly upon all occasions, which has saved them from many wars and massacres, wherein the other colonies have been indiscreetly involved. The truth of it is,

a people whose principles forbid them to draw the carnal sword were in the right to give no provocation.[2]

Thus wrote William Byrd II, who derived much of his wealth from trade with the Indians of western Virginia.

When the chieftains and colonists had gathered in Lancaster's courthouse on June 22, Governor Thomas had a clerk come forth to keep a written record of the talks. This was printed later in the year by the young Philadelphia printer, Benjamin Franklin.

Pennsylvania's Governor Thomas, known as "Onas" to the Iroquois, first scolded the Delaware tribesmen for murdering the Pennsylvania trader John Armstrong and two others near the Warriors' Path. Onas demanded that the Delawares deliver up the culprits and return the stolen goods to Armstrong's wife and children.

"That what I have said may have its due weight with you," the Governor said, holding up a gift of colorful beads, "I give you this string of wampum."

The Indians assented with the cry, "Yo-ha, Yo-ha."

Maryland's spokesman, Governor Jenings, known to the Indians as "Tocarry-Hogan," next came forward and offered the Iroquois a gift of 300 pounds sterling in goods and currency if they would renounce all claim to lands in that colony. "And as a broad road will be made between us," he said, gesturing to show the friendly corridor, "we shall always be desirous of keeping it clear, that we may from time to time take care that the links of friendship be not rusted." Then, accepting a handsome belt of beads from his aide, he told them, "In testimony that our words and hearts agree, we give you this belt of wampum."

"Yo-ha, Yo-ha," cried the Indians. Marylanders then began to spread the goods out for the Indians to see. There were 200 shirts, much cloth, 47 guns, a pound of vermilion for war paint. 1,000 flints to light their gunpowder, four dozen Jew's harps, a dozen wooden boxes, 102 quarters of bar lead, two quarters of gunshot, and seven half-barrels of gunpowder. The Pennsylvanians said it was worth £220 15s in Pennsylvania currency.

Murmuring to each other as they fingered the articles, the great sachems finally shook their heads and agreed to take the goods. However, they were not yet ready to give up their land.

Councilor Lee of Virginia next came forward. Dressed in the dignified style of a Virginia planter, he had come to Lancaster with strong misgivings. Since the settlement of Jamestown in 1607, Virginia had warred chronically with the red men. Many settlers had been massacred along the James River in 1622 and 1644, almost destroying the young colony. Frontier attacks in 1676 led to Nathaniel Bacon's assault on Virginia's southern Indians. Despite the diplomatic efforts of Nicholson and Spotswood, the bloodshed had continued.

Lee came to the heart of the matter. He asked the Iroquois to give up the Great Warriors' Path altogether and to move farther west. To this, an Indian spokesman replied that they had won the land by conquest and deserved to hold it. But "Brother Assaragoa," as Lee was called, persisted:

> If the Six Nations have made any conquest over Indians that may at any time have lived on the west side of the Great Mountains of Virginia, yet they never possessed any lands that we have ever heard of. That part [the Valley of Virginia] was altogether deserted, and free for any people to enter upon, as the people of Virginia have done, by order of the Great King [of England], very justly . . . and free from any claim of you, the Six Nations, our Brethren, until within these eight years.[3]

He reminded them of the chain of friendship which had been made with them in Albany in 1685 by Virginia's Governor, Lord Howard of Effingham, and in 1722 by his successor, Colonel Alexander Spotswood.

To this the Iroquois answered that Spotswood's treaty had bound Virginians not to settle west of the Blue Ridge, leaving the Great Warriors' Path beyond it to the Indians.

> You have not recited [it] as it is [Thomas Lee contradicted them]. For the white people—your brethren of Virginia—are in no article of that treaty prohibited to pass and settle to the westward of the Great Mountains. It is the Indians tributary to Virginia that are restrained, as you and *your* tributary Indians are from passing to the eastward of the same mountains, or to the southward of the Cohongoroaton [Potomac].[4]

Lee pulled the hand-written treaty of 1722 out of his papers. From it he read these words:

> That the Great River of the Potowmack and the high ridge of mountains, which extend all along the frontiers of Virginia to the

westward of the present settlements of that colony, shall be for ever the established boundaries between the Indians[,] subject to the dominions of Virginia, and the Indians belonging and depending on the Five Nations; so that neither our Indians shall not, on any pretense whatsoever, pass to northward or westward of the said boundaries without a passport in like manner from the Governor or Commander in Chief of New-York.[5]

After the chiefs conferred, the spokesman told the Englishmen that they needed the Great Warriors' Path to communicate with the Catawbas and Cherokees in Carolina. A link was needed between the tribes of North and South, and this was theirs.

Again Thomas Lee arose. He reminded the Iroquois that they had promised Spotswood at Albany twenty-two years earlier that they would make peace with the southern tribesmen. However, "It seems, by your being at war with the Catawbas, that it has not been kept between you," he rebuked them. Brother Assaragoa told them, assuming a fatherly and forgiving tone, Virginia would recognize the Indians' right to use the Great Warriors' Path if the Six Nations would "behave themselves orderly, like friends and brethren."

After more negotiations, the Iroquois renounced their right to hunt in Maryland except in the uplands near the Potomac. However, the Indians were clearly resentful of the whites' continued pressure. Chief Gachradadow of the Cayugas, an eloquent and powerful man, rose at length and, with the aid of the interpreter, painted this picture of his tribesmen's gradual loss of their homeland:

Brother Assaragoa:
The world at the first was made on the other side of the Great Water different from what it is on this side, as may be known from the different colors of the skin and our flesh, and that which you call justice may not be so amongst us. You have your laws and customs, and so have we. The Great King [of England] might send you over to conquer the Indans, but it looks to us that God did not approve of it; if He had, he would not have placed the sea where it is, and the limites between us and you . . .

You know very well, when the white people came first here, they were very poor; but now they have got our lands, and are by them become rich, and we are now poor. What little we have had for the land goes soon away, but the land lasts forever. You told us that you had brought with you a chest of goods and that you have the key in

[47]

your pockets, but we have never seen the chest, nor the goods which are said to be in it. It may be small and the goods few ...

The day was Saturday. The Virginians promised to open the chest as soon as the conference resumed on Monday. Meanwhile, on Saturday night, the three colonial delegations feasted the chiefs and the "leading men" of Lancaster at a rich banquet, offering them brandy and rum which they had brought with them from Philadelphia, Annapolis, and Wiliamsburg.

It was a memorable feast, seldom equaled in the annals of colonial America. By the light of candles and lightwood, the unsmiling chiefs and the colonial dignitaries sat down before tables piled high with meat and drink. Each of the chieftains of Six Nations first offered thanks, punctuated by the others with cries and murmers of "Yo-ha, Yo-ha-ha." Then Chief Gachradadow, from his high seat at the head table, spoke. According to the Pennsylvania clerk who wrote the record for Benjamin Franklin's press, he was a formidable figure, standing "with all the dignity of a warrior, the gesture of an orator, and in a very graceful posture." He told of his vision of lasting peace between red man and white. The feast ended and the Indians signed a deed releasing their claims to all of Maryland's lands.

After the treaty-makers had devoted Sunday to rest and worship, they gathered on Monday for Thomas Lee to open Virginia's treasure chest. The thirteen chiefs and their naked warriors gathered around while the Virginia negotiators spread out their array of clothing, firearms, and baubles. To this, Thomas Lee said, Virginia would add £200 in gold on condition that the Iroquois sign a deed recognizing the right of the King of England to the uninhabited Appalachian lands.

Speaking for the Iroquois, Chief Canasatego asked that Brother Assaragoa promise to let the Iroquois continue to pass peacefully through the Warriors' Path. Lee and Beverley agreed, but said the colony must maintain control of the road.

Besides their official treaty, Lee and Beverley took occasion to arrange a treaty with the Indians which sold to them and other wealthy Tidewater land speculators about 500,000 acres beyond the Appalachians which became Jefferson and Columbiana counties in Ohio, and Brooke County in West Virginia.

The colonists devoted the closing days to an effort to strengthen their alliance with the Iroquois in the recurring warfare with France. "I need not put you in mind how much William Penn and his sons have been your friends," said Governor Thomas of Pennsylvania. Giving the Indians a belt of wampum, he reminded them of their treaty to assist Pennsylvania in any war with France. "In this time of war with our common enemies, the French and Spaniards," Brother Onas told them, "it will be the wisest way to be at peace."

The thirteen chiefs and their braves murmured "Yo-ha, Yo-ha."

When the written treaties were about to be signed on July 3, Councilor Thomas Lee of Virginia gave the chiefs another £100 in gold and a belt of wampum. This, he explained through Conrad Weiser, was:

> to make our Chain of Union and Friendship as bright as the sun, that it may not contract any more rust forever; that our children's children may rejoice at and confirm what we have done; and that you and your children may not forget it.[7]

Governor Thomas concluded with an appeal for the future:

> Our friend, Conrad Weiser, when he is old, will go into the Other World, as our fathers have done. Our children will then want such a friend to go between them and your children to reconcile any difference that may happen to arise between them.
>
> The way to have such a friend is for you to send three or four of your boys to Virginia, where we have a fine house for them to live in, and a man on purpose to teach ... the religion, language, and customs of the white people.[8]

He referred to the Indian school which had been established in 1673 at the College of William and Mary, in Virginia, to educate and Christianize the sons of the chiefs. However, few Indians had enrolled, and most who did soon quit and returned to their tribes.

Tocarry-Hogan, speaking for Maryland, urged the Indians: "Let not our chain contract any rust; whenever you perceive the least speck, tell us of it, and we will make it clean."

During the three weeks of meetings, Chief Canasatego had acted as the Indians' principal spokesman. Tall and muscular, he had "a surprising liveliness" in his speech. As the meeting approached its adjournment, he asked that a dram of rum be poured for each Indian. The colonials agreed and passed around small wineglasses. Then, rising in his full regalia, Canasatego addressed Onas, Brother Assaragoa, and Tocarry-Hogan:

We shall never forget that you and we have but one heart, one head, one eye, one ear, and one hand.... In proof of our case we told Onantio [the governor of French Canada] our Father, as he is called, that neither he nor any of his people should come through our country to hurt our brethren the English, or any of the settlements belonging to them.[9]

Canasatego admitted that the Six Nations had obtained the promise of several tribes partial to the French not to aid the French in the impending war. He also promised that the Iroquois stood ready to make peace with the Catawbas whenever they would come up the Warriors' Path from Carolina for that purpose.

Politely, he declined to send his sons to the College of William and Mary. "We love our children too well to send them so great a way," he said, "for the Indians are not inclined to give their children learning. We allow it to be good, and we thank you ... but our customs differing from yours, you will be so good as to excuse us."

Canasatego's wineglass was now empty. When he had first asked for rum, he chided his hosts, "It turned out unfortunately that you gave us it in *French* glasses," holding the small wineglass up for them to see. "We now desire you will give us some in *English* glasses," he said with a wink.

Governor Thomas expressed no surprise that the French "cheat you in your glasses as well as in everything else." He said the commissioners had "enough left to fill our English glasses, and [we] will shew the difference between the narrowness of the French and the generosity of your brethren, the English, towards you."[10] Rum was passed again, and the chiefs and governors drank merrily.

To seal the bargain, the governors distributed one more round of presents. Canasatego proudly wore the scarlet camlet coat he received from Virginia. Gachradadow donned a broad, gold-laced hat from Maryland, and others received gifts from Pennsylvania.

The conference over, Governor Thomas mounted his horse and rode northward to Philadelphia while the other delegates headed south over the Warriors' Path. It had been a fruitful meeting, for when the French and Indian Wars erupted a few months later, the chain of friendship between the Iroquois and the English held fast. Along the St. Lawrence River and Lake Champlain, the Six Nations fought bravely for the Great English King Across the Water, as they had pledged to do.

But the most important result of the Lancaster Treaty was the further withdrawal of the great tribes from the Atlantic coastal plain. Once again the aborigines had been forced westward.

The Great Warriors' Path after 1744 was no longer an Indian trail. It was slowly becoming the Great Philadelphia Wagon Road to the south and the southwest.

CHAPTER 7

Presbyterians in a New Land

Although the Germanic settlers were divided into many sects—Moravians, Mennonites, Lutherans, Amish—the Scotch-Irish who spread along the Great Warriors' Path to the south were nearly all Presbyterians. In a few years William Penn's City of Brotherly Love, which was at first strongly Quaker, became the stronghold of these staunch followers of John Knox in the New World.

Unlike Church of England ministers sent to Virginia and Maryland by the Bishop of London and supported by taxes on their parishioners, the Presbyterian ministers came on their own. In 1718, a minister in northern Ireland exclaimed in alarm that "no less than six ministers have demitted their congregations, and great numbers of their people go with them; so that we are daily alarmed with both ministers and people going off." But this was merely the beginning.

Beset by conflict with both Anglicans and Catholics in Ireland, the Presbyterians chose Pennsylvania as more hospitable to their views than New England, where Congregationalists dominated, or Virginia and Maryland, where the Church of England was established by law. Penn's early insistence on freedom of conscience and his opposition to "looseness, irreligion, and atheism" appealed to the Scots. They found comfort in Pennsylvania's assurance of toleration to all who acknowledged "One almighty God, the Creator, Upholder and Ruler of the World."

Such worshippers were promised that they would never be disadvantaged by their "conscientious Perswasion or Practice, nor be compelled to frequent or maintain any religious Worship, Place or Ministry . . ." Being dissenters against Anglicanism themselves, Quakers favored religious toleration, and word of this had spread to northern Ireland.

Wherever they went, the Scotch-Irish displayed a confidence which carried them far. "Teach me, O Lord, to think well of myself," they prayed, unabashedly.

Philadelphia's first Presbyterian congregation had been formed in 1695 jointly with the Baptists in the waterfront storehouse of the

Barbados Company. Soon others sprang up as new shiploads of Ulstermen surged down the gangway into the growing town. Before 1720, Presbyterians had formed three new congregations westward to the mouth of the Susquehanna, while the next decade saw eighteen more congregations added in Pennsylvania.

As early as 1707, a presbytery or council of elders was formed by ministers of seven pioneer Presbyterian churches in Pennsylvania and New England. Ten years later the Covenanters had increased sufficiently to form the Presbyterian Synod of Philadelphia—the first in America—to direct the growth of new congregations and enlist ministers.

In May 1720, the Presbytery of New Castle reported that the "number of people lately come from Ireland" had grown to such an extent that settlers along the branches of the Elk River had sent commissioners to ask for ministers, with the "design of having the Gospel settled among them." One Presbyterian cleric, the Reverend George Gillespie, reported in 1723 from the head of Christianna Creek, near the later Delaware border:

> As to the affairs of Christ in our parts of the world: There are a great many congregations erected and now erecting; for within the space of five years by gone, near to two hundred Families have come into our parts from Ireland, and more are following: They are generally Presbyterians.[1]

Although many Presbyterian ministers came into Pennsylvania with the Scotch-Irish, they could not keep pace with the denomination's growth. The Reverend Jedidiah Andrews, minister of the Presbyterian Church of Philadelphia, called attention to this problem in 1730.

> Such a multitude of people coming in from Ireland of late years [he wrote] our Congregations are multiplied, in this Province, to the number of 15 or 16, which are all but 2 or 3 furnished with ministers. All Scotch and Irish but 3 or 4. Besides divers new Congregations yet are forming by these new comers, we call ourselves Presbyterians, none pretending to be called Congregational, in this Province.[2]

The beliefs of Scottish Presbyterians and New England Congregationalists were similar, but the two groups followed separate courses. The Congregationalist minister Jonathan Edwards frequently preached to Presbyterians, but he declined to serve as a missionary to Scotch-Irish on Virginia's frontier.

To the handful of hard-working Presbyterian ministers in Pennsylvania, it soon became clear that more clergy were needed. The growing colonists could hardly expect the Scottish universities at Edinburgh, Aberdeen, St. Andrews, and Glasgow to supply these, as they had done in the old country. The first man to try to supply this need was the Reverend William Tennent, pastor at Neshaminy in Bucks County, near the Warriors' Path. In 1726, he began to teach his son William and other youths the Greek and Latin they would need to attend college and prepare for the ministry.

At Tennent's "log college," at Neshaminy, young Scotch-Irish lads lived and worked in the Tennents' household while meeting the arduous intellectual discipline of the Church of Scotland. Soon the Reverend John Blair started another log college at Fagg's Manor, in Chester County. Inspired by the parish schools which John Knox had instituted in early Scotland, the log colleges in the next twenty years led to the creation of the first full-fledged Presbyterian college and theological seminary in the colonies. This institution, the College of New Jersey, eventually became Princeton University. They also led other clergymen to open similar schools along the trail of Scotch-Irish immigration in Maryland, Virginia, the Carolinas, and thence westward through the Appalachians.

Wherever the Scotch-Irish settled, wrote an admirer of those hardy souls,

> they started schools. As the parsons were their best-educated men, they taught the youth as a part of their ministry. In time the schools they started in their congregations grew to be common schools for all. Later some of them became academies, and a few became colleges. In this way these Presbyterians did more to start schools in the South and West than any other people.[3]

The crusading spirit of the Presbyterians was strengthened in 1739 when the Reverend George Whitefield reached Philadelphia from England and aroused great fervor in a series of revival sermons. The minister was only twenty-five, but his golden eloquence and his vivid word-pictures of the hell which awaited sinners stirred Pennsylvania, young and old. Although he was an Anglican, he was at this period an adherent of Charles and John Wesley's Methodists,

[55]

whose popular evangelism, tinged with Calvinism, influenced many other sects.

The normally skeptical Benjamin Franklin was one of the many who heard the Wesleyan and was transported with religious fervor. "It was wonderful to see the change soon made in the manners of our inhabitants," he glowed after hearing the youthful fire-eater. In his autobiography, Franklin described his unsuccessful effort to persuade Whitefield to establish his orphanage in Philadelphia instead of Georgia, and Franklin's resultant decision not to contribute. However, he wrote:

> I happened soon after to attend one of his Sermons, in the course of which I perceived he intended to finish with a collection, and I silently resolved he should get nothing from me. I had in my Pocket a handful of Copper Money, three or four silver Dollars, and five Pistoles of Gold. As he proceeded I began to soften, and concluded to give the Coppers. Another Stroke of his Oratory made me asham'd of that, and determin'd me to give the Silver; and he finish'd so admirably, that I empty'd my Pocket wholly into the Collector's Dish, Gold and all . . .[4]

Although still a nominal adherent of the staid Church of England, Whitefield's eloquent evangelism greatly influenced William Tennent and many other Pennsylvania Presbyterians. Transplanting the emotionalism of Europe's "Great Awakening" to the middle colonies, the young Wesleyan stimulated the growth of evangelical "New Side" ministers like Tennent and his log-college graduates. Many of these went forth to the frontier and planted new churches.

From their hub in Philadelphia, young Scotch-Irish ministers carried the Presbyterian gospel down the Warriors' Path and elsewhere along the frontier. Probably the first Presbyterian church in the Valley of Virginia was organized at Opequon near Winchester in 1737. In the churchyard is a fieldstone slab with its crude, homemade letters still readable:

JOHN WILSON
INTERED HERE
THE BODYS OF
HIS 2 CHILDER &
WIFE YE MOTHER
MARY MARCUS

[56]

WHO DYED AGST
THE 4TH 1742
AIGED 22 YEARS.

In 1740, the Donegal Presbytery directed the Reverend John Craig, who had recently arrived from Ireland, to accept a call to the Presbyterians in the Valley of Virginia. Traveling southward along the path to Augusta County, he established the second church in the Valley at Fort Defiance, eight miles north of the county seat at Staunton. A year later he planted another church at Tinkling Spring, near the future Lexington.

After a preaching trip southward to new settlers along the New and Holston rivers, in southwestern Virginia, Parson Craig brought home to Augusta a long list of church elders he had ordained. For some of them, known as "great sinners," he apologized. "When I cudna get hewn stones," he explained, "I tuk durnaks [brickbats]."

No pioneer Presbyterian, however, equaled the effect of young Samuel Davies, who went south from Pennsylvania in 1748 to preach to frontiersmen in five upland Virginia counties east of the Blue Ridge Mountains. Although only twenty-five at the time, the godly and soul-searching minister—a graduate of John Blair's log college—was soon the most famous preacher in Virginia. He was the leader in the Great Awakening in that Anglican colony and began to stir a demand for greater religious freedom. Rough frontiersmen who grew grain and tobacco in the piedmont uplands gathered by the hundreds wherever Davies came to preach. Anglicans as well as Presbyterians subscribed money to construct seven plain wooden meeting houses which extended his circuit from Hanover to Henrico, Louisa, Goochland, and Caroline counties.

Why did Davies and other Presbyterians exert such strong appeal? Why did so many Americans—especially on the frontier—flock to the Presbyterian meeting in preference to the established Anglican churches? The answer was that the Scottish clerics were freer to follow the pioneers than were the settled Anglican clergy of the coastal plain. Furthermore, Presbyterianism was more democratic and direct than some other faiths: the Scotsman was by nature practical, pragmatic, and impatient of distinctions. All of this appealed to the frontiersman. They were qualities that became part of the American spirit.

The Scottish clergy also appealed to Americans for their Whiggish independence and their skepticism toward British rule. Having chafed under British imperialism in their native Scotland or northern Ireland, they were accustomed to speak out. Many urged disestablishment of the Church of England in the colonies. The Reverend John Witherspoon, who guided American Presbyterianism as president of The College of New Jersey from 1768 to 1794, effectively spoke for separation of Church and state. In essence, Presbyterian preachers on the frontier seemed the most *American* of the religionists until the Baptists and Methodists hit their stride a little later.

Church of England ministers in Virginia eyed Davies' ministry coldly. By attracting so many members of the Established Church in the colony, he was diverting support from settled parish ministers. Furthermore, many dignified Anglicans felt that Davies and other New Side Presbyterians were

> preaching the terrors of the law in such a manner and dialect as had no precedent in the Word of God ... and so industriously working on the passions and affections of weak minds as to cause them to cry out in a hideous manner, and fall down in convulsion-like fits, to the marring of the profiting both of themselves and others ... that they cannot attend to or hear what the preacher says ... [5]

Replying to their "Old Side" or traditionalist Presbyterian critics, the New Siders castigated them as "Dark Lanthorns." Surviving texts of Davies' sermons reveal him to have been an eloquent and sound preacher, who avoided the "hellfire and damnation" of many New Siders. Even so, he was suspect as an itinerant evangelist.

One critic of Davies was Peyton Randolph, the learned and distinguished attorney general of Virginia. He advocated that the colony limit the revival meetings which Davies could hold. It would weaken the Established Church, he protested, if New Side evangelists "are permitted to range and raise contributions over the whole country, when our [Established Church] clergy are confined to a single parish." However, the colony continued to permit Davies to preach at will.

Governor William Gooch, himself partly Scottish and originally sympathetic to the dissenters in Virginia, branded the New Siders as "False teachers ... professing themselves ministers under the pretended influence of new light, extraordinary impulse, and such like fanatical and enthusiastical knowledge ..." His objection also applied to "New Light" Baptists and "enthusiastick" Wesleyans.

In 1747, the Virginia Council ruled that dissenting ministers in the colony must be "settled" and minister to established congregations. It disapproved of circuit riding as destructive of the Anglican concept of orderly parish ministries. It declared:

> It is with Hearts full of the most unfeigned Concern that we observe a Spirit of Enthusiasm introduced among the People by Itinerant Preachers; a Spirit, more dangerous to the common Welfare than the furious Element which laid the Royal Edifice [the Virginia Capitol at Williamsburg, which had just burned] in Ashes; a Spirit, productive not only of Confusion, but of Blasphemy, Profaneness, and the most wicked & destructive Doctrine and Practices . . .[6]

But such Anglican objections merely strengthened Davies' popularity. A boy named Patrick Henry, brought up in the Church of England, heard Samuel Davies in Hanover County, Virginia, and remembered him as the greatest orator he had ever listened to. Reports of such disaffection began to reach the ears of English statesmen with disturbing frequency. In a few years, the writer Horace Walpole would tell a worried British public: "There is no use crying about it. Cousin America has run off with a Presbyterian parson, and that is the end of it."

Another Presbyterian pioneer was the Reverend Hugh McAden, who became one of the first "settled" (as opposed to itinerant) ministers in North Carolina. Graduating from the College of New Jersey in 1753, he was licensed to preach two years later and ordained. In 1759, he accepted a call from Hanover Presbytery, which Samuel Davies had helped establish, serving from Virginia southward to Georgia.

McAden recorded his first preaching mission down the Wagon Road in his journal. Traveling on horseback, he stopped overnight with Presbyterian ministers and laymen "on both sides," referring to the Old Sides and New Sides who divided that denomination. Once he noted: "Alone in the wilderness. Sometimes a house in ten miles, and sometimes not that." Near Augusta Courthouse, later named Staunton, he "stayed for dinner" at Mr. Poage's, "the first I had eaten since I left Pennsylvania."

At the invitation of the Reverend John Brown, he preached at the Timber Ridge Church in the Valley of Virginia. "Felt some life and earnestness in alarming the people of their dangers on account of sin, the procuring cause of all evils that befall us in this life, or in that to come," wrote the Calvinist.

While staying with the family of Joseph Lapsley in Augusta County, McAden's host received the shocking news of General Braddock's tragic defeat in Pennsylvania. "This, together with the frequent account of fresh murders being daily committed upon the frontiers," he wrote, "struck terror in every heart. . . . In short, the whole inhabitants were put into an universal confusion. Scarcely any man durst sleep in his own house—but all met in companies with their wives and children, and set about building little fortifications to defend themselves . . ."

Some frontiersmen urged McAden to return to the safety of Pennsylvania, but he continued southward. Several weeks later he preached at a Presbyterian meeting house on the Yadkin River in North Carolina. "Many adhere to the Baptists that were before wavering," he wrote. "O may the good Lord . . . visit this people!" Passing through the lands of the Catawba Indians, the minister was surrounded and his baggage rifled, but he was unharmed. As a consequence of his trip, McAden became the "settled minister" of two congregations at Duplin and New Hanover, North Carolina, in 1759, and died in 1781 in North Carolina.

Bitterness between Old Side and New Side Presbyterians in Pennsylvania reached such intensity that they split into two groups from 1741 to 1758. During this period, the liberal Presbyterians of New York and of New Brunswick broke away from the more conservative Old Side Presbyterians of the Synod of Philadelphia.

It was during this period that the Synod of New York created a new institution to replace Tennent's log college, principally to train clergymen and schoolmasters. Opening its doors first in 1747 at Elizabeth, New Jersey, it moved five years later to nearby Princeton and became the College of New Jersey. This stronghold of Presbyterian thought soon took over and broadened the log colleges' mission of supplying religious and intellectual leaders to the Scottish immigrants who were infiltrating the Appalachian region. In 1896 it became Princeton University.

As the Scotch-Irish spread, other ministers opened schools like those which Knox had created in Scotland. The first to be established in the Valley of Virginia was taught in 1749 or earlier by the

Reverend John Brown, who had come south on the Warriors' Path and begun his ministry at Timber Ridge, near Staunton. When the Hanover Presbytery twenty-two years later resolved to create a "Seminary of Learning," it decided to take under its patronage the struggling Augusta Academy, then located in Virginia's "Irish tract" at Mount Pleasant. In 1776, the Hanover Presbytery, which served Virginia and much of North Carolina, assumed control of the academy and moved its location to Timber Ridge, on the Wagon Road. It installed as rector the Reverend William Graham, who had graduated from the College of New Jersey in 1773 as a classmate of Henry "Lighthorse Harry" Lee. (Lee later persuaded George Washington to endow the Presbyterian academy with $50,000 of canal stock, and his son, Robert E. Lee, was still later the president of the school.)

Like the pioneer log college at Neshaminy, the academy of Timber Ridge was a rough-hewn institution of high idealism but spartan severity. The building was only twenty-eight by twenty-four feet in size, but its course of study was such as to satisfy the rigorous requisites of Presbyterian education. About 1780 the academy, now named Liberty Hall, was moved to a hill near Lexington.

Describing the first academy, a later head of the school wrote:

> The schoolhouse was a log cabin. A fine forest of oaks, which had given Timber Ridge its name, cast a shade over it in the summer and afforded convenient fuel in winter. A spring of pure water gushed from the rocks near the house. From amidst the trees the student had a fine view of the country below, and of the neighboring Blue Ridge. In short, all the features of the place made it a fit habitation of the woodland muse, and the hill deserved its name of Mount Pleasant.
>
> Hither about thirty youth of the mountains repaired, "to taste of the Pierian spring," thirty-five years after the first settlement of Burden's Grant. Of reading, writing, and ciphering the boys of the country had before acquired such knowledge as primary schools could afford; but with a few late exceptions, Latin, Greek, algebra, geometry, and such like scholastic mysteries, were things of which they knew perhaps to lie covered up in the learned heads of their pastors—but of the nature and uses of which they had no conception whatever . . .
>
> It was a log hut of one apartment. The students carried their dinner with them from their boarding-houses in the neighborhood.

[61]

They conned their lessons either in the school-room, where the recitations were heard, or under the shades of the forest, where breezes whispered and birds sang without disturbing their studies.

A horn—perhaps a real cow's horn—summoned the school from play, and the scattered classes to recitation. Instead of broadcloth coats, the students generally wore a far more graceful garment, the hunting-shirt, homespun, homewoven, and homemade, by the industrious wives and daughters of the land. Their amusements were not the less remote from the modern tastes of students; cards, backgammon, flutes, fiddles, and even marbles were scarcely known among these homebred mountain boys. Firing pistols and ranging the fields with shot-guns to kill little birds for sport they would have considered a waste of time and ammunition.

As to frequenting tippling-shops of any denomination, this was impossible, because no such catchpenny lures for students existed in the country, or would have been tolerated. Had any huckster of liquors, knicknacks, and explosive crackers hung out his sign in those days, the old puritan morality of the land was yet vigorous enough to abate the nuisance.

The sports of the students were mostly gymnastic, both manly and healthful, such as leaping, running, wrestling, pitching quoits, and playing ball. In this rustic seminary a considerable number of young men began their education, who afterwards bore a distinguished part in the civil and ecclesiastical affairs of the country.[7]

The Scottish schoolmaster was a revered and familiar figure in America and in Great Britain throughout these years. Known as "dominie" (from the Latin *dominus*), he did not hesitate to inflict bodily punishment on miscreant students. Such a schoolmaster was the Reverend Samuel Doak, a graduate of Augusta Academy who founded two schools in the territory of Tennessee. This stern old classicist transported his library by packhorse and at commencement presided in the classic garb of the colonial clergyman: powdered wig, long black coat, short breeches with white stockings, and broad-toed shoes with shining buckles.

As they spread southward, Scotch-Irish ministers planted other schools. From such beginnings in Virginia grew Hampden-Sydney and Mary Baldwin colleges. Further south, in North Carolina, Davidson was begun in 1836. In Georgia, Franklin College, begun about 1800, grew into the University of Georgia. Similarly, in the Appalachian territories which they settled after the Revolution, the Scotch-Irish launched Transylvania and Centre colleges in Kentucky and the predecessors of the University of Tennessee, and George Peabody College for Teachers in Tennessee.

Like their parishioners, migrant Scotch-Irish ministers lived with hardship and sudden death. In his journal, the Reverend John Cuthbertson, who came to Pennsylvania in 1751 as the first American missionary of the Reformed Presbyterian Church, described grueling travels on horseback in his thirty-nine-year ministry amounting to 60,000 miles. He preached on 2,400 days, and baptized 1,800 children.

Cuthbertson's energies knew no bounds.

> After being forty-six days at sea from Derry Loch [his journal begins], landed safely at New Castle, Delaware, August 5th, 1751. ... In good health, *laus Deus* [praise God]. Then ... at four, afternoon, took horse and rode twenty miles to Moses Andrews.[8]

Shortly after his arrival in Pennsylvania, Cuthbertson rode down the Appalachian corridor as far south as Opequon and Winchester in Virginia, preaching and baptizing as he went. Such mission journeys were frequent on the Wagon Road.

Another Presbyterian missionary who traversed the Road was the Reverend Philip Vickers Fithian, who in his journal described a mission tour from Philadelphia to York, Hagerstown, Martinsburg, Winchester, and other Valley of Virginia settlements in May and June 1775.

On a preaching trip in 1775, the Reverend David McClure reported an instance of the riotous living which the puritanical Presbyterians sometimes observed along the frontier. He noted disapprovingly:

> Attended a marriage, where the guests were all Virginians. It was a scene of wild and confused merriment. The log house, which was large, was filled. They were dancing to the music of a fiddle ... The manners of the people of Virginia who have removed into these parts are different from those of the Presbyterians and Germans. They are much addicted to drinking parties, gambling, horse racing, and fighting. They are hospitable and prodigal. Several of them have run through their property in the old settlements and have sought an asylum in the wilderness.[7]

[63]

Despite their lonely isolation along the frontier, the Scotch-Irishmen played a steadily larger part in colonial affairs. Critical of English policy before they had left Ireland, most of them were natural adherents to the Revolutionary cause. Thus when Patrick Henry—himself partly Scottish—thundered against the Stamp Act in 1765, his words found response on the Appalachian "Irish tract" and beyond.

Truly, as the English writer Horace Walpole saw, Cousin America in the years before the Revolution was running off with a Presbyterian parson.

CHAPTER 8

Mapping the Great Mountains

As colonists moved westward to the foothills and highlands of the Appalachians, surveyors were repeatedly called on to extend the boundaries which separated the colonies. Border disputes between adjoining settlers absorbed much of the attention of governors and assemblies in these years of frantic growth.

In Virginia, the far-spread upland claims of Lord Fairfax complicated the colony's westward growth. Based on early grants by Stuart kings to lords Culpeper and Arlington, they were resented by Virginians as an unwarranted exercise of royal favor. Inherited by the Fairfaxes, the claims embraced a vast tract from Tidewater westward to the mountains. It was an empire in itself.

Part of the problem was that no one knew the upland headwaters of the Potomac and Rappahannock rivers, whose "first heads or springs" were designated by King James II in 1685 as the westward boundaries of the Fairfax tract. Governor Gooch of Virginia in 1729 protested the claim, and the House of Burgesses asked King George II to reconsider it, but King George II refused.

Disturbed by protests, Lord Fairfax himself arrived in Virginia in 1735 with an order from the King to have the western bounds of the Fairfax lands surveyed. When the Governor and Fairfax disagreed on survey methods, each sent his own survey party out. On the strength of the surveys, the court in 1745 confirmed Fairfax's claim to 6,000,000 acres, making up most of northern and western Virginia. Nineteen counties of Virginia and five in West Virginia were carved from this kingly domain.

The settlement enabled Virginia at last to extend its government to the disputed area, which embraced several hundred miles of the Great Warriors' Path. The colony at first divided the region into two vast counties, which it designated as Frederick and Augusta—Frederick in honor of the eldest son of King George II and Augusta for Princess Augusta of Saxe-Gotha, Frederick's wife. Their county seats were the tavern-stop towns of Frederick Town (later Winchester) and Staunton, which were among the uplands' earliest settlements.

[65]

In charge of the surveys for the Fairfax grant settlement was Thomas Lewis, a bespectacled Scotch-Irishman whose father had settled near Staunton about 1730. His assistant was Peter Jefferson, a descendant of lowland Virginia pioneers who had moved upland into Albemarle County. The surveys which they laboriously made were soon the basis for large land sales to the incoming Scotch-Irish and German immigrants.

Working with Lewis and Jefferson was Joshua Fry, a versatile Oxford graduate who had come to Virginia about 1720 and taught mathematics at the College of William and Mary. Seeking land for his growing family, Fry moved to the frontier and put his geometry to use as a surveyor.

Beginning his survey near the Rappahannock River's source, Thomas Lewis and his party of forty men worked from September 1746 until February of the following year. Lewis's journal lists many hardships. Though winter made forest travel easier, it inundated the surveyors with rain and snow, retarding the movement of men and horses. Describing a mountain creek, Lewis wrote:

> This River was Calld Styx from the Dismal apperance of the place Being Sufficen to Strick terror in any human Creature[;] ye Lorels [laurels] Ivey & Spruce pine so Extremly thick in ye Swamp through which this River Runs that one Cannot have the Least prospect Except they look upwards[.] the Water of the River of Dark Brownish Cooler & its motion So Slow that it can hardly be Said to move[.] its Depth about 4 feet the Bottom muddy & Banks high, which made it Extremely Difficult for us to pass[.] the most of the horses when they attempt'd to asend the farthest Bank tumbling with their loads Back in the River. most of our Bagage that would have been Damaged by the water were Brought over on mens Shoulder Such as Powder, Bread and Bedclothes &c ... we Could not find a plain Bieg enough for one man to Lye on no fire wood Except green or Roten Spruce pine[,] no place for our horses to feed[.] And to prevent their Eating of Loral tyd them all up least they Should be poisoned.[1]

The surveyors erected a stone monument at the beginning of the line, marking it with their names.

On October 30, Lewis and Jefferson and their party celebrated George II's birthday. "This Being his majesty Birth Day," Lewis wrote, "We Concluded the Evening in meriment [.] Drank his majesty health which was Followed by a Discharge of nine guns."

Lewis's narrative uncomplainingly describes the winter's cold, the chilling rains, and the beds of wet leaves on which they sometimes slept. When their job had been completed, the surveyors were paid by Lord Fairfax and the Virginia colony. Then they hastened home to their farms to plow up their newly cleared lands in readiness for the spring plantings of tobacco, wheat, and corn.

Three years after surveying the Fairfax grant, Peter Jefferson and Joshua Fry accepted a commission to extend further west the boundary between North Carolina and Virginia. (John Lewis, by this time a dignified member of the Virginia Council, was busy handling western Virginia land sales as chief agent of the Loyal Company.) William Byrd II had surveyed the line with North Carolinians in 1728, but now it needed to be carried further west.

Peter Jefferson and Joshua Fry were again chosen in 1750 when the Lords of Trade in London directed the Governor of Virginia to have a map drawn of the inhabited portions of Virginia.

By this time the two men had become leaders of the frontier which was growing along the Great Warriors' Path. Fry was Albemarle County's presiding magistrate, the head of its militia, and its county surveyor. As such, he ranked as its first citizen. Not far behind was his neighbor Jefferson, who was also a magistrate, or justice of the peace. At his rustic plantation, Shadwell, Peter's son Thomas Jefferson was born in 1743, the eldest son of the family.

Peter Jefferson was largely self-taught, but he possessed a working knowledge of mathematics and surveying. His son Thomas, who was only fourteen when his father died in 1757, wrote of him:

> My father's education had been quite neglected; but being of a strong mind, sound judgment and eager after information, he read much and improved himself insomuch that he was chosen with Joshua Fry ... to continue the boundary line between Virginia & N. Carolina which had been begun by colo Byrd, and was afterward employed with the same Mr. Fry to make the 1st map of Virginia ... that of Capt. [John] Smith being merely a conjectural sketch."[2]

The two map makers returned to the Appalachian trail with their surveying instruments, and by the autumn of 1751 they had completed their map. Received by the Virginia Council in Williamsburg, it was approved and each man was paid £150 for his work and expenses. In 1754, the map was printed in England. So useful did it prove that several later editions were issued in the twenty years leading to the Revolution.

Titled "A Map of the Inhabited part of Virginia, containing the whole Province of Maryland, with Part of Pensilvania, New Jersey and North Carolina," it showed the Great Wagon Road from Pennsylvania crossing the Potomac at Watkins' Ferry (later Williamsport) into Virginia. Then, slanting southwestward through the Valley, the map projected the "Indian Road by the Treaty of Lancaster," signed in 1744.

By the time the 1775 edition of the map had been issued in London, this Appalachian pathway was labeled "The Great Wagon Road from the Yadkin River through Virginia to Philadelphia distant 435 miles." From the Yadkin, several extensions of the road led southward, one as far as the Indian trading town of Augusta, on the upper Savannah River in Georgia.

Boundary disputes created many problems for settlers along the Pennsylvania-Maryland border in these same years. These resulted from ambiguous grants made by the Crown to the original proprietors of these two early colonies. In the first of these, King Charles I in 1632 gave to Lord Baltimore the land north of Virginia, to a point "which lieth under the Fortieth degree of north latitude" and westward to the Potomac River. However, Charles II in 1681 granted some of the same property to William Penn, who established the proprietorship of Pennsylvania to the north of Maryland.

In an effort to resolve the Maryland-Pennsylvania dispute, James II in 1685 ordered the contested territory to be divided equally and the western half given to Pennsylvania. Nothing was done, however, and the boundary remained undefined. Emigrants coming south from Philadelphia found the land claimed by both colonies. Hostility threatened to burst into flame unless the confusion could be ended.

To resolve the issue, Lord Chancellor Hardwick ruled in England in 1750 that the dividing line should be drawn due west from a point slightly north of New Castle, Delaware. Two English surveyors, Charles Mason and Jeremiah Dixon, were engaged to do the work. Starting in 1765, they established the Mason-Dixon line westward, marking it with milestones. Every fifth one was a "crown stone," bearing the Penn family arms on the Pennsylvania side and those of the Baltimores on the Maryland side. The 233-

mile boundary was completed in 1768. At last the long controversy was ended.

The growing emigration south from Philadelphia gave colonists an increasing awareness of the trail through the Appalachians. The Virginia Assembly in 1744 ordered a ferry kept on the Potomac, where the road had crossed by a shallow ford from Maryland into Virginia. The act specified that it be "On Patomack river from Evan Watkins landing opposite to the mouth of Anagochego creek to Edmund Wade's land in Maryland, the price for a man 3 pence and for a horse 3 pence."

Watkins' Ferry made the Potomac crossing safer and faster. Soon the growing movement southward justified a larger boat, which could transport wagons as well as horses and cattle. Ferryman Evan Watkins was kept busy from dawn to dusk poling his boat back and forth across the river. As trade grew he expanded his services and became a prosperous figure, well known to travelers along the road. He typified the ferrymen who became prominent and prosperous along the early road.

Watkins and his wife Mary had settled by the Potomac about 1741. The river landing was then known as Maidstone in honor of an English town familiar to Lord Fairfax, who owned the area. Watkins first built a one-room log cabin. As his family grew, he added to it, renting beds overnight to travelers. He also built a forge to make hardware and implements and a riverfront store to supply travelers. His ledger book listed ferriage rates, blacksmithing charges, and prices for such refreshments as wine slings, toddies, and "cideroyl." Watkins' Ferry in time became Light's Ferry, then Lemen's Ferry, and finally Williams' Ferry. Eventually the site became Williamsport, Maryland.

Further south along the Wagon Road, other settlers began to ferry travelers across the streams. In 1749, a few western Virginia settlers petitioned their House of Burgesses for a ferry across New River, not far from Big Lick, which later became Roanoke. In response, the Burgesses chose as ferryman a thirty-three-year-old Englishman, William Ingles, who had come to the frontier with his father and uncle.

Ingles at first poled his ferry. Later he pulled it by a cable suspended across the stream. Like Evan Watkins, he also kept a public house, which passed after his death to his descendants. The ferry was replaced by a covered bridge in 1842 but was resumed after the bridge was burned in the Civil War. Ferry service at Ingles' Crossing did not end until 1948.

Mile by mile, the Wagon Road spread further into the Deep South. After Ingles' Ferry was established, travelers by horse and wagon could travel with some assurance down the Appalachians as far as the Yadkin River in North Carolina, though the road grew progressively worse.

Once the Yadkin River was reached, the road branched into several old Indian trails which had developed in earlier days between the villages of the Occonneechee, Tuscarora, Catawba, Shawnee, Cherokee, and other tribes. The growth of the Moravian settlement of Wachovia after 1753 increased travel from Virginia south to that region. So many settlers were now coming into piedmont North Carolina that the frontier county of Rowan was created in 1753 and the county seat of Salisbury established thirty miles south of Wachovia, at the juncture of the old Catawba and Cherokee paths.

Traveling west to view his farthest frontier, North Carolina's Governor Arthur Dobbs in 1755 wrote glowingly to England of his colony's progress.

> Yadkin ... is a large, beautiful river where is a ferry [he wrote]. It is nearly 300 yards over, it was at this time fordable, scarce coming to the horses' bellies. At six miles distant I arrived at Salisbury, the county seat of Rowan. The town is but just laid out, the courthouse built, and seven or eight log houses erected.[3]

Most Salisbury householders operated public houses, taking in travelers for the night. So great was the demand that their number had grown to sixteen by 1762. Among Wagon Road travelers, Salisbury enjoyed a reputation as the first important trading center of the Carolina frontier. There a Germanic pioneer, John Lewis Beard, built a tavern about 1757 and operated it and a tanyard until after the Revolution. Hudson Hughes became an innkeeper there in 1766, later playing host to Colonel Banastre Tarleton at his hostelry during the Revolution. Andrew Jackson later lived at the Hughes House while studying law, and George Washington put up there during his Presidential tour in 1792.

Another Salisbury tavern was Thomas Gillespie's, which was operated after his death by his widow. When the Revolutionary general, Nathanael Greene, arrived at Elizabeth Shields' in 1781, "hungry, penniless, and without a friend," she gave him a bounteous meal and a bag of specie. "Now," she said, "you are no longer without food, money, nor friends." The grateful soldier never forgot her.

Several stores in Salisbury supplied the frontier, and a shoe manufactory, prison, hospital, and armory grew up there before the Revolution. One merchant, John Mitchell, in 1767 supplied Governor William Tryon with a large quantity of goods to trade with Indians. Another, William Nesbit, sold Daniel Boone the powder, shot, and yellow ribbon which he took on his trading missions to the Indian territories of Tennessee and Kentucky.

Other early merchants in Salisbury were William Montgomery, Archibald Craige, Thomas Bashford, James Bowers, John Verrell, Luke Dean, James Berry, and Henry Horah. They enjoyed a growing trade. As Governor Tryon wrote the Board of Trade in England, more than a thousand immigrants' wagons had passed through Salisbury in the fall and winter of 1765.

Thirty miles south of Salisbury, the hamlet of Charlotteburgh grew similarly. Settled about 1750, it attracted a few innkeepers and shopkeepers. As the seat of the large frontier county of Mecklenburg, it grew so steadily that by 1768 it was chartered as a town, largely by Scotch-Irish traders.

As it had done in Pennsylvania and Virginia, the Great Wagon Road in the Carolinas forced the Indians to move farther west.

> Like most of our historic highways [historian Carl Bridenbaugh has pointed out] the Great Philadelphia Wagon Road followed the meanderings of old Indian trails.... Year after year, along this narrow-rutted intercolonial thoroughfare coursed a procession of horsemen, footmen, and pioneer families "with horse and wagon and cattle." In the last sixteen years of the colonial era, southbound traffic along the Great Philadelphia Wagon Road was numbered in tens of thousands; it was the most heavily traveled road in all America and must have had more vehicles jolting along its rough and tortuous way than all other main roads put together.[4]

The tempo of settlement to the south increased after the Treaty of Lancaster cleared the way for European settlers in 1744. It was stimulated further by the victory of British and colonial forces over the French and their Indian allies in 1763, which made Britain the greatest naval power in the world. The decisive triumph of British redcoats and American frontiersmen over the forces of King Louis XV turned the eyes of many colonists toward the Appalachians and beyond.

The rumble of wagon wheels along the Great Philadelphia Wagon Road mounted in the 1750s and '60s. An irrepressible confidence in America's destiny drove men forward, creating ever new frontiers.

CHAPTER 9

Bethabara and New Salem

Having planted themselves early in Pennsylvania and Georgia, the devout Moravians in 1750 looked for other places where they might spread their austere gospel. After much searching and prayer they chose western North Carolina, where they bought 98,985 acres from Lord Granville.

Thus began the great undertaking which they named *Der Nord Carolina Land und Colonie Etablissement.*

Bishop August Spangenberg, known as Brother Joseph, led a small group from Pennsylvania over part of the Wagon Road in 1752 to choose the site for the first buildings. After passing south of Augusta Courthouse (later Staunton), Virginia, on October 24, he observed that "there the bad road began. It was up hill and down, and we had constantly to push the wagon, or hold it back by ropes that we fastened to the rear."

On reaching the Catawba River, the bishop wrote: "Hitherto we have been on the Trading Path, where we could find at least one house a day where food could be bought; but from here were to turn into the pathless forest."

At Quaker Meadows on November 24, he observed:

> The land is very rich, and has been much frequented by buffalo, whose tracks are everywhere, and can often be followed with profit. Frequently, however, a man cannot travel them, for they go through thick and thin, through morass and deep water, and up and down banks so steep that a man could fall down but neither ride nor walk. ... The wolves here give us music every morning, from six corners at once, such music as I have never heard. They are not like the wolves of Germany, Poland, and Livonia, but are afraid of men, and do not usually approach near them. A couple of Brethren skilled in hunting would be of benefit not only here but at our other tracts, partly to kill the wolves and panthers, partly to supply the Brethren with game. Not only can the skins of wolves and panthers be sold, but the government pays a bounty of ten shillings for each one killed.[1]

Once they reached the Catawba River, near the lands of the Catawba Indians, Spangenberg and his followers were invited to stay at the house of Andrew Lambert, a Scotsman. Here they gave final approval for the purchase of Lord Granville's land.

"Our land lies in a region much frequented by the Catawbas and Cherokees, especially for hunting," Spangenberg wrote.

> The Indians in North Carolina behave quite differently from those in Pennsylvania. There no one fears an Indian, unless he is drunk. Here the whites must needs fear them. If they come to a house and find the men away, they are insolent, and the settler's wife must do whatever they bid. Sometimes they come in such large companies that a man who meets them is in great danger. Now and then a man can do as Andrew Lambert did: a company of Senecas came on his land, injured his corn, killed his cattle, etc. Lambert called in his bear hounds, of which he had eight or nine, and with his dogs and his loaded gun drove the Indians from his place.[2]

The Moravians named their tract Wachau for the ancestral estate of Count Nikolaus Ludwig von Zinzendorf, reviver of the Moravian faith in Austria. Later it was changed to the more musical Wachovia, a term which was to embrace the original village of Bethabara and the larger towns of Salem and Bethania.

When word of the land acquisition reached Bethlehem, prayers and song rang through the Congregation of Saints there. Leaders of Moravian colonies from Lititz, Nazareth, and Bethlehem gathered at the Single Brothers' Farm at Christiansbrunn and carefully chose the pioneers to go south in advance of the main group.

Two ministers were chosen to lead it: Bernard Adam Grube, who would direct spiritual life, and Jacob Loesch, who would manage business affairs. Thirteen others were selected, four of them to return to Pennsylvania after a few months to guide others to the new mission field.

Hitching the horses to their homemade wagon, the fifteen men left Bethlehem on October 8, 1753, and were soon headed south on the Wagon Road. Crossing Watkins' Ferry over the Potomac, they admired the reddening of the great maples along the Valley hillsides. By mid-November they had entered North Carolina and reached the initial Moravian settlement site, which they named Bethabara, or House of Passage.

In ten days they cleared three acres of densely forested land and cultivated it with a plow built by Brother Henrich Feldhausen.

Within five months they were growing wheat, corn, potatoes, flax, cotton, tobacco, barley, rye, oats, millet, buckwheat, turnips, and pumpkins. In a fenced garden, to keep out rabbits and squirrels, they cultivated "salat" greens.

Winter was confining, but in spring the Brothers visited neighbors to buy apple and peach trees, livestock, and poultry. They branded their cows with an M on one flank and a mark on the left ear. They hollowed tree trunks into barrels. Except for a few items—glass, nails, salt, and coffee among them—they supplied their own wants.

To Carolina frontiersmen the newcomers were an enigma, but they found them helpful. A Scotsman came to have a tooth pulled. Others asked them to make leather breeches or shoes. Others wanted nails from the smith, brandy from the distiller, or cooking ware from the potter.

Brother Hans Peterson was named *fremden diener,* or foreign worker, to receive visitors. Brother Adam Grube looked to the day when they could offer more hospitality. "It is very inconvenient for us to entertain strangers," he explained, "for our space is small and we have nothing for them to sleep on. Nearly every day we have some extra people to feed."

Soon the Moravians opened a store and brought a gunsmith and other craftsmen from Pennsylvania. When a neighbor, Abraham Wilson, cut his foot, Brother Kalberlahn doctored him for a fee of two cows. Two other visitors felled 100 trees and rived 3,000 shingles in exchange for two pairs of shoes. Soon settlers were coming sixty miles to trade.

Within a few months the Brothers built the log-cabin guesthouse which Brother Grube had advocated. Even so, visitors often outnumbered beds, impelling the Moravian hosts to sit up all night to accommodate them.

When the first spring came, the Brethren laid out their garden, orchard, and cow pasture.

The usual and best food of the Brethren [one of them wrote] has been milk and mush and whatever can be made from cornmeal. The garden did well, and from May 8 to July 5 we had salat every day for midday dinner and often at evening meal. When salat came to an end we had cucumbers for three weeks, with three or four meals of sugar peas, beans several times, occasionally cabbage, and squash twice. Meat has been scarce, and we have had only four

[75]

deer and two small bears—the bears generally are smaller than in Pennsylvania. Hunting has not proved profitable, and we give little time to it.[3]

The diary of John Jacob Friis, who came from Bethlehem as Bethabara's pastor in 1754, reflects the industry of the Moravians. One day he noted that he had hunted strayed pigs for a whole afternoon. On another he carved intricate claw feet for a table, meanwhile musing, "One day I am a joiner and the next day a carver; what could I not learn if I was not too old?" With rueful humor he proclaimed himself "your first cowherd in North Carolina."

In one two-week span Pastor Friis harvested flax, served as community cook, picked blackberries for vinegar, tended the chickens, cleaned the dormitory and yard, and cured tobacco.

Soon Bethabara was complete, and plans were considered for a larger village. Its principal buildings were a *gemeindehaus,* or meeting house, a two-story Single Brothers' House, blacksmith shop, cooperage, grain mill, brick kiln, toolmaking house, pottery, tannery, washhouse, and tailor shop. The Brethren had also cleared roads to the Yadkin River and the Wagon Road and surrounded their whole town with a wooden palisade against the Indians.

Laying the cornerstone for the Single Brothers' House, the Moravians offered up this hymn:

> The Corner-stone of a new house we're laying,
> And for Thy presence, Lord, we're humbly praying;
> May Thy dear blood, for our salvation given,
> Our work and rest, our thoughts and actions, leaven.
>
> O Jesus, grant our prayer: may every Brother
> Here live in joy and peace, one with the other,
> And Thou with us; and every day and hour
> Show us Thy wounds, and their redemptive power.[4]

The second village was named Bethania and placed three miles from Bethabara in Black Walnut Bottom. Eight Moravian couples from Pennsylvania and eight other couples who wished to adopt the Moravian way of life set to work building it in 1759. Fear of Indian attack had forced the sect to abandon its plan for a scattered farming community, like those in Pennsylvania.

Constantly guiding the destiny of the Wachovia settlements was

Bishop Spangenberg, an able and godly man who was second-in-command to Count Zinzendorf among the Moravians. Born in Germany in 1704 and trained for the Lutheran ministry, he had deserted that sect at twenty-nine in objection to its formalized doctrine. Though highly educated, he patiently accepted the hardships of travel between Moravian settlements from Pennsylvania to Georgia.

John Wesley, one of the founders of Methodism, became acquainted with Spangenberg as a fellow missionary in Georgia. He was amazed and impressed that a bishop who preached the gospel one day would demean himself as the village cook the next.

Bishop Spangenberg was constantly dismayed by the godlessness of frontiersmen. "There are many cases of murder, theft, and the like, but no one is punished," he complained. "Land matters in North Carolina are in unbelievable confusion. A man settles on a piece of land, does a good deal of work on it—from the Carolina standpoint—and then another comes and drives him out."

He also disapproved of North Carolina's laws. "No Christian brought into this land can be a bond servant," he wrote. "Yet a man who helps another's slave to escape must serve the slave's owner for five years."

Like William Byrd II, who had found Carolinians shiftless and ignorant, Spangenberg painted a dark picture of the colony:

> The inhabitants of North Carolina are of two kinds. Some have been born in the country, and they bear the climate well but are lazy, and do not compare with our northern colonists. Others have moved here from the northern colonies or from England, Scotland, or Ireland, etc. Many of the first comers were brought by poverty, for they were too poor to buy land in Pennsylvania or Jersey, and yet wished to have land of their own; from these the Colony receives no harm. Others, however, were refugees from debt, or had deserted wives and children, or had fled to escape punishment for evil deeds, and thought that here no one would find them, and they could go on in impunity. Whole bands of horse thieves have moved here, and constantly show their skill in this neighborhood; this has given North Carolina a very bad name in the adjoining Provinces...[5]

Like Bethabara before it, Bethania prospered from the hard work of its settlers. Five years after it was started, word came from Count

Zinzendorf that the time had come to build the principal town, which he directed be called Salem.

The Brethren in North Carolina were not convinced that this was a wise move and appealed to the Governing Board in Saxony. That body accordingly "referred it to the Lord" through the lot. Back came word from Saxony: "We are to tell our Brethren in America that the Savior wills that Salem shall be the town of our Brethren in Wachovia for trade and the professions and they shall be moved thither from Bethabara."

Salem's location was chosen by lot, and in May 1765 the site was surveyed. Money was raised by selling some of Wachovia's acres, and the Moravians agreed that the new town would be given 3,159 acres rent-free for five years.

Artisans to build Salem were brought down the Wagon Road from Pennsylvania. By 1766 they had raised the population of Bethabara to 130 and of Bethania to 87.

As Salem took shape in brick, clapboard, and shingles, its congregation began to move in. The first building, a *gemeindehaus* or meeting house, was consecrated in 1771. Others followed rapidly: a Single Brothers' House, Single Sisters' House, store, tavern, pottery, homes for the blacksmith and gunsmith, an apothecary, mill, sawmill, and a farm with a barn for ten cows. As the town took shape, more Moravians came by wagon from Pennsylvania to take their places in the new mission.

Just as the Pennsylvanians had done, the people of North Carolina found the Congregation of Saints a remarkable group. In the tough and amoral environment of the frontier, they miraculously preserved some of the Christian virtues of medieval monasticism: altruism, self-denial, meditation, industry, frugality, and selfless submission to discipline.

Shunning the moral relativism of politics, they refused to take an oath or to bear arms. "It does not accord with our character as Brethren," they told the Carolinians, "to mix in such political affairs. We are children of peace and wish peace of all men. Whatever God lays upon us, that we will bear." When passage of the Stamp Act incensed the Carolinas, a Wachovian exclaimed: "We sigh and pray: 'From tumult and uproar, deliver us, oh God!'"

In lieu of the Catholics' mass and the Anglicans' eucharist, the Moravians periodically observed a "love feast." Here the congregation sat down to share their bounteous food and drink as primitive Christians did. Observing their simple brotherhood, the poet Goethe concluded that "the Moravian doctrine has something magical in that it appeared to continue . . . the conditions of those first times."

The most glorious event of Moravian life was their observance of Easter. Before sunup the congregation gathered in God's Acre, where the bodies of their dead lay buried in choirs—men in one section and women in another, each marked by a simple stone to signalize the democracy of death. At the sight of the sun's first rays, the cry, "The Lord has risen indeed!" provoked a glorious choral outburst, accompanied by the majestic chords of the massed bands.

Originated at Herrnhut, Austria, in 1732, the sunrise service brought the worshippers of Salem in a body to their *hutberg*, or watch hill. Each Moravian congregation had such a hill, celebrated by Count von Zinzendorf in one of his many hymns:

> If in this Darksome wild I stray,
> Be Thou my light, be Thou my way;
> No foes, no evils need I fear,
> No harm while Thou, my God, art near.
>
> Savior, where'er Thy steps I see,
> Dauntless, untired, I follow Thee:
> O let Thy hand support me still
> And lead me to Thy holy hill![6]

Brother Grube and other musicians at Salem continued to add to the treasury of great Moravian hymns—many of which were later adopted by countless other churches. Describing his arrival at Salem, Brother Seidel told of the zeal with which he sang the stanza which Grube had written to honor the newcomers:

> We hold arrival love feast here,
> In Carolina land;
> A company of Brethren true,
> A little pilgrim band,
> Called by the Lord to be of those
> Who through the whole world go,
> To tell of Jesus everywhere,
> And naught but Jesus know.[7]

Outside, wolves howled in the night and owls screeched a counterpoint to the music.

The constant journeys of Moravians back and forth from Pennsylvania to North Carolina were typified by the experience of Anne Catherine Antes, who wrote on arriving in Salem:

> In the latter part of April, 1759, we set out for North Carolina, accompanied by the other five Brethren from Bethabara and their wives. It was not a long journey, only one month, for our big wagon was drawn by six horses, and we had others for riding; so we made good time. It was a pleasant experience; the country was new to me, and the budding trees and balmy air made us forget the bad stretches of road. Even the night camps had their charm, though we began to hear of renewed Indian activity. Cherokees, who had accompanied General Forbes in the campaign against Fort Duquesne, were returning home along the mountains and were involving themselves in quarrels with the back settlers of Virginia and Carolina. We were taking the lower road by Frederick, Maryland, and Orange Court-house, Virginia; so we were not in great danger and saw no red men.[8]

Incited by the French, the Carolina Indians made widespread attacks against the Carolina frontier in 1760. It was the worst danger the Moravians had known in America. In February of that year, several settlers were killed by Cherokees near the Yadkin. Nine days later, frightened refugees rushed into the safety of Salem, aghast at the Indian atrocities. But Wachovia escaped Indian attack.

Singing and praying together, the Moravians made light of their labor.

> As intimate converse turned washday into almost a pleasure [wrote Anna Catherine Antes], so did the pulling and retting of the flax have its happy side as we worked together in the fields, singing sometimes, and thinking of the shirts and towels and other things which our flax would make when it had been broken and swingled and hackled and spun and woven. The Brethren did the heavy work of breaking and hackling, and some of the weaving, but the rest of it fell to us.[9]

Many visitors came to Salem's church, and Moravian ministers went out to preach to frontiersmen. One wrote in 1766: "The Baptists are the only [other] ones who go far and wide preaching and caring for souls." Brother Utley was the itinerant minister, preaching in English and German.

As at Bethabara and Bethania, the Moravians made Salem into a prosperous settlement. By 1772 it housed 120 persons. Around this central market town clustered the two earlier villages plus the later Friedland and Friedberg. Far-seeing Bishop Spangenberg saw Salem as the principal trading center of its region, sparing North Carolinians the trouble of sending their produce north to Virginia:

> A good deal of tobacco is raised, but it is generally taken to Suffolk or Norfolk [he wrote]. Thus it is shipped by the Virginia merchant, and the Carolinians must accept whatever prices he chooses to pay. Many cattle also are sold outside of North Carolina, but the profit is in Virginia, not here. They are not killed, salted and exported from this province but are driven to Virginia and sold on the hoof, at a loss rather than a profit.[10]

In all their deliberations, the Moravians sought direct guidance from God. In this effort they depended on the lot, which earlier Brethren had used in the fifteenth century to select bishops. Seeking a decision on a congregational matter, they would submit their question in prayers "Dear Savior, I have nothing. I make no choice. Show me Thy will and I will be obedient thereto."

Three choices, on identical ballots, would answer yea, nay, and in blank, which meant that the question was unanswerable. Once drawn, the lot's answer was accepted.

Not all Moravians could constantly adhere to the abstinence and celibacy which their faith required. In 1762, Brother Feldhausen, the Salem distiller, was expelled when he "yielded to carnal desires and fell into all kinds of sin and shame." Young members who became engaged to outsiders without permission of village elders were dismissed. It was a faith which demanded one's whole soul.

Despite their puritanism, the Moravians had no scruples against temperate use of alcoholic beverages. In their Salem taverns they sold brandy, whiskey, and other spirits. Tavern fights were not unknown, but they were usually provoked by Scotch-Irish customers.

To protect themselves against Indian attack, North Carolina's Moravians eventually had to overcome their lifelong scruples and begin carrying guns. Brother Jacob Loesch trained a militia unit to protect the Wachovia settlement when the watchman sounded his trumpet or rang the village bell. When peace came, however, the Brethren put away their guns and sent missionaries to the Cherokees. Many Indians were thus converted to Christianity.

[81]

Over the years, the Moravians contributed greatly to the peace and upbuilding of the frontier which lay along the Great Road. As Bishop Spangenberg believed, the settlement at Salem grew, ultimately becoming part of the city of Winston-Salem. But in the aggressive capitalism of frontier America, the monastic idealism of his faith found fewer converts with each generation.

Even so, the gentle spirit of the *Fratres Unitas* was perpetuated in song and legend. The village of Salem remained a monument to a remarkable people. And in the great Easter litany and in countless soaring hymns, Zinzendorf and his followers left an undying legacy:

> Jesus, lead the way
> Through our life's long day
> And with faithful footsteps steady,
> We will follow, ever ready.
> > Guide us by Thy hand
> > To the Fatherland
>
> Order Thou our ways,
> Savior, all our days.
> If Thou lead us through rough places
> Grant us Thy sustaining graces
> > When our course is o'er
> > Open heaven's door.
> > > Amen[11]

CHAPTER 10

The Threat from the French

Once the English colonies in 1744 took over the Great Warriors' Path, the stage was set for a new westward surge of settlement. In this effort, which set off the French and Indian Wars in 1754, the north-south Appalachian road became a strategic link binding the six southern colonies, from Pennsylvania southward to Georgia.

The murderous conflict between Great Britain and France for control of eastern North America was to end in a great victory for the British, but it was won only at great loss of life to frontier settlers. It also thrust the British government deeply in debt, leading to King George III's efforts to tax the thirteen colonies which brought on the Revolution. For the frontier dwellers, however, the French and Indian Wars brought immediate gains: a sense of colonial unity, new lands to the south and beyond the Appalachians, and less danger from the Indians.

The Virginians' incessant westward drive brought on the war. Emboldened by a 1609 grant from King James I to the Virginia Company of territory "from sea to sea," the tobacco barons of Tidewater believed with Alexander Spotswood that Virginia should possess the lands west and north of the Appalachians. Land—the symbol of wealth and family position to the English country-dwellers who were the ancestors and models of Virginia's tobacco planters— became their consuming passion.

The coming of the French into the Ohio Valley pricked Virginia's pride. Sir Walter Raleigh had dreamed of "a new English nation" in North America. Virginia's Governor and Council agreed the French must be combatted. In this heroic and lengthy struggle, the Wagon Road became a vital colonial supply line.

To seize the Ohio Country, the wealthy Thomas Lee and other Virginia investors formed the Ohio Company and in 1749 obtained from England a grant of 500,000 acres on the Ohio River, which they planned to populate. Learning this, the Marquis Duquesne, Governor-General of New France (Canada), sent a party of soldiers and Indians southward to resist Virginia's encroachment and hold the Ohio country for France. The French in 1753 built three forts in the Ohio Valley, west of the Wagon Road, and manned them with 1,000 soldiers to hold the land.

Virginia countered France's move by dispatching to one of the French forts, Le Boeuf, the Virginia militiaman, George Washington, to warn the French to withdraw. The twenty-one-year-old Washington proceeded from Frederick Town (later Winchester) up the Wagon Road, crossing the Potomac on Evan Watkins' Ferry, over land he had surveyed for Lord Fairfax. As the principal artery for the British frontier, the Road was already familiar to Washington. His knowledge of the frontier was to serve him well.

When the French at Le Boeuf ignored Washington's warning, Governor Dinwiddie sent a force to Virginia's Northwest Territory to fortify the strategic point where the Monongahela and Allegheny rivers join, and to hold back the French. Virginia claimed this unpeopled area as part of her Northwest Territory. However, the French forced the Virginians' surrender and built their own Fort Duquesne on the spot. Now alarmed, Virginia's government sent Colonel Joshua Fry and Colonel Washington at the head of 300 men to regain the strategic site.

To outfit the force, Washington went to Winchester on the Wagon Road and began buying and impressing wagons, horses, and foodstuffs. He found them almost impossible to obtain. "Out of seventy-four wagons impressed at Winchester," he complained to Dinwiddie, "we got but ten after waiting a week, and some of those so badly provided with teams, that the soldiers were obliged to assist them up the hills, although it was known they had better teams at home."

Fortunately, Benjamin Franklin was more successful in obtaining wagons in Pennsylvania. A broadside he printed at Lancaster and distributed to German farms produced 150 in the next two weeks. Franklin's appeal, dated at Lancaster on April 26, 1755, called for 150 wagons of four horses each, plus 150 saddle or packhorses. In a letter to the inhabitants of Lancaster, York, and Cumberland, he held out the prospect of ready cash.

> The People of these back Countries have lately complained to the Assembly that a sufficient Currency was wanting; you have now an Opportunity of receiving and dividing among you a very considerable sum; for if the Service of this Expedition should continue (as it's more than probable it will) for 120 Days, the Hire of these

Waggons and Horses will amount to upward of Thirty thousand Pounds, which will be paid you in Silver and Gold of the King's money.[1]

Leaving the Wagon Road and heading west across the Alleghanies, George Washington's regiment surprised a French party on May 28 and killed all but one man. Five weeks later, however, his force was attacked and forced to surrender at Fort Necessity, on the Pennsylvania border. When General Edward Braddock was sent from England the next year to command the colonials, his army was ambushed by French and Indian forces and Braddock killed. France was then in control of the Ohio country.

While the two great powers built up their forces for the decisive North American battle, Indians and settlers along the Appalachian frontier continued the war. The years 1756, 1757, and 1758 were stained with the blood of many German and Scotch-Irish settlers along the Wagon Road and in the settlements beyond it. Fear of the French and their Indian allies drove many Pennsylvania settlers southward in these years, adding to the traffic along the Wagon Road.

Turned against the English colonists by the French, the Indians of the Appalachians converted the frontier into a war zone in these years. "All the frontiers of Virginia have been reduced to one universal waste by the burning, murdering and scalping committed by the Indians," wrote Lewis Evans in 1755. "In Virginia the enemy was fetched to the door and left there, without any body to oppose him; there no forces were left to cover the militia, while they formed themselves into an army for their own defense."

From Winchester, one of George Washington's officers wrote him on October 4, 1755, that the Indians "go about and commit their outrages at all hours of the day and nothing to be seen or heard of, but desolation and murder heightened with all barbarous circumstances, and unheard of instances of cruelty. They spare the lives of young women, and carry them away to gratify the brutal passions of lawless savages. The smoke of the burning plantations darkens the day, and hides the neighboring mountains from our sight."

The Shawnees were France's chief allies. Occupying the high land of the Appalachian range, they resented the brunt of the colonists' steady movement beyond those mountains. In strike after strike, they inflicted bloody death on pioneer households along the Wagon

Road. Against them, the English colonies turned the Cherokees, who had carried on much of the fur trade in the South. Anxious to keep their loyalty, the English in 1763 sent seven Cherokee chiefs to England, where they had pledged their faith to "the Great King over the Waters." But before the war was over, even the Cherokees were to prove traitorous allies.

When the western Indians began to attack, the colonies were poorly prepared to resist them. Hurriedly, they built a series of Indian forts and blockhouses along the Wagon Road and the passes which led from the road through the Appalachians to the west. In Virginia, Major Andrew Lewis led an expedition against Shawnee strongholds in these mountains, while Colonel George Washington directed the frontier defense and strung a chain of forts along the Wagon Road and its western perimeter.

The Indian raids first hit the western reaches of Virginia settlement. In 1755, Shawnee from the Scioto Valley of the Ohio country crept through the forests and massacred the settlers at Draper's Meadows, later to be known as Blacksburg. There they killed Colonel James Patton, a pioneer Scotch-Irish settler, and three others, wounded another, and captured five more. One of those captured was Mary Draper Ingles, who was carried to a Shawnee town on the Scioto and then to Big Bone Lick, where she made her escape and returned after a hair-raising journey through several hundred miles of wilderness to her home.

When news of General Braddock's defeat filtered through the colonies, fear enveloped the frontier. A German settler in the Valley of Virginia wrote:

> One terrifying message after another came in that the General Braddock had been completely beaten with all his men by the French and Indians, raising such alarm and horror among the people that it is hard to express while we daily fear to be fallen upon by the Wild Men.[2]

No crueler war has ever been fought in America than the French and Indian Wars. To win the Indians' support, the colony of Virginia paid them for scalps of French and enemy Indians. At Winchester, where he desperately trained Virginia's frontier defenders during the spring and summer of 1756, Colonel Washington literally whipped soldiers into fighting condition. For drunkenness, they received 100 lashes; for profanity, 25 immediately and more on the next offense; for malingering, 50 with a cat-o'-nine-tails; and for a sergeant for "running away with his party" a second time before the enemy, death by hanging. Washington timed the hanging so that "the newly draughted recruits for the regiment may be here by that time to see it executed, and it will be good warning for them."

Many settlers fled south to the supposed safety of North Carolina, whose western flank was protected by the friendly Cherokees. Describing "the wretched and unhappy situation" of the western frontier in a letter to the Governor of Virginia in 1756, George Washington wrote that the Appalachian frontiersmen were "in a general motion towards the southern colonies" and that Virginia's westernmost countries of Frederick, Hampshire, and Augusta would soon be empty. Previous defense steps were "evidently insufficient for the security and safety of the Country," and the young colonel recommended "a vigorous and offensive war" to "remove the cause" of the trouble.

In the Valley of Virginia, settlers built community blockhouses and forts and fled to them on word that the Indians were coming. Such was Fort Harrison, erected about 1749 in Rockingham County, near the present Dayton. The stone house was built with an underground passage that led to a spring by the nearby Cook's Creek. During this period, several villages of Germanic settlers grew in the lower Valley of Virginia as farmers left their lands and sought safety. From this era of Indian raids date the villages of Stephensburg, Woodstock, Strasburg, and Staunton.

Many pioneers lost their lives. Captain Robert McKenzie attempted to visit a Dunker settlement in the Valley in 1757 but "found nothing on the Spot they inhabited but some Spears, broken Tomahawks, and the Ashes of Their Hutts. The Spears are of French make."

In March and April 1758, Shawnees took nearly fifty captives from Germanic settlements in the Valley. As a consequence, most German neighborhoods were abandoned. Some moved east of the Blue Ridge, while others returned to eastern Pennsylvania over the Wagon Road.

Four members of a colony at Massanutten wrote to Europe:

We were 39 Mennonite families living in Virginia. One family was murdered and the remaining of us and many other families were forced to flee for our lives, leaving all and going empty-handed.

[87]

Last May, the Indians murdered over 50 Persons and more than 200 families were driven away homeless.[3]

The building of forts gave greater security to the Wagon Road after the outbreak of the French and Indian Wars. Hastily thrown together, the forts were similar to the wooden palisade which Virginia's first settlers had erected at Jamestown in 1607. Such was Fort Loudoun, for example, which the colony of South Carolina built on its western extremity, later a part of Tennessee. Built of rough-hewn logs, spiked at the top and inserted into the earth, they were protected on the outer side by an earthwork and a hedge of thorny honey-locust bushes.

Inside the fort was a blacksmith shop, guardhouse, barracks for the colony's soldiers, storehouses, a powder magazine, quarters for a half-dozen officers, and a well. The smith's shop was the most important building in the fort, serving also as guardhouse, council house, and chapel. The guardhouse held arms and ammunition and a station for the officer of the guard. To protect Fort Loudoun, nearly a dozen small cannon were carried over the Wagon Road and the Great Smoky Mountains by packhorses, and mounted in the fort.

Built near the Indian village of Chota, which was the chief seat of the Cherokees beyond the Appalachians, Fort Loudoun maintained a friendly alliance between South Carolina and the Cherokee until 1759. In that year, French influence succeeded in winning the sympathies of the Overhill Cherokees away from the British and their American colonists. The Indians laid siege to the fort, forced its surrender, and then violated their surrender terms to kill most of the garrison and to ransom the others to their governments.

Another Wagon Road fort attacked by the Indians was Fort Evans, near Winchester, Virginia. In the spring of 1756, when its garrison of men was away, it was surrounded by a force of Shawnees. The women and children inside were alarmed, but one soldier's wife, Polly Evans, ran inside the fort from one gunport to another, firing one gun after another. Misled into thinking the fort was strongly garrisoned, the Indians retreated.

By the year 1758, England had sent troops and ships to North America in readiness to launch her great offensive against France for control of the New World. In three successful offensives, the English commanders in the north colonies and Canada wrested control of the continent from France. Most important to Pennsylvania and the southern colonies, Great Britain's General John Forbes at last took Fort Duquesne from the French in 1758, eliminating the threat of French expansion eastward into the Appalachians. Frontier troops under General Andrew Lewis of Augusta County, Virginia, played a part in the victory.

Indians still remained a danger along the Wagon Road, but the skillful diplomacy of Sir William Johnson, who served as a sort of roving British ambassador to the western tribes, gradually reduced their threat. Border troops under Johnson's command destroyed French forts. By keeping the covenant chain between the British colonies and the Six Nations bright, Johnson restored a shaky peace along the Appalachian frontier. The loyalty of the Iroquois was again pledged to King George II of England, "the Great King Who Rules Across the Water."

But peace with the Indians did not last long. Though Great Britain in 1763 expelled the French from the trans-Appalachian region, warfare with the red men continued. The very next year Chief Pontiac of the Ottawas—one of the Six Nations—renewed attacks on white settlers. Shawnees again ravaged the Valley of Virginia, annihilating a whole settlement on the Greenbrier River and harassing others on Kerr's Creek, near the later site of Lexington.

Again the valley's settlers fled into their chain of forts, leaving the unprotected frontiersmen in Pennsylvania to feel the Indians' fury. As Francis Parkman, the historian, wrote: "The country was filled with the wildest dismay. The people of Virginia betook themselves to their forts for refuge. But those of Pennsylvania, ill supplied with such asylums, fled by thousands . . ."

Anger against the tribes impelled Pennsylvania frontiersmen, known as "the Paxton boys," to invade the peaceful Conestoga Indian settlement in Lancaster County in 1762 and slay fourteen in cold blood. When local officials placed the surviving Conestogas in Lancaster jail for safekeeping, the Paxton boys stormed it and murdered them, cutting off their hands and feet and removing their scalps.

Similar attacks on the Christianized Indians of Nequetank and Nain, Pennsylvania, were barely averted by action of that colony.

By the time news reached North America in 1764 that a treaty had been signed in Paris between France and Great Britain, the Appalachian frontier was more peaceful. In the eleven years since George Washington had gone up the Wagon Road to discourage French settlement on the Ohio River, villages had developed around several English forts. Paths between the upcountry and the seacoast had improved. Trade had increased between western farmers and coastal towns like Annapolis, Baltimore, Alexandria, Fredericksburg, Williamsburg, and Charles Town, South Carolina. Continued western warfare had compelled the frontier to look east for its guns and ammunition instead of to Philadelphia.

The exposed western settlements of Pennsylvania had suffered a loss of population from Indian threat, but the western reaches of Virginia and the Carolinas had grown in consequence. Edmund Burke, the great British advocate of the colonists' rights, wrote in his *Account of the European Settlements in America* in 1761:

> The number of white people in Virginia is . . . growing every day more numerous by the migration of the Irish who, not succeeding so well in Pennsylvania as the more frugal and industrious Germans, sell their lands in that province to the latter, and take up new ground in the remote countries in Virginia, Maryland and North Carolina. These are chiefly Presbyterians from the northern part of Ireland, who in America are generally called Scotch-Irish.[4]

In the Germanic and Scotch-Irish influx of the French and Indian Wars, the Carolinas actually gained more settlers than Maryland or Virginia. Contributing to this southern growth was King George III's prohibition of further trans-Appalachian settlement, which he proclaimed shortly after peace was reached between the French and British in 1764. The King decreed that no American settlers were to advance westward beyond the sources of the rivers emptying into the Atlantic. For the sake of peace with the Indians, the King's subjects were to stay east of the Appalachians. Thus another complaint was added to Americans' grievances against His Majesty's government.

Word now spread that the best lands available east of the Appalachians were along the headwaters of the Holston, the Watauga, the Yadkin, the Catawba, and the Savannah rivers.

> In Carolina [wrote a chronicler of those colonies], large tracts of the best land as yet lay waste, which proved a great temptation to

the northern colonists to migrate to the South. Accordingly, about this time above a thousand families, with their effects, in the space of one year resorted to Carolina, driving their cattle, hogs and horses overland before them.[5]

The Great Wagon Road was expanding, and English America along with it. Victory over the French and Indians made the diverse peoples of the thirteen colonies realize their unity of interest. The Americanization of people once English, Scottish, or Germanic was underway. Out of this sense of purpose was to come a yearning for independence.

CHAPTER 11

Life in the Appalachians

Hardly had the Treaty of Paris been signed in 1763 and peace restored along the American frontier than new rumblings were heard in the seacoast capitals of several of the colonies. Confronted by Parliament with a Stamp Tax in 1765 to help pay the enormous cost of driving France from Canada and the Ohio Valley, bold spirits like John Adams and Patrick Henry strongly objected. Soon colonial assemblies in Boston and Williamsburg bristled with protests.

Being far removed from legislative halls, the farmers of the Appalachians were slow to take up the cry of "Liberty or Death." They were tired of war. Once they saw the French and Indians beaten, they hitched up their oxen and began again to cultivate their wheat and tobacco fields. But not for long.

These years which followed the Treaty of Paris saw great growth along the Wagon Road. In a few short years it was extended from the Yadkin River in North Carolina to the newest British colony in North America: Georgia, once the domain of Creeks and Cherokees but claimed in 1733 in the name of King George II. The southern terminus of the Road now became the English fur-trading center of Augusta, laid out by Governor James Oglethorpe in 1735 along the upper Savannah River.

Riding along the Great Wagon Road in the decade before the American Revolution, visitors from Europe expressed amazement at the rapid growth of the interior. Stretched from Philadelphia to Georgia were endless farms, punctuated by an occasional fort, tavern, or village. In simple meeting houses along the trail, sectarians from England, Ireland, and the Germanic lands gathered each Sunday to worship God.

By 1765, most of the road had been cleared to accommodate horse-drawn vehicles. To maintain it, county courts appointed "overseers" and "viewers" who were responsible for keeping up segments of the thoroughfare at county expense. To fill the holes and lay new gravel over last year's mud, local farmers were employed in the fall, after they had gathered their crops. "Road work" remained a source of off-season income for rural Americans for many years thereafter.

A military officer thus described the Great Road as his soldiers found it in the neighborhood of Winchester:

> ... on our march to this place the men experienced such distresses as were severe in the extreme; the roads were exceedingly bad from the late fall of the snow, which was encrusted, but not sufficiently to bear the weight of a man, so we were continually sinking up to our knees, and cutting our shins and ancles, and, perhaps, after a march of sixteen or eighteen miles in this manner, at night the privates had to sleep in the woods; after their arrival at the place of destination, the officers had to ride five or six miles to find a hovel to rest in.[1]

Such roads were difficult for men and packhorses; they often became impossible for two-wheeled carts and especially for the Pennsylvania wagons, which sometimes carried as much as ten tons of goods. Developed to their highest form in the Conestoga Valley, near Lancaster, these vehicles were eventually built to such size that five or six horses were required to pull them, harnessed in pairs. To relieve the horses' burden, the driver and his companions often walked alongside or behind the wagon.

A family cow, an ox, a herd of sheep, or a pig or two were sometimes tethered to such a wagon. Chickens and other fowl were transported in pens suspended from the tailgate.

To the uplander, the goods wagon served as the principal means of transport. It was the cargo ship of the Appalachians. "Liners" were freight-hauling wagons operated from town to town on fixed schedules, while "tramps" moved at will; the terms were later applied to ships.

Southward along the road two-wheeled carts outnumbered the larger wagons. Lacking the German wagonsmiths of Pennsylvania, southern farmers built homemade "carriages" with wooden axles and wheels which were cross sections of large tree trunks. A single ox or horse pulled such a vehicle.

As the prosperity of the uplands increased, the two-wheeled "chair" or "chaise" was used for short hauls along the Wagon Road, but the elegant carriages of Philadelphia and New York were non-existent on the frontier.

Packhorse trains vied with wagons as carriers of the frontier's goods. Each horse in the train was fitted with a pack saddle, which was strapped to its back. Cargo weighing as much as 600 pounds was sometimes carried. A rider on the lead horse led as many as ten or twelve horses in procession, the bridle of each being attached to the saddle of the preceding horse. When staked out to forage at night, packhorses were often belled so they could be followed if they strayed. Many pack-train leaders wrote of the trouble of rounding up a pack train dispersed by storm or Indian attack.

Besides wagoners and packhorse drivers, the Great Road in summer swarmed with drovers who led or drove livestock to market. Boys were often hired to assist, and a boy's first trip to town was a thrill he long awaited. Aided by vigilant shepherd dogs, the drover kept his animals together until they could be sold and delivered to the butcher, bawling and squealing in protest.

In the Wagon Road's early days, Philadelphia was the market for most livestock. However, the growth of upland market towns in Virginia and the Carolinas gradually diminished the drovers' journeys to the City of Brotherly Love. Such towns as Lancaster, Winchester, Salisbury, and Camden—originally way stations for travelers—eventually became trading centers.

Besides ferrymen and wagoners, many other tradesmen made their living on the Great Philadelphia Wagon Road. Foremost was the taverner or pub-keeper, who kept a house for the traveling public. Licensed by his town or county court, the owner obligated himself to perform specified services at rates approved by the local licensing body. The term "public house" included the roadside boardinghouse and the "ordinary" (so called because guests dined simply, at the host's table) as well as the larger inn or tavern. One English visitor found accommodations hardly to his liking as he progressed southward into Virginia:

> . . . all taverns and public houses are, in Virginia, called ordinaries, and faith not improperly, in general; they consist of a little house placed in a solitary situation, in the middle of the woods; and the mode of describing the roads is from such an ordinary to such a one, so many miles; the entertainment you meet with is very poor indeed, seldom able to procure any other fare than eggs and bacon, with Indian hoe-cake, and at many of them not even that; the only

liquors are peach brandy and whiskey. For this miserable fare they are not remiss in making pretty exorbitant charges . . .[2]

A German visitor in the same period left a similarly jaundiced account of southern inns:

In the item of public houses Virginia and the other southern provinces are worse off than the northern. The distinction between Private and Public Entertainment is to the advantage of the people who keep the so-called Private Houses, they avoiding in this way the tax for permission to dispense rum and other drinks and not being plagued with noisy drinking-parties. Other public houses lacking, travellers are compelled to seek out these and glad to find them. Here, one eats with the family both thick and thin hominy (a preparation of Indian corn), drinks water at pleasure, is not free to demand and has no right to expect what he wants, but pays quite as much as elsewhere . . . On the other hand, it must be said for these "private houses" that in them one has to submit to a general interrogation but once, on the part of the family, whereas in the taverns every person coming in must be thoroughly answered . . .[3]

Typical of local ordinances fixing tavern prices was one adopted by the justices of the peace of Botetourt County, Virginia, in 1773, setting rates in that section of the Great Road:

For West India Rum, 10s gallon
For Rum made on This Continent, 2s 6d per gallon
Madeira wine, 12s per gallon
French Brandy, 5s per gallon
Claret, 16s per gallon
Teneriffe wine, 10s per gallon
Peach brandy, 4s per gallon
Virginia Strong Malt Beer, bottled 3 months, 7½d the bottle
Virginia Strong Malt Beer, not bottled 3 months, 1s 3d per gallon
Bumbo with 2 gills rum to the quart, made with White sugar, 1s 3d
Same made with Brown Sugar, 1s per quart
Whiskey Bumbo made with white sugar, 7½ d per quart
Virginia cider, 1 shilling 3d per gallon
Bristol strong beer, 1 shilling 3 pence per bottle[4]

In addition to these potations, the public-house keeper was permitted to charge ninepence for "a warm diet with small beer"; sixpence for "a cold diet with small beer"; sixpence for "lodging in clean sheets, one in a bed"; and threepence three farthings apiece for "same, two in bed." No charge was added for more than two persons in a bed.

To feed his horse the traveler paid sixpence for twenty-four hours' pasturage. Stableage "with plenty of hay or fodder, one night," cost 7½ d. Oats by the sheaf were threepence.

The operation of ferries over heavily traveled routes was similarly controlled by law. The Virginia Assembly at its September 1744 session specified that ferries be kept at Evan Watkins' landing on the Potomac, sometimes called Maidstone, and at several other Virginia rivers. The statute concluded:

> And the courts of the several counties, wherein such ferries are kept, shall have the power to appoint proper boats to be kept ... for the convenient Transportation of coaches, waggons, and other wheel carriages, that when any such boat shall be so provided and kept, it shall be and may be lawful for the keepers of such ferries to demand and take, for the ferriage of such wheel carriages, the following rates, to wit, for every coach, chariot, or wagon, and the driver thereof, the same as for the carriage of six horses. And for every cart, or four-wheel chaise, and the driver of such chaise, the same as for the ferriage of four horses; and for every two-wheeled chair or chaise, the same as for the ferriage of two horses; according to the rates herein before settled at such ferries, and no more.[5]

A similar Virginia enactment in November 1762 authorized William Ingles to operate his ferry across New River in lower Augusta County. It authorized these rates:

> Price for man, 3 pence; horse, same;
> coach and driver, same as six horses;
> cart or four-wheel chase, same as four horses;
> two wheeled cart, same as two horses.
> Every head of neat cattle: same as one horse.
> Goat or sheep: 5th part of a horse
> Hog: 4th part of a horse.[6]

Next to the houses and churches along the road, nothing was more important than the inns. County justices of the peace often held court there before courthouses could be built in new counties, and public meetings assembled on tavern steps. A German traveler, Johann David Schoepf, commented on the notices and advertisements tacked to tavern doorways:

It is not always the custom to hang shields before taverns, but they are easily to be identified by the great number of miscellaneous papers and advertisements with which the walls and doors of these publick houses are plaistered; generally, the more the bills are to be seen on a house, the better it will be found to be. In this way the traveller is afforded a many sided entertainment, and can inform himself as to where the taxes are heavy, where wives have run away, horses been stolen, or the new Doctor has settled . . .[7]

Most inns were small and uncouth, but they gave backwoodsmen a sense of identification with the larger world of Philadelphia and the East Coast towns. Indeed, the rural inn served for several centuries as the countryman's gathering place, marketplace, political forum, and newspaper.

The greatest number of Wagon Road taverns were found in the heavily traveled sixty-three miles between Philadelphia and Lancaster, which served not only southbound travelers to Maryland and Virginia but also westbound traffic to Harrisburg and Wheeling. Usually run by Germans, the southern Pennsylvania inns served hearty meals which were famed throughout the colonies. From the *hausfrau's* tidy kitchen came such dishes as *sauerbraten, schmorbraten, spanferkel, kalbsbraten, hinkel, apfelklose, bratwurst,* apple cake, coffee cake, and other German delicacies. Their hearthside ovens exuded the aroma of yeast bread that braced the tired traveler.

Inns often catered to specialized clientele as their numbers grew. There were drovers' inns, packhorse inns, and wagoners' inns, each equipped to handle its users' needs. As sentiment divided on the Stamp Tax issue after 1765, certain Pennsylvania inns became known as "loyalist houses" and others as "Whig houses." Later, when mail coaches and stagecoaches began to operate from Philadelphia, the best inns became regular stops, known as "stage stands." At some of these the coach regularly changed horses.

Most inns or taverns proclaimed themselves in bright roadside signs, painted in a style familiar in Europe and bearing a symbol to illustrate the tavern's name for the benefit of those who could not read. Among the several score hostelries between Philadelphia and Lancaster in these years were such familiars as The Black Horse, The Buck, The Plough, The Ball, The Sign of Admiral Warren, The Ship, The Wagon, and Widdow Caldwell's Hat. Germanic settlers knew The Brown Fox as *Die Braun Fuchs* and similarly translated other names.

One of the best-known early Wagon Road inns was originally named The Admiral Vernon for Great Britain's Sir Edward Vernon, hero of the battle of Porto Bello in South America in 1739. However, its name was changed in 1747 in a surge of enthusiasm for Admiral Peter Warren, who defeated a French fleet that year in the War of the Austrian Succession.

The Admiral Warren became a rendezvous for Pennsylvania militiamen after its first owner, George Aston of Northampton County, had organized a militia company to defend his neighborhood against the French and Indians. When Aston grew old, The Admiral Warren was taken over by Peter Valleau. In 1763, it was bought by Lynford Lardner, a Welshman and brother-in-law of Richard Penn, son of Pennsylvania's founder. Under Lardner the inn became a gathering place for Tory sympathizers, just as the nearby General Paoli Inn attracted the neighborhood Whigs.

The most celebrated Pennsylvania tavern-keeper was undoubtedly the kindly German, Casper Fahnestock, who bought the Warren about 1786. He and General Joshua Evans, who owned and operated the competing Paoli, were household names along the Great Road, just as was Evan Watkins at Maidstone on the Potomac. In the Valley of Virginia, innkeeper Thomas Harrison in 1779 deeded his lands to become the town of Harrisonburg, county seat of Rockingham County. At nearby New Market, the Huguenot emigrant Valentin Sevier—father of Tennessee's early leader John Sevier—kept a popular inn.

Another well-known Valley inn was Lincoln's, which was established by John Lincoln at Lacey Spring in Rockingham County after he had come to Virginia over the Great Road from Berks County, Pennsylvania, in the mid-eighteenth century. One of his five sons was Abraham Lincoln, grandfather of the President, who emigrated westward with three of his four brothers into Kentucky, Tennessee, and Ohio.

In several cases, the presence of an inn dictated the location of a county seat, for county justices needed a place to meet before newly authorized courthouses could be built. On "court days"— pronounced "co't days" in the Deep South—the inns of Lancaster, York, Gettysburg, Hagerstown, Salisbury, Charlotte, and other county seats swarmed with lawyers and litigants. County farmers also came to town on such days to trade livestock and produce. Tavern greens and courthouse yards were enlivened with contests of strength and skill: wrestling, foot racing, quoit pitching, bowling, and other simple sports. Cockfighting was also popular in the South.

Lawyers waiting for their cases to be called often acquired skill at these inn-yard sports. John Marshall, who was heard as a young lawyer in cases in the Valley of Virginia, took modest pride in his skill at quoits.

The uncouth flavor of American taverns was lampooned by Ebenezer Cook in 1708 in "The Sot-Weed Factor; or a Voyage to Maryland." Typical were these stanzas:

> Soon after hearty Entertainment
> Of Drink and Victuals without Payment:
> For Planters Tables, you must know,
> Are free for all that come and go.

> While Pon and Milk, with Mush well stoar'd,
> In Wooden Dishes grac'd the Board;
> With homine and Syder-pap
> (Which scarce a hungry dog would lap.)

> Well stuff'd with Fat from Bacon Fry'd,
> Or with Mollossus dulcify'd.
> Then out our Landlord pulls a Pouch
> As greasy as the Leather Couch

> On which he sat, and straight begun
> To load with Weed his Indian Gun...

> His Pipe smoak'd out, with aweful Grace,
> With aspect grave and solemn pace,
> The reverend Sire walks to a Chest,
> Of all the furniture the best.

> From thence he lugs a Cag of Rum
> And nodding to me, thus begun:
> I find, says he, you don't much care,
> For this, our Indian Country Fate; ...

> Not yet from Plagues exempted quite,
> The Curst Muskitoes did me bite:
> Till rising Morn and blushing Day
> Drove both my Fears and Ills away;[8]

The tavern-keeper was a good man to know along the road. Not only could he forewarn you of dangers or discomforts but he provided medical aid, advice to the potential buyer or seller, and sympathy for the homesick. "There is nothing which has yet been contrived by men," Dr. Samuel Johnson aptly put it, "by which so much happiness is produced as by a good inn." Not many inns along the Wagon Road were really good, but they beat camping out.

Ferrymen also helped the wayfaring. Such men as William Ingles on New River or James Patton on Looney's Mill Creek—later Buchanan, Virginia—welcomed the company of travelers. Lord Adam Gordon of England attested in 1755 that such men "assist . . . all strangers with their equipages in so easy and kind a manner, as must deeply touch a person of any feeling. The ferries, which would retard in another country, rather accelerate [in America]," he observed.

The chief hazard to ferries was the floodwater which followed heavy rains. A nervous horse might break a leg in a rocking boat, despite the blinders they sometimes wore to limit their vision. Upcountry ferries were usually no more than flat-bottomed scows or barges, seldom longer than thirty feet, with sloped end and high gunwales or railings to restrain livestock from going overboard. Most ferries were poled from the stern or pulled forward from the bow by a rope pulley.

Where streams were shallow, the traveler simply forded them. Such was the intention of William Brown when he reached New River in Virginia in 1782. "The ford of New River is rather bad," he observed on arrival. "Therefore we thought it advisable to cross in the ferry-boat. . . . The fords of Holstein and Clinch are both good in dry weather, but in a rainy season you are often obliged to raft over."

For such reasons, traffic on the early Wagon Road rose and fell with the seasons, as the streams themselves rose and fell. A dry spell was best for travel, when mud roads turned to dust and creeks narrowed to a trickle. But drovers had no choice but to drive their pigs or cattle to market whenever they were fattened.

At any season travel was uncomfortable and often hazardous. Even so, the adventurers steadily increased. For these were visionary people, entranced by the promise of new and unknown lands. No dangers were too bloody to discourage them for long.

"Those who explore and settle new countries," John Marshall observed, "are generally bold, hardy, and adventurous men, whose minds, as well as bodies, are fitted to encounter danger and fatigue; their object is the acquisition of property, and they generally succeed." The Chief Justice spoke knowingly, for his father and several brothers went west from Virginia into Kentucky.

Of such tough-fibered men and women was frontier America made.

BOOK THREE

The Wilderness Trail

1774-1789

CHAPTER 12

The Wagon Road Turns West

Despite a proclamation by King George III in 1763 to restrict English settlement to the eastern slope of the Appalachians, the bold procession of western pioneers refused to be held back. So great was the pressure that the King was forced to modify his dictum. In 1768, he permitted Sir William Johnson, Great Britain's agent to the northwestern Indians, to negotiate a new treaty with the naive tribesmen. By the Treaty of Fort Stanwix, New York, the area of British settlement was moved westward across the Applachians as far west as the Tennessee River. It was a great advance, but it was to cost many lives.

This was the verdant country soon to become known as Kentucky and Tennessee. To many pioneers, however, it was to become "The Dark and Bloody Ground," as a Cherokee chief, Dragging Canoe, warned North Carolina land speculators who came in 1768 to buy his tribal acres. "We have given you a fine land, Brother," he declared as the last covenant chain gifts were exchanged, "but you will find it under a cloud—*a dark and bloody ground.*"

Little was known of the new land at first. "The country beyond the Cumberland Mountains still appeared, to the dusky view of the generality of the people of Virginia, almost as obscure and doubtful as America itself to the people of Europe before the voyage of Columbus," wrote John Marshall in these years. "A country there was . . . but whether land or water, mountain or plain, fertility or barrenness preponderated—whether inhabited by men or beasts, or both, or neither, they knew not. If inhabited by men, they were supposed to be Indians—for such had always infested the frontiers. And this had been a powerful reason for not exploring the region west of the Great Mountains, which concealed Kentucky from their sight."

Such was the general ignorance of the lands beyond the Appalachians for nearly fifty years after the Great Philadelphia Wagon Road had its beginning. Not until 1750, when Dr. Thomas Walker of Albemarle County, Virginia, rode west to explore the area for the Loyal Land Company, was the nature of Kentucky's terrain known.

As one of the incorporators of the Loyal, the adventurous Walker hoped to leave his family rich. Along with Councilor John Lewis of Augusta, who had surveyed western Virginia with Peter Jefferson and Joshua Fry, Walker and a few other influential Virginians had received title from the Virginia Council in 1748 to extensive western lands. These he naturally wished to explore.

Leaving his Castle Hill plantation in Albemarle in the spring of 1750, Walker and five companies rode west for several days over the Wagon Road. They were awed by the great Natural Bridge, once worshipped by the Monacan Indians as "the Bridge of God." Then, leaving the Road and plunging through the mountains, they followed an ancient buffalo trail which the Indians had discovered to press through the rocky Cumberland range.

Small, blue-eyed Thomas Walker shared the Virginian fever for westward settlement which Alexander Spotswood had generated when his Knights of the Golden Horseshoe first climbed the Blue Ridge. Educated at the College of William and Mary and trained in "physic," he had married a wealthy cousin of George Washington's and moved to her 11,000-acre estate in Virginia's piedmont. Intoxicated by prospects of trans-Appalachian riches, he largely quit medical practice to explore, to map, and to write of his discoveries.

With typical zest, Walker described the colony of Dunkards, or German Baptist Brethren, whom he came upon in the Valley after their exodus from Pennsylvania.

> The Duncards are an odd set of people [he wrote], who make it a matter of Religion not to Shave their Beards, ly on Beds, or eat Flesh, though at present, in the last, they transgress, being constrained to it, as they say, by the want of a sufficiency of Grain and Roots, they having not long been seated here I doubt the plenty and deliciousness of the Venison & Turkeys has contributed not a little to this. The unmarried have no private Property, but live on a common Stock. They dont baptize either Young or Old, they keep their Sabbat on Saturday, & hold that all men shall be happy hereafter, but first must pass through punishment according to their Sins.[1]

Leaving the westernmost Virginia settlement, Walker's explorers passed into the Tennessee territory, which was then part of North Carolina's claim. Then, following the indistinct trail worn down by buffalo and Indians, Dr. Walker and his horsemen came upon a narrow and rocky mountain pass hitherto unknown to white men in North America. A gateway to the west had been found. Naming the defile Cumberland Gap in honor of the son of King George II, the Duke of Cumberland, he pushed on through the Appalachians to the "Dark and Bloody Ground" of Kentucky.

It was an important discovery, for Cumberland Gap would soon become one of the three main routes through the Appalachians into the Ohio Valley. The most northerly route, already discovered, led from the Hudson Valley in New York through the Mohawk River to the Great Lakes. A second route led northward along the Potomac River to western Maryland and thence through Pennsylvania to the juncture of the Ohio and Monongahela, where the town of Pittsburgh was to grow. But Cumberland's gateway—the new route—was easiest for Great Road travelers.

For military purposes, the colonies found Cumberland Gap an immediate strategic advantage in warring with the French and Indians on the Ohio River. Louis XVI's forces there were far from their Canadian base of supplies, and they lacked in the South the powerful Iroquois allies who fought with them in the North. Accordingly, colonial militia in the years 1754–1763 made good use of the Cumberland Gap and of the nearby Holston and Watauga river valleys to force the French from the Valley and gain Britain's great North American victory.

Not until 1768, when "The Dark and Bloody Ground" was bought from Dragging Canoe and other chieftains, did settlement begin to push through Cumberland Gap in force. Leading the van was a thin-lipped Carolina backwoodsman named Daniel Boone, who in May 1769 took the first of his many expeditions through Cumberland Gap, bound for Kentucky.

The son of a Pennsylvania Quaker who had led his family down the Wagon Road in 1750 to the Yadkin River near Bethabara, Daniel Boone became the all-time hero of Kentucky frontiersmen. Serving as a boy wagoner in General Edward Braddock's tragic expedition to dislodge the French at Fort Duquesne in 1755, he knew the woods and its language as well as any Indian brave. Ill-educated and a failure at farming, he never reaped the riches from furs or lands which a few other frontiersmen did. Yet Dan Boone embodied the spirit of the early frontier as did no other American.

Dressed in coonskin cap, buckskin jumper, and leggings, Boone disappeared for weeks at a time into the dense Kentucky wilderness, always to return. He set the style for the western outdoorsman for the centuries to follow, from Lewis and Clark to the cowboy heroes of the movies and television. He was the model, consciously or otherwise, for Davy Crockett, Buffalo Bill, Teddy Roosevelt, and Tom Mix. To Europeans, Daniel Boone created an American image: the natural man of Jean-Jacques Rousseau, living in total freedom amid the beauty of nature.

Typical of his naive heroics was the inscription he cut into a beech tree along the Watauga River in Tennessee. It read:

> D. Boon
> cilled A BAR on
> The Tree
> in YEAR
> 1770[2]

After a youth in Pennsylvania and Virginia, Boone at twenty-two married dark-eyed Rebecca Bryan and settled down near the Great Road in North Carolina. But the lure of the frontier tugged at him. John Finley, an itinerant peddler, who traveled the Road from Pennsylvania selling his wares, first roused Boone's interest in finding the Cumberland Gap which Thomas Walker had first traveled in 1750. "There's a big gap in the mountain range which the Indians use," Finley told Boone one day in 1768.

That was all Daniel Boone needed to hear.

Leaving a settlement called Castle's Woods—then the farthest western village in Virginia—Boone and Finley and four companions followed the Valley of Virginia almost into North Carolina before turning west, as Thomas Walker had eighteen years earlier. Describing the trip, Boone wrote:

> We found every where abundance of wild beasts of all sorts, through this vast forest. The buffaloes were more frequent than I had seen cattle in the settlements, browsing on the leaves of the cane, or cropping the herbage on those extensive plains, fearless, because ignorant, of the violence of man. Sometimes we saw hundreds in a drove, and the numbers about the salt springs were amazing.[3]

Hacking their way through dense underbrush, Boone's explorers followed a Shawnee trail to the Cumberland River and a nearby buffalo wallow known as Flat Lick, where Indians collected salt. Then, steadily climbing upward over rocky terrain, they at last gazed down through virgin pine forest to the rich land of Kentucky. It called forth Boone's purplest prose:

> Just at the close of day the gentle gales retired and left the place to the disposal of a profound calm. Not a breeze shook the most tremulous leaf. I had gained the summit of a commanding ridge, and, looking around with astonishing delight, beheld the ample plains, the beauteous tracts below. On the other hand I surveyed the famous Ohio River, that rolled in silent dignity, marking the western boundary of Kentucky with inconceivable grandeur. At a vast distance I beheld the mountains lift their venerable brows, and penetrate the clouds.[4]

The magic of cheap land now lured many to follow the Great Wagon Road as far south as Fort Chiswell, a palisade built by the colony of Virginia in 1768 to protect the western frontier and strategically important lead mines of John Chiswell. From this fort (near the later site of Wytheville, Virginia) the narrow horse path which led down the Valley of Virginia now became known as the Wilderness Road.

To extend the road through Cumberland Gap to the new settlement lands in Tennessee and Kentucky, Colonel Richard Henderson sought out Boone and contracted with him to do the work.

Henderson, a shrewd North Carolina lawyer, had studied the British treaties acquiring the Tennessee-Kentucky lands from the Indians, and he concluded that the Cherokees still legally owned valuable lands on the Ohio in Kentucky. Accordingly, Henderson formed the Transylvania Company and bought a 20,000,000-acre Kentucky tract from Cherokee chiefs for 10,000 pounds of serviceable goods. To cut a trail through Cumberland Gap to provide access to this area, which Henderson named Transylvania, Daniel Boone was offered 2,000 acres and each of his thirty workers a smaller tract.

Henderson's purchase immediately aroused rival Virginia investors in the Ohio and Loyal land companies. Thus, as the fearless Daniel was hacking his way into Kentucky and fighting off Shawnee attacks, Colonel William Preston of Draper's Meadows (later Blacksburg) was notifying Virginia's Governor Dunmore of the unexpected "invasion" of Virginia's Kentucky territory:

A great number of Hands [Preston wrote] are employed in cutting a Waggon Road through Mockeson & Cumberland Gaps to the Kentucky which they expect to compleat before planting time; & at least 500 people are preparing to go out this Spring, from Carolina besides great Numbers from Virga. to Settle there.[5]

Dunmore quickly protested Henderson's move, calling it illegal and terming his investors "disorderly persons." Even the dispassionate George Washington, who had invested in other frontier lands, conceded that "there is something in that affair which I neither understood, nor like, and I wish I may not have cause to dislike it worse as the mystery unfolds."

Boone completed the Cumberland Gap road in a surprisingly short time, thereby unleashing a rush of immigration through the Appalachians. One of the old frontiersman's road-builders paid this tribute to his leadership:

I must not neglect to give honor to whom honor is due. Col. Boone conducted the company under his care through the wilderness with great propriety, intrepidity, and courage, and was I to enter an exception to any part of his conduct, it would be on the ground that he appeared void of fear and its consequence—too little caution for the enterprise. But let me, with feeling recollection and lasting gratitude, ever remember the unremitting kindness, sympathy, and attention paid to me by Col. Boone in my distress. He was my father, my phisician, and friend: he attended me as his child, cured my wounds by the use of medicines from the woods, nursed me with paternal affection until I recovered, without the expectation of reward.[6]

Once through Cumberland Gap, Daniel Boone's company pushed northward to the Kentucky River and built a fort called Boonesborough. This was the beginning of what Henderson intended as a proprietary colony, like William Penn's Pennsylvania. Soon other settlements were planted at Harrodsburg, Boiling Spring, and Logan's Station, and Henderson organized a provisional Transylvanian government. However, the Virginia and North Carolina colonies in 1776 persuaded the first Continental Congress to refuse Transylvania's plea to be admitted as the fourteenth colony. Suddenly, Henderson's dream died overnight.

Instead, Virginia made Kentucky its huge westernmost county, placing the county seat in the little log town of Fincastle, not far from Ingles' Ferry on the Wagon Road.

Though the storm of Revolution was about to burst, the Wilderness Road immediately attracted pioneers as word spread of the new road into Kentucky through Cumberland Gap. Known also as Boone's Trail, the Kentucky Road, and the Virginia Road, it diverted westward many land-hunters coming down the Valley of Virginia. As one chronicler of the Wilderness Road wrote:

> Through the great trough between the Alleghany and Blue Ridge ranges passes the pioneer route to which we of the central West owe as much as to any thoroughfare in America—that rough, long, roundabout road which, coming down from Lancaster and York, crossed the Potomac at Watkin's Ferry and passed up the Shenandoah valley by Martinsburg, Winchester, and Staunton; and on to the headwaters of the New River, where it was joined by the thoroughfare [road] through central Virginia from Richmond. Here, near the meeting of these famous old-time Virginia thoroughfares, stood Fort Chiswell, erected in 1758 and situated 200 miles east of Cumberland Gap. Beyond Fort Chiswell ran the Indian trail toward the Gap and, within 50 miles of the Gap, stood Fort Watauga on a branch of the Holston.[7]

Once Boone had cut the Wilderness Road, enterprising merchants built fortified "stations" like Castle's Woods to sell ammunition, hardware, provisions, and overnight accommodations to pioneers. These stations were small palisades, each enclosing a blockhouse and outbuildings to protect against attack from Shawnees and Cherokees who resented the sale of their lands.

Many of the migrants went west in pursuit of land bounties granted by the colony of Virginia for military service in the French and Indian Wars. Lacking money to pay pensions, the Old Dominion was persuaded by George Washington to thus repay the militiamen who had fought with Braddock at Fort Duquesne or elsewhere on the frontier. Each veteran received from 50 to 3,000 acres, based on his rank and length of service.

Always alert to opportunity, many Scotch-Irish went west to the new territories. One was John Brown, the pioneer Presbyterian minister who had taught the first classical school in the Valley of Virginia near Lexington after 1749. To his father-in-law, the influential Colonel William Preston of Draper's Meadows, Brown wrote on May 5, 1775:

> What a buzzel is amongst people about Kentuck! To hear people speak of it one would think it was a new found paradise; and I

doubt not if it be such a place as represented but ministers will have thin congregations, but why need I fear that? Ministers are moveable goods as well as others and stand in need of good land as others do, for they are bad farmers.[8]

Among others who soon moved to Kentucky was Thomas Lincoln, who went out from Virginia, married Nancy Hanks, and fathered Abraham Lincoln. To the Tennessee wilderness went a young North Carolina couple whose son, Davy Crockett, was born in 1786 there. About the same time, James Knox Polk, aged 11, helped his parents build their humble cabin in the Duck River Valley in the Tennessee territory of North Carolina.

From Spotsylvania County, Virginia, a Baptist minister led his congregation over the Wilderness Road to Kentucky, singing hymns and praying hourly along the way.

Moving west over the Wagon and Wilderness roads from Pennsylvania in 1783 was John Filson, a young school teacher who glowingly described his travels in *The Discovery, Settlement, and Present State of Kentucky,* published in 1784. He measured the mileage from Philadelphia to Fort Nelson—later Louisville—at 826 miles. Among his stops he listed Botetourt Courthouse, Virginia, which became the town of Fincastle; and "Fort Chissel," as most travelers spelled Chiswell.

One of the Wilderness Road's earliest forts was Martin's Station, built by Captain Joseph Martin about 1774 near the eastern entrance to Cumberland Gap. Martin was appointed as Virginia's Indian agent in the region. His usefulness in promoting the Tennessee and Kentucky settlements is illustrated by a letter which Richard Henderson, the land speculator, wrote him in 1775 from Kentucky's chief settlement:

> Boonesborough
> 12th June 1775

Dear sir:

Mr. Ralph Williams, David Burney, and William Mellar will shortly apply to you for salt and other things which we left with you and was sent for us since we came away—Please to deliver to them, or those they may employ, what they ask for, and take a receipt—Also write me a few lines informing me, what you have sent &c by them and by whom—I long much to hear from you, pray write me at Large, how the matter goes with you in the valley, as well as what passes in Virginia—If the packhorsemen should want any thing which you see is necessary, please to let them have it on our acct.—All things goes well hitherto with us, I hope they do with you would have sent your Mares but am afraid they are not done horsing. They will be safely brought by my brother in a few weeks.

I am Dr. Sir your

Mr. Joseph Martin in the Valley   Hble Servt

Rich. Henderson.[9]

At the outbreak of the Revolution in 1776, settlers were again exposed to the murderous Indian attacks of the French and Indian Wars. The heaviest casualties were among settlers beyond the Appalachians. These included Daniel Boone's Kentuckians as well as the hardy few who had emigrated through the Holston, Watauga, and Clinch River valleys into eastern Tennessee.

Like Kentucky's pioneers, these Tennessee settlers had plunged westward without awaiting the protecting arm of government. Mistakenly assuming they were in Virginia—until a survey in 1780 proved otherwise—they followed the statutes of that colony. Chief among their leaders was John Sevier, who had come west with his brother from Virginia.

Against the Watauga settlements, Cherokee warriors made the first of a series of bloody attacks in July 1776, to drive the white men east of the Appalachians. It was a critical moment in the western migration of Americans. Years later, one historian wrote:

> The opening scene of the Revolutionary War in the West was the most important phase of the war in the history of Boone's Wilderness Road; for at the very outset the question was decided once for all whether or not that thin, long, priceless path to Kentucky through the Watauga settlement was to be held or lost. If it could not be held, there was no hope left for the brave men who had gone to found that western empire beyond the Cumberland mountains. . . .[10]

Embittered by the sale of their lands, the Cherokees were now persuaded by the British to join forces against the rebellious colonists. To assist the Indians, the British sent fifty packhorses loaded with ammunition to the Indians of the Carolina and Georgia uplands. "Kill the Long Knives!" was now the war cry.

To justify this warfare against The Great King Over the Water (as Britain's monarch was known to the Indians), the colonies' Indian agent read this parable to warriors assembled in the tribal villages of the Cherokees, Creeks, Choctaws, and Chickasaws:

> Suppose a father had a little son whom he loved and indulged while young, but growing up to be a youth, began to think of having some help from him; and making up a small pack, he bid him carry it for his father. The boy cheerfully takes this pack up, following his father with it. The father, finding the boy willing and obedient, continues in this way; and as the boy grows stronger, so the father makes the pack in proportion larger; yet as long as the boy is able to carry the pack, he does so without grumbling.
>
> At length, however, the boy, having arrived at manhood, while the father is making up the pack for him, in comes a person of an evil disposition, and, learning who was to be the carrier of the pack, advises the father to make it heavier, for surely the son is able to carry a larger pack. The father . . . makes up a heavy load for his son to carry. The son addresses the father:
>
> "Dear Father, this pack is too heavy for me to carry . . ."
>
> The father orders his son to take up his pack and carry it off or he will whip him.
>
> "So," says the son, "am I to be served thus for not doing what I am unable to do? . . . then I have no other choice left me but that of resisting your unreasonable demand and thus, by striking each other, learn who is the strongest."[11]

The survival of the trans-Appalachian settlements in the Revolution was due chiefly to George Rogers Clark's heroic campaign against the British and Indians in the Ohio and Mississippi valleys, beginning in 1776. Persuading Virginia's governor, Patrick Henry, that "If a Cuntrey was not worth protecting, it was not worth Claiming," Clark marched his 500 Virginia militiamen into Virginia's Northwest Territory. With four companies of frontiersmen which he had enlisted in the Holston River and Kentucky settlements, the fearless Clark captured British forts at Kaskaskia, Illinois, and Vincennes, Indiana, thus shattering British military power in the northwest.

To cap the victory, the Virginia frontiersmen captured Britain's Lieutenant Governor Henry Hamilton at Detroit. After returning him to Virginia via the Wilderness Road—a distance of 840 miles—they imprisoned him in the colony's jail at Williamsburg. "The Hair-Buyer" (so-called for the bounty he paid Indians for colonists' scalps) found the trip grueling. At one frontier station, His Excellency was "accosted by the females especially in pretty coarse terms." Of the Wilderness Road, he wrote:

> The difficulty of marching through such a country as this is not readily imagined by a European. The Canes grow very close together, to the height of 25 feet and from the thickness of a quill to that of one's waist. As they are very strong and supple, the rider must be constantly on the watch to guard his face from them, as they fly back with great force. The leaves and young shoots are a fodder horses are exceedingly fond of and are eternally turning to right and left to take a bite. The soil where they grow is rich and deep so you plod thro in a narrow track like a cowpath, while the musketoes are not idle.[12]

The revival of emigration over the Wagon and Wilderness roads came immediately after the Revolution. Writing from Mahanaim, a Dunkard colony near Fort Chiswell in 1782, William Christian urged better protection against Indians for the pioneers traversing Cumberland Gap:

> The Gap is near half way betwixt our settlement on Holston and Kentucky, and a post there would be a resting place for our poor citizens going back and forward, and would be a great means of saving the lives of hundreds of them. For it seldom happens that Indians will kill people near where they trade; & it is thereabouts the most of the mischief has been done . . . I view the change I propose as of great importance to the frontier of Washington [County], to our people journeying to & from Kentucky, particularly the poor families moving out . . ."[13]

During the Revolution and for several years after, travelers from the Wagon Road usually went to Kentucky and Tennessee in groups, armed with rifles. The scheduled departure of such companies was advertised so that prospective travelers might join up. A Kentucky newspaper carried this announcement of a group forming up at Crab Orchard, a Kentucky way station, to return to the Valley of Virginia:

> Notice
>
> Is hereby given, that a company will meet at the Crab Orchard, on Sunday the 4th of May, to go through the wilderness, and to set out on the 5th, at which time most of the Delegates to the state convention will go.[14]

[115]

Another read:

Notice

A large company will meet at the Crab-Orchard the 19th of November in order to start the next day through the Wilderness. As it is very dangerous on account of the Indians, it is hoped each person will go well armed.[15]

Indian attacks continued in Kentucky and Tennessee for several decades, usually by Shawnees but occasionally by renegade Cherokees. After one ambush near Cumberland Gap in the winter of 1787, an armed group of men formed and followed the Indians' footprints through heavy snow. Near dusk, they saw the marauders drying themselves around their campfire. When the frontiersmen charged, the surprised braves fled naked into the night. Most of them died of exposure in the bitter cold.

Boone's Wilderness Road remained an important offshoot of the Great Philadelphia Wagon Road for many years. By 1790, when the first United States Census was taken, nearly 70,000 people had climbed on foot or on horseback over that steep path. When Kentucky was admitted as the fifteenth state of the union in 1792, the stream of immigrants increased. Some came by keelboat down the Ohio River from Pittsburgh or Wheeling, but the majority took the safer overland route.

The fabled fertility of mid-Tennessee and mid-Kentucky drew countless farmers from the worn-out tobacco lands of the east. Whole villages of people pulled up stakes and went west. "The more pious companies as they traveled along," one writer observed, "would now and then give up in despair, sit down, raise a hymn, and have prayers said before they would go further."

Cumberland Gap continued to offer a challenge. "While yet some miles away," one traveler exclaimed, "it looms up, 1675 feet in elevation, some half-a-mile across from crest to crest, the pinnacle on the left towering to the height of 2,500 feet." After Kentucky became a state the footpath was improved and widened to accommodate wagons.

To do this work, Colonel John Logan and James Knox hired surveyors and road cutters at two shillings six pence daily. When the Kentucky Assembly decided to widen the remaining portion of the road to thirty feet, tough old Daniel Boone, now sixty-one, wrote Governor Isaac Shelby and asked to be placed in charge:

Feburey the 11th 1796

Sir

After my Best respts to your Excelancy and famyly I wish to
inform you that I have sum intention of undertaking this New Rode
that is to be Cut through the Wilderness and I think My Self in-
titeled to the ofer of the Bisness as I first Marked uot that Rode in
March 1775 and Never Re'd anything for my trubel and Sepose I
am No Statesman I am a Woodsman and think My Self as Capable
of Marking and Cutting the Rode as any other man. Sir if you think
with Me I would thank you to wright mee a Line by the post the
first oportuneaty and he Will Lodge it at Mr. John Miler son hinks-
ton fork as I wish to know Where and When it is to be Laat [let]
So that I may atend at the time.

I am Deer Sir your very omble sarvent.

[Daniel Boone][16]

The opening of Tennessee and Kentucky deflected much of the
former traffic of the Wagon Road for several decades, but the road
continued to grow in importance. Indeed, the great years of the
Deep South's settlement were yet to come. The ancient path which
led through the Carolinas to Georgia would continue to lead to
green lands and golden opportunity. The Great Philadelphia Wagon
Road would grow with the years.

CHAPTER 13

The Saga of Castle's Woods

The Wilderness Road was well named, for those who traveled its lonesome miles saw little evidence of civilization. The southwestern extremity of the Valley of Virginia, through which it ran, was a rugged land of cliff and forest, dotted only occasionally with a log hut.

One of the first settlers of this wilderness was Jacob Castle, who moved westward from Augusta County, Virginia, about 1746, and bought a small tract from the Indians on the Clinch River, paying for it with a butcher knife and rusty musket. He gave the area the name Castle's Woods. Insignificant as it was, it gained a minor repute as the westernmost settlement along the Wilderness Road to Kentucky. It later became the town of Saltville.

Jacob Castle was a roving hunter, living for months in the woods with no companionship save that of the Cherokees and Shawnees. From them he traded deerskins, which he bartered or sold to wagoners trading along the Great Road.

Leaving his cabin in the fall, Castle would disappear for months into the pine forests. Dressed in deerskin hunting shirt with buckskin moccasins and leggings, he might have been mistaken for an Indian but for the beaver cap he wore, its tail hanging down to the nape of his neck. In a sling over one shoulder he carried hatchet, knife, shot pouch, and such provisions as meal, salt, jerked beef, and pemmican. Over the other he slung his rifle, which was always with him.

This weapon was the familiar long-barreled rifle made by Germanic gunsmiths in eastern Pennsylvania, Maryland, and along the road. Known by its early makers as the *jaeger* or hunter's rifle, it became known in these times as the Pennsylvania rifle. Kentuckians were soon to call it their own.

In 1769—about twenty years after Jacob Castle settled in western Virginia—other pioneers cleared patches at Castle's Woods and moved in as squatters. So vast were the western landholdings of the Loyal Company that emigrants to this section simply set up housekeeping without the formality of buying or renting property. If it proved poor, they moved on; if fertile, they continued to squat until confronted by the owner and forced to buy.

Indian threats compelled Castle's Woods pioneers to live close together, though they had little in common. Some of its squatters came from nearby Virginia and North Carolina, while at least one group—William and John Cowan and their families—had emigrated from County Down, in Ireland.

To protect themselves, the settlers about 1770 built a protective wooden palisade, calling it Snoddy's Fort for William Snoddy, who was in command, in case of attack. Within the palisade stood a two-story wooden blockhouse, stoutly built and containing small gunports, in lieu of windows. From these second-story openings riflemen could fire down on Indians besieging the fort.

To warn the villagers of danger, the lookout fired a gun or rang the fort's bell. The frontiersmen soon learned that the chance of attack was greatest in summer and early fall, when the Indians roamed farthest from their mountain camps. The lazy September days of Indian summer were especially dangerous, especially if there were an autumnal haze over the hills to cloak the stealthy approach of the attackers.

By the time the newly formed frontier Virginia county of Botetourt had extended its operations to Castle's Woods in 1770, the area had attracted more than eighty families. The county's tithable list for the year 1772, which enumerated all white males over sixteen years for purposes of taxes and militia rolls, numbered sixty-three. Each tithable in that year paid twenty-five pounds of tobacco, valued at one penny per pound.

Several of Castle's Woods's settlers had fought for the Virginia colony in the French and Indian Wars and were therefore entitled to a land grant. Such grants were not at first recognized at Castle's Woods because the land was owned by the Loyal Land Company, but Virginia's Council in 1773 voted in Williamsburg to award veterans' grants wherever they chose, provided the land had not been previously cleared. (The veterans thanked George Washington for this measure, for he had argued their right to such reward.)

When new settlers arrived and increased the population, another protective palisade, Moore's Fort, was built a mile from Snoddy's Fort. One of the new men who helped build it was William Russell, who had come out from coastal Virginia. Russell was the son of an English immigrant to Culpeper County, Virginia, who had served as a militia colonel in the French and Indian Wars. His son, William, had attended the College of William and Mary a year, had fought against the French, and had then moved his wife, children, and several slaves to Castle's Woods in 1770.

"My hands are so sore at work about the fort," Russell recorded in 1774, "I can scarce write."

About twenty families were protected in Moore's Fort. To garrison it, the militia assigned twenty-five soldiers from 1774 until 1778, when the threat of Indian or British assault from the west was reduced by George Rogers Clark's conquest of British forts at Kaskaskia and Vincennes. Castle's Woods in these days was a typical frontier mixture of English, Scotch-Irish, and Germanic descendants, together with a few Negro slaves.

To provide for unified defense of southwestern Virginia and the growing Kentucky settlement, the Virginia colony in 1773 placed this vast territory in the new county of Fincastle. A county seat was established near Fort Chiswell and the Wagon Road, and William Russell of Castle's Woods was appointed one of fifteen justices of the peace to administer the vast territory.

Heightened importance was attached to this area by the colonies' urgent need in the Revolution for the lead produced by Colonel John Chiswell's mines, not far from Castle's Woods. In July 1775, the Virginia Assembly sternly directed the Fincastle Committee of Safety to contract with the mines for "such quantities of lead as may be judged necessary." Should the owner be uncooperative, the Committee was directed to operate the mines "at the charge of the colony."

Young William Russell had been attracted to the frontier by the prospect of riches, and he cast covetous eyes toward Kentucky. However, his effort brought him only grief.

Knowing Daniel Boone's familiarity with that region, Russell engaged Boone in October 1773 to lead a group of Castle's Woods settlers to Kentucky. Dividing into three detachments, they set forth. In the first went women, children, cattle, and baggage, while the second group contained the eldest sons of Russell and Boone with other settlers and slaves. Russell and several other men brought up the rear.

But Indians attacked the caravan the first night out. Russell's son Henry and Boone's son James were shot through the hips and stabbed repeatedly. Young Boone died in agony begging to be killed, after his tormenters pulled out his fingernails and toenails. Several other boys were killed instantly, together with one of Russell's two slaves.

After they buried their dead, the families met and decided to return to Castle's Woods. Boone, who had sold his farm on the Yadkin River before heading west, would have been homeless but for the loan of David Gass's cabin at Castle's Woods.

Russell had the attackers hunted down. Found to be two Shawnee chiefs, they were put to death.

When British Indian agents unleashed the wholesale fury of their Cherokee and Shawnee allies in 1774 against the Appalachian frontier, several of Castle's Woods families fled east toward safety. To meet this threat the Fincastle County militia was mobilized, and garrisons were strengthened at Fort Chiswell, Castle's Woods, and elsewhere along the thin line of settlement.

Daniel Boone and Michael Stoner, another Castle's Woods resident, were sent into Kentucky to warn that area of expected Indian attack. Not far behind them marched Colonel William Christian, commanding a company of Fincastle County's militia sent westward to attack the Shawnees in their Kentucky villages.

Crossing the Appalachians, Christian's troops joined those from Augusta and Botetourt counties under Colonel Andrew Lewis to defeat Chief Cornstalk and his naked Shawnee warriors in the battle of Point Pleasant. This triumph over the most militant of the Appalachian tribesmen opened up a large part of what later became West Virginia.

William Russell represented Castle's Woods on the Fincastle County Committee of Safety when it met in January 1775, and expressed the western frontier's growing hostility to British rule. Despite its "love" for King George III, it refused to submit "liberty or property to the power of a venal British Parliament, or to the will of a corrupt ministry." Its members pronounced themselves "deliberately determined never to surrender" their freedoms to any power on earth.

William Russell was sent by Fincastle County to Virginia's historic Constitutional Convention in Williamsburg in 1776, and he became one of the county's first ten representatives to the new House of Delegates.

The thin-spread militia units of the frontier were moved frequently, often leaving villages like Castle's Woods exposed to Indian attack. Such was the case in 1783, when seventeen Indians assailed one of its two forts. With their men gone off to war, the women and children were unprotected. Capturing Ann Bush Neece, who had survived an earlier scalping at Indian hands, they tomahawked and killed her. Attempting to breach the fort, they were fought off by the remaining women. With only two guns left to them, the women killed two Indians and dispersed the others.

When Captain William Russell returned home after the Revolution, his wife had died, and he soon married Elizabeth Henry Campbell, sister of Patrick Henry and widow of General William Campbell, who had commanded frontiersmen in their victory over the British at Kings Mountain, South Carolina. Elected again to the Virginia House of Delegates in 1785, he was honored by having the new county of Russell named for him.

Life at Castle's Woods reflected the easy-going morality of the frontier. In the first years after the Revolution, before the advent of Baptist and Methodist evangelists, householders commonly danced, played cards, and imbibed beer and whiskey without guilt. Sex morality was liberal, and bastardy was not uncommon. The names of Mary Culberson, Prudence Osbourn, and Abigail Beavers appear in early records as mothers of illegitimate children. Prudence Peppers had hers taken from her and placed with a family. Frances King was dismissed after trial for murdering her "base-born child." Other offenses were profanity, drinking on the Sabbath, "breaking open a letter," and selling "bad corn liquor."

Indians remained an occasional threat. In 1785, Castle's Woods was alarmed by the attack nearby on the family of Archibald Scott and his wife, Fannie Dickenson Scott. The tribesmen first killed Scott and the three youngest children, then stabbing the eldest child as she clung to her mother. They then abducted Fannie Scott and carried her northward. After eleven days, the wiry young woman eluded her captors and made her way through the Appalachian Mountains. After a month in the forest with no food except berries, leaves, and cane juice, she reached Castle's Woods and was slowly nursed back to health.

The usual fare of Castle's Woods cabins was "hog and hominy," the two staples of frontier diet. This was usually served with cornbread. Milk and mush were eaten for supper, and mush was sometimes accompanied by sweetened water, molasses, bear's oil, or gravy. Pork was preferred to venison and beef, and chicken was a delicacy usually reserved for "company."

Throughout the colonial years, the frontier men along the Appalachians usually wore deerskin hunting shirts, fringed with colored cloth, together with leggings and moccasins. In the nineteenth century, men began to adopt the European fashion of long trousers. Frontier women wore homemade cotton or wool dresses, topped by sunbonnets or poke bonnets.

Negro slaves were uncommon along the frontier, but a few farmers and artisans owned them. At Castle's Woods the Russells and Dickensons each had several. More commonly found were indentured white servants, who were bound by their guardians or impoverished parents to serve a master for a given period of time. Meanwhile they were to serve faithfully and "not commit fornication nor contract matrimony during the said term . . . play at cards, dice, or any unlawful game."

Castle's Woods adopted use of decimal currency in 1792, along with the rest of the United States. The Russell County Court prescribed the permissible prices which county taverns could charge: a warm dinner, twenty-five cents; breakfast, eighteen cents; a half pint of whiskey, nine cents; a quart of cider, nine cents; and overnight lodging "between clean sheets," nine cents.

Like most frontier towns, Castle's Woods, was strongly Protestant. Most of the earliest settlers were nominal Anglicans or Presbyterians, though no church served them for many years. Baptists were the most numerous and active denomination, building Brick Church in 1774 or 1775. The tradition long persisted in Castle's Woods that Daniel Boone had a hand in building it, but there is no evidence that Daniel was a church-going man.

Unlike nearby Abingdon, which became the county seat of neighboring Washington County in 1776, Castle's Woods did not attract many Scotch-Irish settlers. The largest denomination after 1788 was the Methodist, which had split off from the Anglican or Episcopal church four years earlier, after growing for fifty years as an Anglican reform movement. During the revival services conducted along the frontier by Bishop Francis Asbury and other circuit-riding spellbinders, many frontiersmen left other sects to join the Methodists.

("I left the navy of the Lord," explained one lapsed Baptist who heeded Asbury's appeal, "to join the army of the Lord.")

Part of Methodism's success on the Wilderness Road was the work of the Reverend John Tunnel. In Tunnel's congregation one Sunday in 1788 were Brigadier General and Mrs. William Russell, now approaching old age. At the end of the service, Mrs. Russell came forward to the pulpit and confessed to the evangelist that she was "the veriest sinner upon earth." After several hours of earnest prayer with Tunnel and her husband, Elizabeth Henry Russell was converted. The General soon followed.

Like many other Americans of their time, they left the Episcopal Church, which once had been powerful but which had suffered in the Revolution from its association with hated Toryism. The change was symptomatic of the rise of Calvinism and revivalism in post-Revolutionary America.

Methodism's acceptance in Castle's Woods did not come overnight. Indeed, Francis Asbury was dismayed when he held a service there at Charles Bickley's tavern in 1790 and drew seventy people. Deciding to try again the next day, Asbury and his fellow evangelist, Bishop Richard Whatcoat, were again chagrined at the small turnout. Whatcoat expressed amazement that people living in such danger of death from the Indians should have "no more religion than the savages."

But the great revivalism of the age was beginning to stir even the remote frontiersmen of Castle's Wood. When Francis Asbury made his next visit to the region, he found 200 people waiting to hear him preach at Russell County Courthouse. After the suffocating Presbyterianism of Abingdon, he gasped, he felt as if he were "escaping from a prison!"

On his final visit to Castle's Woods in 1801, the aging Methodist pioneer could begin to see the fruition of his many and arduous frontier trips. "I was amazed at the goodness of the Lord to this western country generally," Asbury wrote in his journal, "and was surprised and gratified to observe the improvements made in Russell County particularly."

Like many other villages along the Wagon and Wilderness roads, Castle's Woods suffered from the pioneers' mystic belief that a better opportunity somehow lay in wait for them a little further down the road. This naive optimism of the frontier was to continue to beckon the young, the hopeful, and the ambitious throughout the life of early America. The prospect of "a second chance" hung like a golden rainbow over the trail, pointing to riches beyond the far horizon.

As great as the lure of the frontier had been before the American Revolution, it became even greater after the Treaty of Paris was signed and peace returned in 1783. Then, with the territories of Tennessee, Kentucky, Ohio, and the Northwest to beckon them, Americans set out in unprecedented numbers for the lands beyond the Appalachians.

"All of the young men are going west," mourned one Virginian after the Revolution. It was true: Americans *were* going westward, as well as to new lands in the Northwest and the South, to the future homeland of Henry Clay, of Andrew Jackson, of Abraham Lincoln, and of other Americans to come. The West was the land at the end of the rainbow.

CHAPTER 14

Apostle of the Frontier

As the fever of independence spread along the frontier, religious emotionalism also seized its settlers. This was the Great Awakening, which the fervent preaching of Jonathan Edwards had first stirred in New England in the 1730s. George Whitefield, the great Methodist evangelist, had brought it to Pennsylvania and the southern colonies in 1739. In the next forty years it had been spread along the Great Wagon Road by Moravian evangelists and a sprinkling of Baptists and Presbyterians.

Steadily, as reaction against Great Britain and its dignified Anglican establishment deepened, the lurid evangelism of the new age spread. With dramatic shouts and gestures, "enthusiastic" preachers depicted the terrors of hell which awaited sinners. Like a forest fire, the Great Awakening spread southward through the colonies along the road from Philadelphia. To the unsophisticated frontier dwellers, its simple Calvinism preached the clear-cut doctrine of eternal life through faith.

The new religion spoke chiefly to the common man. No wonder, then, that its most powerful preachers were often farmers or artisans who heard the call to preach God's word—and responded without waiting to go to college or theological school. In the changing era of the Revolution, the circuit-riding Baptist or Methodist preacher became a familiar figure to the Appalachian back country. Dressed in black and carrying his Bible, and extra shirts in a saddlebag, he rode the upland trails, preaching to hastily assembled crowds in barns and shaded pine groves.

In this spiritual revival, a tough-minded Englishman named Francis Asbury became the best-known apostle to the upland farmers and traders of the frontier. Reared in the Church of England, the serious and introspective young man was influenced early by John and Charles Wesley, who led a reform movement called Methodism to inject evangelical Calvinism into the English establishment.

Young Asbury fell under the spell of Methodist eloquence when he heard a former baker, Alexander Mather, preach in a Staffordshire village in his native England.

[Asbury wrote], the word of God soon made deep impressions on my heart, which brought me to Jesus Christ, who graciously justified my guilty soul through faith in his precious blood, and soon showed me the excellency and necessity of holiness. About sixteen I experienced a marvellous display of the grace of God, which some might think was full of sanctification.[1]

After serving several years as a Methodist minister in England, Francis Asbury volunteered to go to America as a missionary. He sailed from England in 1771. In his journal he set down his reasons:

Sept. 12. I will set down a few things that lie on my mind. Whither am I going? To the New World. What do to? To gain honour? No, if I know my own heart. To get money? No; I am going to live to God, and to bring others so to do. In America there has been a work of God; some moving first among the Friends, but in time it declined; likewise by the Presbyterians, but among them also it declined. The people God owns in England are the Methodists. The doctrines they preach, and the discipline they enforce, are, I believe, the purest of any people now in the world. The Lord has greatly blessed these doctrines and this discipline in the three kingdoms; they must therefore be pleasing to him. If God does not acknowledge me in America, I will soon return to England. I know my views are upright now; may they never be otherwise![2]

John Wesley soon placed Asbury in command of all Methodist activities in America, and the evangelist set out on a tour of the colonies. In the ranks of Methodist converts he was pleased to have reformed "swearers, liars, cock-fighters, card-players, horse-racers, drunkards, etc." He exulted: "The Lord has done great things for these people." By 1776, the ranks of Methodists equaled those of the Roman Catholics, Moravians, and Lutherans. However, they remained far smaller than those of the Church of England, Presbyterian, or Baptist churches.

In 1780, Asbury rode south over the Wagon Road to preach to Methodists in Maryland, Virginia, and the Carolinas. "I dwell as among briers, thorns, and scorpions," he wrote after preaching along the Haw River, in North Carolina.

The people are poor, and cruel one to another; some families are ready to starve for want of bread, while others have corn and rye distilled into poisonous whisky, and a Baptist preacher has been guilty of the same; but it is no wonder that those who have no compassion for the non-elect souls of people should have none for their bodies. These are poor Christians.[3]

The hardships of the Wagon Road caused Asbury much suffering. Sometimes he did not have enough to eat, and often he slept out-of-doors. At the Tar River, in North Carolina, his legs became so swollen he could not mount his horse. But two members of his flock lifted him into his saddle and tied him so that he could ride on to the next settlement.

In South Carolina, Asbury in 1780 found the colony overrun with the English troops of General Cornwallis, who had undertaken to quell the Revolution in the southern colonies. Once he unknowingly rode between British and American troops who were firing at each other from the woods adjoining the sides of the Wagon Road. One bullet pierced his hat, but he was unharmed.

Opposition to slavery was a Methodist principle, but Asbury and his Methodists made little headway against it. In South Carolina he wrote:

> My spirit was much grieved at the conduct of some Methodists who hire out slaves to the highest bidder, to cut, skin, and starve them; I think such members ought to be dealt with; on the side of the oppressors there are law and power, but where are justice and mercy to the poor slaves: What eye will pity, what hand will help, or ear listen to their distresses? I will try, if words can be drawn swords, to pierce the hearts of the owners."[4]

After Great Britain had recognized American independence in 1783 and American Methodists had broken away from John Wesley's control and organized the Methodist Episcopal Church at Baltimore in 1784, Asbury was named its first bishop. To his rivals, who accused him of a thirst for power, he answered:

> I pity those who cannot distinguish between a pope of Rome and an old worn man of sixty years who had the power given him of riding five thousand miles a year, at a salary of eighty dollars, through summer's heat and winter's cold; travelling in all weather, preaching in all places; his best covering from rain often but a blanket; the surest sharpener of his wits hunger, from fasts voluntary and involuntary; his best fare for six months of the twelve coarse kindness; and his reward from too many suspicion, envy, and murmurings all around.[5]

Asbury made another tour of the Wagon Road in 1788, as a part of a 6,000-mile trip through his circuits. On that journey he met with Methodist ministers and laymen in New York, Philadelphia, Uniontown in Pennsylvania, Baltimore, Virginia, North Carolina, South Carolina, and Georgia.

In Georgia he was anxious to observe the results of mission work which George Whitefield had begun fifty years earlier. At the forks of the Broad River, near the Wagon Road, he held his first Georgia conference with that colony's six itinerant ministers and four "probationers."

Returning northward along the Wagon Road, he obtained a packhorse and in April 1788 crossed the Alleghanies into the Tennessee territory. To cross the Watauga River, he swam his horses. He spent one night in a hunter's cabin in the Alleghanies, huddled in his greatcoat for lack of dry wood for a fire. After crossing the Holston River, he reached the home of General and Mrs. William Russell at the later site of Saltville in southwest Virginia. There Asbury held a conference of Kentucky and Tennessee preachers.

For want of settled churches and schools, the lonely pioneer families were especially receptive to Methodism and its message. Although nearly all frontier settlers had come from Christian families in Europe or along the Atlantic Coast, they had little time for organized worship in their first years on the rough and remote frontier. Early travelers spoke of "Godless" frontiersmen, of raffish morality. Many settlers were said to be fugitives from the lowland counties or escaped Negro slaves. Some were part Indian. Asbury thought that the materialism of land claimants was his chief obstacle. He wrote:

> I am of the opinion that it is as hard or harder for the people of the West to gain religion as any other. When I consider where they came from, where they are, and how they are, and how they are called on to go farther, their being unsettled with so many objects to take their attention, with the health and good air they enjoy, and when I reflect that not one in a hundred came here to get religion; but rather to get plenty of good land, I think it will be well if some or many do not eventually lose their souls.[6]

Francis Asbury and his fellow itinerants stirred up their hearers to a fever pitch of religious enthusiasm which rocked the Christian world. Stimulated by the preacher's vision of hellfire, congregations listened wide-eyed and fearful. The earnest bishop pleaded with them to repent and join the forces of the Lord. His rhythmic eloquence, coupled with his exhortations to heaven in his theatrical voice—now quavering, now pleading, now shouting the grisly terrors of Judgment Day—had an electric effect. One by one, his listeners began to jerk, to bark, to rise from their campstools with cries of "Hallelujah!" and "Amen." Some writhed in the aisle, falling even into cataleptic trances.

Wrote the Reverend Peter Cartwright, a frontier Methodist circuit-rider, of a service near Cumberland Gap in the Kentucky territory:

> There was a very great work of religion in the encampment. The jerks were very prevalent. There was a company of drunken rowdies who came to interrupt the meeting. These rowdies were headed by a very large drinking man. They came with their bottles of whisky in their pockets. This large man cursed the jerks, and all religion. Shortly afterwards he took the jerks and he started to run, but he jerked so powerfully he could not get away. He halted among some saplings, and although he was so violently agitated, he took out his bottle of whisky and swore he would drink the damned jerks to death, but jerked at such a rate that he could not get the bottle to his mouth, although he tried hard. At length he fetched a sudden jerk, and the bottle struck a sapling and was broken to pieces and spilled his whisky on the ground. There was a great crowd gathered round him, and when he lost his whisky he became very much enraged, and cursed and swore profanely, his jerks still increasing. At length he fetched a very violent jerk, snapped his neck, fell, and soon expired, with his mouth full of cursing and bitterness . . . I always looked upon the jerks as a judgment of God.[7]

Cartwright wrote that he had seen more than 500 people jerking at one Methodist meeting. At a camp meeting in Kentucky, the Reverend Lorenzo Dow said that a hundred men and women at one time could be seen clinging to the saplings in the grove and "jerking violently." Most ministers encouraged such demonstrations, some believing that the more violent they were, the more blessed they were. However, others realized that sexual relations between excited penitents often resulted from such services.

Rhythmic jerking often gave way to barking. Frenzied converts made noises like dogs. A Kentucky minister wrote that:

It was common to hear people barking like a flock of spaniels on their way to meeting. There they would start up suddenly in a fit of barking, rush out, roam around, and in a short time come foaming back. Down on all fours they sometimes went, growling, snapping their teeth, and barking just like dogs.[8]

A camp meeting in Bourbon County, Kentucky, lasted six days without intermission and was addressed by seventeen Methodist and Presbyterian preachers. It was estimated that 3,000 people lay unconscious at one time during the service. Nearly 500 were said to have barked and jerked rhythmically together. This was indeed the highwater mark of frontier revivalism.

Part of the Methodists' appeal lay in their hymns, whose simple melodies and lyrics were later adopted by nearly all denominations. Next to Moravians and Lutherans, Methodists were the most musical of the sects in eighteenth-century America. At camp meetings along the frontier, hundreds of voices would unite to sing:

> Alas! and did my Savior bleed,
> And did my Sovereign die?
> Would He devote that massacred head
> For such a worm as I?[9]

Even when he grew old and infirm, Francis Ashbury continued to ride the roads of the Appalachians, bringing the Methodists' gospel. "I seldom mount my horse for a ride of less distance than twenty miles on ordinary occasions," he once wrote, "and frequently have forty or fifty, in moving from one circuit to another. In travelling thus I suffer much from hunger and cold." As he grew older, his journals of his travels were filled with accounts of his ailments. "Oh, my jaws and teeth!" he once wrote. "Oh, the rocks, hills, ruts, and stumps! My bones, my bones!" On another occasion he explained, "I could only speak sitting ... I took a pew near the pulpit and preached from there."

But the old man persisted. "My horse trots stiff," he wrote, "and no wonder, when I have ridden him upon an average of five thousand miles a year for five years successively!" In four months he covered 2,575 miles.

Although his ministry was characterized by an unhealthy emotionalism, Bishop Asbury and his fellow circuit-riders brought Christianity to the frontier at a time when it was needed. Above all, the circuit-riders' selflessness was a needed counterweight to the land-hungry materialism of frontier America. As his biographer, Herbert Asbury, wrote of him:

> He had no place he could call home, but carried his belongings, always pitifully small, in his saddle-bags, and slept where night found him. He became the best-known man in the whole of the United States, and for almost half a century his gaunt figure, encased in black or gray homespun and surmounted by a low-crowned beaver hat, was a familiar sight along the country roads from Maine to the southern border of Georgia, and from the sea to the territory beyond the Alleghenies. As he rode, he sang hymns at the top of his voice, or prayed aloud for the salvation of the Methodists; again he was silent as he peered, from deep-set eyes that burned beneath bushy brows from a lined and weather-beaten face, into a book, for it was on horseback that he did most of his reading . . .[10]

Such was the gospeler of the frontier. From the admixture of nationalities and faiths along the Great Wagon Road, a peculiarly American faith was beginning to emerge.

Indian attacks were frequent along the Wagon Road as it wound through western Virginia and the Carolinas. Settlers often travelled in groups for protection.

The early limestone Abram's Delight is typical of the stout houses built at Winchester and elsewhere along the Wagon Road by 18th century Germanics.

George Washington's militia headquarters in his 1750s campaigns against French and Indians in the Ohio Valley are preserved at Winchester along the Wagon Road.

Colonial Williamsburg

Some Wagon Road settlers travelled in covered wagons built at Conestoga, Pennsylvania.

Virginia Division of Tourism

The Wagon Road in mid-Virginia neared Natural Bridge, an arch over a stream. Rockbridge County was created in 1778, settled largely by Scotch-Irish immigrants.

American Road Builder

Frontiersman Daniel Boone cut a wagon trail through Cumberland Gap from western Virginia into the Kentucky Territory. It became the Wilderness Roads

Virginia Division of Tourism

From Pinnacle Overlook at Cumberland Gap National Park are visible Virginia, Kentucky, and Tennessee. The Gap is part of the Wilderness Road.

Ohio River

Fort Nelson
[Louisville]

Lexington

Boonesborough

Harrodsburg

Danville

Cumberland Gap

MOUNTAINS

ALLEGHENY MOUNTAINS

Staw

Lexin

Fincastle

Big

Christiansburg

Wytheville

Abingdon

Roc

To Nashville

CUMBERLAND

Knoxville

THE WILDERNESS ROAD

RIDGE

Bethania

Bethabara

Salem

BLUE

Salisbury

NORTH

Charlotte

Rock Hill

Chester

Newberry

Camden

SOUTH CAROLI

Augusta

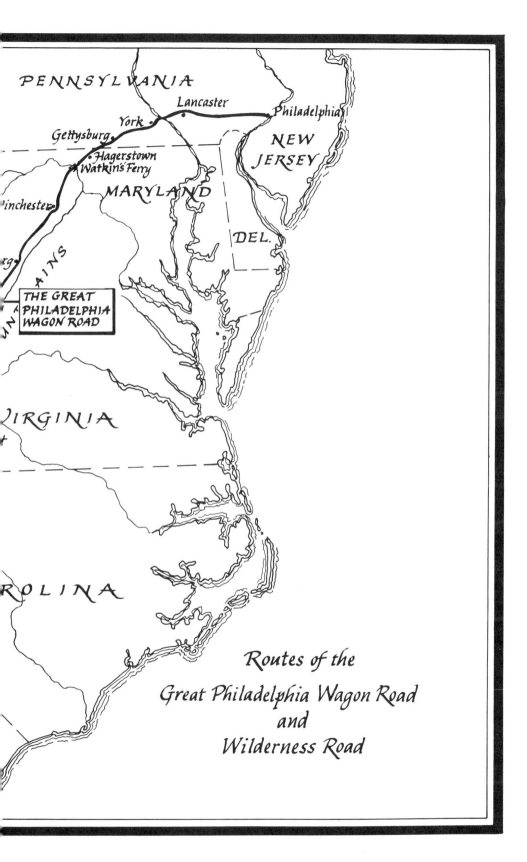

Routes of the
Great Philadelphia Wagon Road
and
Wilderness Road

Countless gristmills arose along up-country streams in the 18th century, like this Virginia water-turned mill which converted corn into meal and wheat into flour.

Virginia Department of Agriculture

18th century Wagon Road settlers often raced their horses at county court days. Owners of stallions advertised their services occasionally in colonial newspapers.

In 19th century Maryland and Virginia farmers sent produce downriver by the Potomac and James river canals. Here the James canal approaches Lynchburg amid Piedmont foothills.

Fearnought,

WHO is now perfectly recovered, and in high spirits, will cover the ensuing season at NEW-MARKET, at EIGHT POUNDS a mare. The money to be paid before the mares are taken away.

I   JOHN BAYLOR.

Newmarket, April 20, 1767.

Advertisement from The Virginia Gazette

Edward Beyer lithograph

Travelers of the Wagon Road at first forded rivers but later crossed some by ferries poled by ferrymen or pulled by cable. The ferryman often ran an inn.

American Road Builder   National Park Service

At Harper's Ferry on the upper Potomac River, many Wagon Road travellers came southward. A 19th century town grew up along the narrow river gorge.

American Road Builder

A stagecoach halts at a Lancaster, Pennsylvania, tavern in this 1795 depiction of the Great Wagon Road. In the distance a Conestoga wagon heads southward.

Barns and fences built by early Wagon Road settlers are reproduced at the Museum of American Frontier Culture, built along the route at Staunton, Virginia.

Museum of American Frontier Culture

Germanic settlers after 1700 travelled the Wagon Road and claimed fertile valley lands for farms, while Scotch-Irish newcomers usually preferred hilly uplands.

North Carolina Department of Commerce

BOOK FOUR

A Frontier in Danger

1776-1789

CHAPTER 15

Andrew Jackson
of the Waxhaws

The triumph of the Americans in the Revolution set off a noisy rush of settlement beyond the Appalachians. Though the ownership of Ohio and Mississippi Valley lands was to be argued for many years between Great Britain and the United States, this did not deter Revolutionary veterans from claiming bounty acreage there. The rise of the frontier—the major fact of nineteenth-century America—had begun.

Among the pioneers who traveled westward were hundreds of men who would guide the destinies of the states. Many of these left the Wagon Road area. "All the young men are going west," lamented a Virginian, and it was almost true. From that sprawling commonwealth alone, 329 men who emigrated to other states rose to national political prominence in the 150 years beginning with the Revolution. To Kentucky went Henry Clay. To Tennessee went John Sevier and Sam Houston, later to move on to Texas. Hundreds of others held major offices, from congressmen up to president. Thus the old states became seedbeds for the new.

Easily the most dashing figure in this exodus was a rawboned North Carolinian who moved from the Great Wagon Road into Tennessee and became the seventh president of the United States. He was Andrew Jackson.

Old soldiers in the back country recognized Jackson as the spittin' image of themselves: a shrewd, tough, strong-willed, self-made man of endless endurance. He was at heart a fighter, though he acquired the amiable ways of a country lawyer. Like many of that first wave of pioneers, the Jacksons were Presbyterians, coming from Carrickfergus in north Ireland to Pennsylvania in 1765. Here was the hardiness of Daniel Boone plus a military and political astuteness which Americans admired.

After a brief stop in the Scotch-Irish settlement along Conowingo Creek in Lancaster County, the elder Andrew Jackson and his wife, Elizabeth Hutchinson, started south over the Wagon Road with their two small sons. Their goal was the Waxhaw settlements in

North Carolina, where four of Betty Jackson's sisters lived on small farms with their husbands and children, a few miles below the future site of Charlotte and along the South Carolina line.

To ex-tenant farmers like the Jacksons, the area seemed to promise good crops. It was known locally as "The Garden of the Waxhaws," while a Moravian diarist called it "Cow Heaven." Though close to the Catawba Indians, no trouble was expected from this small and vanquished tribe. From their reservation along the Catawba River, this section of the road had acquired its name—the Catawba Path.

To reach Waxhaw, the Jacksons had to come south through the Valley of Virginia before fording the Yadkin River and resting their horses close to the log courthouse at Salisbury. Then they pushed on over the post road which could be followed eastward to Camden and to Charles Town, whose 12,000 people made it the metropolis of the southern colonies.

In the Waxhaw region, Andrew Jackson settled his family on land near the farms of his wife's kinsmen, the Crawfords, McKemeys, and Lessleys, about four miles from the Wagon Road. Despite the region's good repute, however, the red soil of the Jacksons' farm proved thin, bearing little more at first than a stand of scrub pine. Furthermore, a man named Thomas Ewing was already occupying the property. Nevertheless, Jackson and Ewing made a deal by which the new emigrant would occupy the 200 acres as if it were his own, eventually acquiring title to it.

In 1767—two years after the Jackson family arrived in Carolina—young Andrew Jackson was born, just after the death of his father. Left with three small sons and no money, Elizabeth Jackson moved into the home of relatives. Young Andrew, the brightest of the three boys, was sent to a school conducted at Waxhaw Church by William Humphries. At five he could read, and at eight he wrote "a neat, legible hand" and could understand maps. His mother, described by a woman who knew her as "very conversive" and industrious ("She spun flax beautiful. She spun us heddie-yard for weaving and the best and finest I ever saw"), wanted Andrew to become a minister.

Many years later, ex-President Andrew Jackson recalled long winter evenings before the hearth, when his mother told him and his brothers of "the sufferings of their grandfather at the siege of

Carrickargus [Carrickfergus] & the oppression by the nobility of Ireland over the labouring poor."

One of the diversions of life along the Great Road was the occasional passing of the post-rider, bearing a copy of the Pennsylvania or Virginia or South Carolina *Gazette*. Then neighbors would gather at the house of Andrew's prosperous uncle, Robert Crawford, to hear the news read aloud, column by column. Nine-year-old Andy was "selected as often as any grown man in the settlement," he later wrote, to read the week's news. Though his voice was high, he "could read a paper clear through without getting hoarse ... [or] stopping to spell out the words."

At twelve years, Andrew had grown into a tall, blue-eyed boy with a shock of reddish hair which seemed always to stand on end. He had a quick temper, too, and was frequently involved in schoolyard fights. A schoolmate, George McWhorter, who was larger than Andy, said the young redhead "would never give up, although he was always beaten" because McWhorter was the stronger of the two. Another added: "I could throw him three times out of four, but he would never *stay throwed*. He was dead game, and never would give up."

The young man took readily to the frontier sports: wrestling, horse racing, logrolling, cockfighting. When he was twelve he wrote "A Memorandum, How to feed a Cock before you him fight Take and give him some Pickle Beaf Cut fine ..." Andy was hardly preacher-material.

When Charles Town fell to the British in 1780—thereafter to be known as Charleston—its Patriot defenders who survived retreated to the back country. Andrew's uncle, now Major Crawford, returned to his home on promise that he not rejoin the Patriot forces. Once back at Waxhaw, however, Crawford re-formed his militiamen and returned to service.

On May 29, 1780, Colonel Banastre Tarleton's British cavalrymen reached Waxhaw and caught up with a retreating Virginia regiment commanded by Colonel Abraham Buford. Buford's force was nearly obliterated. Dozens of wounded men were brought into Waxhaw Church, where Andy and Robert Jackson helped their mother stanch their blood on an improvised straw floor. Some months later they witnessed General Horatio Gates' retreat up the road towards Charlotte after Cornwallis' victory at Camden.

[139]

When Cornwallis moved into Waxhaw country, its Patriot sympathizers followed Gates. A Mecklenburg County woman one day in September 1780 saw a tired-looking boy coming up the road on an underfed pony. Seeking news of her soldier family, she asked where he came from.

"From below."

"And where are you going?" she persisted.

"Above."

Slowly she elicited the information from the close-mouthed youth that he was Andrew Jackson, that Horatio Gates's army had reputedly been virtually wiped out at Camden. When Andrew and his mother and surviving brother reached Charlotte, they found it apparently deserted. On closer approach, however, they saw North Carolina militiamen hidden behind garden walls, waiting to delay Cornwallis' northern advance. Thus the Charlotte hornets protected their nest.

After the Mountain Men's victory at Kings Mountain and Daniel Morgan's at the Cowpens, the Jacksons and other evacuees cautiously returned to Waxhaw. Andrew and Robert Jackson rejoined the ranks of Uncle Robert Crawford's mounted militia. They were among forty local militiamen assembled at Waxhaw Church on April 9, 1781, when a company of British dragoons attacked with sabers drawn. Eleven of the forty were captured and the church set in flames.

Andy Jackson, now fourteen, mounted his horse and fled with his cousin, Lieutenant Thomas Crawford, pursued by a dragoon. Jackson escaped but Crawford's horse was overtaken and Crawford captured. Andy found his brother, and the two boys lay in hiding overnight. Detected by a Loyalist informer, the boys were overtaken at breakfast and Andrew directed to clean the officer's boots.

The fourteen-year-old refused. He said he expected the treatment properly given a war prisoner. The officer lifted his sword and smote Andy's left hand and forehead, gashing both.

Ordered next to lead the British to the house of a Patriot sympathizer named Thompson, Jackson did so by a circuitous route which permitted Thompson to escape unseen. For this the youth was forced by the British to march forty miles without food or drink to Camden, there to be confined to prison with his brother and other militiamen on bread and water. When smallpox swept the prison stockade, Brigadier General Lord Rawdon, the British commander, acceded to Elizabeth Jackson's request that her sons be included in an exchange of prisoners.

Robert Jackson died and Andrew bade his mother good-bye for the last time when she set out for Charleston to nurse American soldiers imprisoned by the British there. "Wiping her eyes with her apron," Andrew Jackson wrote later, his mother gave some parting advice.

"Make friends by being honest, keep them by being steadfast," she said. "Andy . . . never tell a lie, nor take what is not your own, nor sue . . . for slander . . . *Settle them cases yourself*"[1]

A few months later she was buried with other victims of prison fever in an unrecorded grave at Charles Town Neck, not far from the floating British military prison. Along with the news of her death, Andrew received his mother's last few effects. "I felt utterly alone," he declared.

When the Revolution ended, Andrew Jackson was bereft of family and most property, except his father's 200 acres. But suddenly it looked as though his fortune might change, for his grandfather Hugh Jackson, a weaver and merchant, died in Ireland and left Andy a legacy of £400. Setting out from Waxhaw in March 1783, Andrew Jackson rode to Charleston (as the General Assembly now decreed it be spelled) and collected the money at the Quarter House Tavern.

Should he return to rustic Waxhaw or enjoy the horse racing of the spring season at Charleston? Andy showed his Celtic high spirits: he stayed and bet on the races. Being a fancier of horses, a keen sportsman, and a born gambler, his legacy dissolved amid the pleasures of South Carolina's capital. He soon lacked money to pay his landlord. On his last night in Charleston he wagered his horse in a game of "Rattle and Snap" and won.

Next day he paid his landlord and left for the Waxhaw settlements with "new spirits infused into me."

Back through the Pine Barrens of North Carolina he followed the Great Road, there to attend school briefly at Charlotte and then to teach. In his mind, plans had begun to take shape: the west needed lawyers of practical mind and strong body, and he had both. During Christmas at the Rowan House at Salisbury, young Andrew persuaded Spruce Macay to let him read law in his office.

Meanwhile, he continued to enjoy the pleasures he had known in Charleston. "Andrew Jackson was the most roaring, rollicking, game-cocking, horse-racing, card-playing, mischievous fellow, that ever lived in Salisbury," one inhabitant said of him. "The head of the rowdies hereabouts . . . more in the stable than the office."

A slave woman who worked at Hughes' Hotel when young Jackson boarded there never saw him studying his law books. "All I ever saw him do," Mama Judie later recalled, "was clean his pistols, fight cocks, and chase yellow women."

Like other early Wagon Road towns of the Appalachian frontier, Salisbury after the Revolution enjoyed prosperity and a new urbanity. Though Andrew Jackson was whispered to have lived a riotous life of liquor, cards, and mulatto mistresses, such stories, if true, did him no great hurt on the frontier. "We all knew that he was wild . . . that he gambled some and was by no means a Christian young man," wrote the half-enamored Nancy Jarret. Nevertheless, "there was something about him I cannot describe except to say that it was *a presence . . .*"

At the elaborate Christmas ball his second year in Salisbury, Andrew Jackson was manager. Suddenly the party stopped when Molly and Rachel Wood, the only white prostitutes in town, presented their cards of invitation at the door. Young Andrew stepped up and apologized to them. Oh, yes . . . he had sent them invitations as "a piece of fun." Out they went. The dance went on.

Soon after his brutal practical joke, Andrew Jackson shifted his apprenticeship in the law to the office of Colonel John Stokes. Admitted to the bar, he began to follow the trial circuit with the county judges of upland North Carolina: Salisbury, Charlotte, Wadesboro, Martinsville, and other stops.

But all the young men were now going west. Like Virginia, North Carolina claimed lands westward to the Mississippi. Much of it was unexplored, but the area of settlement already reached well past the Appalachians. Through the Wilderness Road and other mountain passes, settlers were daily going out to profit from the river-bottom lands of the Western District.

When the North Carolina General Assembly in 1787 chose Jackson's friend, John McNairy, to become first judge of the Superior Court of the newly formed Western District of North Carolina, the two young men agreed that Jackson should go along and accept

McNairy's appointment as public prosecutor. To reach the area, they would have to ride far to the west of the Great Wagon Road, through the pine forests of the Great Smokies. And this would take them into the armed domain of "Nolichucky Jack" Sevier, so called for his career along Tennessee's Nolichucky River.

Sevier, twenty-two years older than Jackson, was the strong man of the Tennessee territory in these years. Tall and magnetic, like Jackson, he was already a legend for his strength and skill as an Indian fighter and a politician. He had led settlers in forming the State of Franklin in 1784, after North Carolina had ceded its western lands to the United States—an act which North Carolina awkwardly rescinded seven months later. Back east on the Wagon Road, it was said that Nolichucky Jack's Franklinians would rudely turn back any North Carolinians headed for the Western District.

Even so, Jackson and John McNairy saddled up and headed west over the pack trail. Andrew rode a fine horse and led another, followed by his foxhounds. By the time Jackson arrived at Morganton, he found that the state of Franklin had collapsed and Sevier was feuding with his erstwhile allies. When the North Carolina militia in 1788 opened up the first wagon road from east Tennessee to the infant town of Nashville, Andrew Jackson joined the first wagon train to pass over it. A guard of sixteen soldiers gave protection against Indian attack.

By the time North Carolina in 1790 finally ceded her western country to the United States, Jackson was well established as a lawyer and land speculator. Besides these sources of riches, he had set up a country store near his Hermitage plantation and was profitably exchanging goods from Philadelphia for furs and cotton.

The French botanist François André Michaux was impressed with the commerce of Andrew Jackson's Tennessee when he came through it collecting material for his study of American trees, *The North American Sylva.* "The tradespeople get their provisions by land from Philadelphia, Baltimore, and Richmond in Virginia," he wrote, "and they send in return, by the same way, the produce of the country, which they buy of the cultivators, or take to barter for their goods . . ."

When Tennessee was admitted to the Union in 1796, Andrew Jackson was a member of its constitutional convention. His rise to the Presidency in 1829 was rapid.

The admission of Kentucky in 1792 and Tennessee four years later moved the American frontier westward to the Mississippi River. No longer was the Great Wagon Road a "western" thoroughfare. Still, it continued to pour an undiminished stream of adventurers into the hills and hollows beyond the mountains.

CHAPTER 16

The Exodus of the Quakers

The American Revolution brought new agonies along the Wagon Road, which had so recently been menaced by the French and Indians. County militiamen were called back into action, and tensions arose between Britain's apologists and those who favored a war for American independence.

One of the somber effects of the conflict was the dispersion of a group of prominent Philadelphia Quakers, whose pacifism and whose trade with the Mother County made them increasingly suspect. Ardent revolutionists were convinced that many of these peace-loving burghers were King's men, or Tories. As a result, a number of leading Quaker merchants and traders were forced southward from Philadelphia to Winchester in 1777.

Their experience illustrated the plight of many sectarians—Mennonites, Amishmen, Sabbatarians, and others—whose scruples against bearing arms resulted in their harassment or conscription during America's fight for freedom.

Members of the Society of Friends from Great Britain had been the first settlers of Pennsylvania when it was founded in 1682 by William Penn, himself a leading Quaker. In England, these adherents of George Fox had been severely persecuted for opposing the Church of England and its priesthood. Claiming that no minister and no outward rite were needed to establish communion between the soul and its God, Fox taught that everyone could receive understanding and guidance toward divine truth from the "Inward Light" supplied in his heart by the Holy Spirit.

William Penn's decision to accept land in America in lieu of money which the Crown owed to his father's estate provided a welcome haven of religious freedom for the Quakers in America. Large numbers of industrious middle-class English artisans thereupon crossed the Atlantic to settle along the Schuylkill and the Susquehanna. The colony's utopian appeal to religious minorities in the British Isles, in Germany, and in Switzerland had increased the population of Penn's colony by the time of the American Revolution to a level exceeded only by Virginia.

Among Pennsylvania's settlers, the Quakers were for many years the wealthiest and most powerful. When Germanic and Scotch-Irish settlers began to pour into Philadelphia after 1730, they found the Quakers in possession of the best lands and the highest political offices. Along Philadelphia's Front and Market streets, a coterie of Quaker merchants dominated the colony's trade.

Being pacifists, the Quakers refused to take up arms when the Pennsylvanians revolted in 1776, just as they had refused earlier to war against the Indians. These conscientious scruples naturally turned many Pennsylvania patriots against them.

Hostility was provoked especially in December 1776, when a paper bearing the signature of John Pemberton, a prominent Quaker, was circulated in Philadelphia. It was addressed "To our friends and brethren in religious profession in these and the adjacent provinces," in behalf of the Meeting of Sufferings held in Philadelphia in that month.

Reading this pacifist statement, delegates to the Continental Congress who were then meeting in Philadelphia passed a resolution recommending to the Pennsylvania government that it "apprehend and secure" Pemberton and others who signed the petition. Fearing disloyalty in its midst, the Congress ordered that the colonies should immediately disarm and imprison all citizens "notoriously disaffected" against the Revolutionary cause.

In the ensuing arrests, seventeen Quaker merchants and businessmen were taken into custody and confined temporarily to the Masons' Lodge in Philadelphia.

To remove the suspects from the center of Revolutionary planning, Pennsylvania's Executive Council decided to send them under guard to a region remote from the war, where they could be watched. It was finally decided to dispatch them down the Wagon Road to Staunton or Winchester, which were chosen internment sites for war prisoners because of their remoteness from the embattled coast.

Shocked and aggrieved, the suspected Tories demanded a hearing by the Continental Congress, but that hard-pressed body declined on account of the pressure of other business. On September 8, 1777, it ordered the Quakers moved immediately to Staunton unless they would swear allegiance to Pennsylvania in the war with Great Britain.

The Congress' concern was justified, for the British under General Sir William Howe were hourly advancing on Philadelphia. After their victory over Washington's forces at Brandywine on September 11, Philadelphia itself was threatened, and the Congress was forced to move hastily to York, where it met in the York County Courthouse for the next year, while the British occupied Philadelphia—"the capital of the rebellion."

Six Light Horse guards under Colonel Jacob Morgan of Bucks County were assigned to move the suspects down the Wagon Road to Virginia. To add to the Quakers' sense of injury, they were ordered to pay the expenses of their arrest, confinement, and transportation. Only to several of the men who were ailing would the Pennsylvania Council show mercy. "It is reported that several of those gentlemen are in a low state of health and unfit to travel," it wrote to Morgan.

> If you find this to be the case, they must be left where they are for the present. Those of them who are in health you are to bring with you, treating them on the road with that polite attention and care which is due from men who act from the purest motives to gentlemen whose stations in life entitle them to respect, however they may differ in political sentiments . . .[1]

Thus began the journey of the Quakers: Israel, John, and James Pemberton; Elijah Brown; William and William Drewes Smith; Charles Jervis; Miers, Thomas, and Samuel Fisher; John Hunt; Thomas Affleck; Thomas Pike; Edward Penington; Thomas Gilpin; Samuel Pleasants; Charles Eddy; Owen Jones, Jr.; Henry Drinker; and Thomas Wharton.

On September 9, 1777, the movement of the prisoners from Masons' Lodge to Virginia began. Though many of their fellow-citizens protested the treatment of the seventeen, they were forced into wagons and driven westward beyond the Schuylkill River and down the Wagon Road toward Downington and Lancaster. Of their departure, one of them wrote:

> On the day of our removal, not only the house in which we were confined but the streets leading to it were crowded by men, women, and children, who by their countenances, sufficiently though silently expressed the grief they felt on the occasion.[2]

[147]

After a stop at Palmer's Tavern, which lay a day's journey from Philadelphia, the conscientious objectors were again rounded up and their journey resumed. Halting again at the Black Horse Tavern, they went on in hopes of stopping for the night at the Widow Lloyd's, about thirty miles from Philadelphia. Finding no rooms there, the group was carted on to Pottsgrove, where they spent the night in four households.

Some passers-by were hostile. In the town of Reading several patriots stoned the Quakers. To avoid further mischance, the prisoners were now placed under close guard. Their Quaker friends, Isaac Zane, Sr., and James Starr, were pulled away and stoned when they attempted to visit the seventeen at the Widow Withington's Tavern. Of the indignities they received, Thomas Gilpin wrote:

> Very false ideas and information are spread through the country concerning us, by which people are grossly imposed upon and made to believe that we are the cause of distress and bloodshed, instead of those who are *really* the cause of it; and which false opinion ought to be set right.[3]

Word now reached the prisoners that their place of internment had been changed from Staunton to Winchester, through the efforts of a well-to-do Winchester Quaker named Isaac Zane, Jr. This was good news, indeed, for other members of the Society of Friends lived in Frederick and Loudoun counties near Winchester, many of them having emigrated there from Philadelphia in the 1730s. From these fellow sectarians they could expect kinder treatment than from the militant Scotch-Irish of Staunton.

Passing through Maryland to Evan Watkins' ferry, the wagons bearing the Quakers were ferried across the Potomac while their horses were led across the ford. On September 29—three weeks after leaving Philadelphia—the conscientious objectors reached the town of Winchester, where most of them were lodged at Philip Bush's inn. There the hospitable Isaac Zane, Jr., met and consoled them.

The Philadelphians found Winchester a village much like their own Lancaster or York. Made up chiefly of one main street—the Wagon Road—it was lined with inns and taverns to serve Valley travelers. Founded in 1744, it had at first been called Frederick Town until renamed to avoid confusion with nearby Frederick in

Maryland. Situated in Lord Fairfax's immense Northern Neck tract, it was given the name Winchester by Colonel James Wood, the first clerk of Frederick County in 1743, who came from the English town of that name.

Like Lancaster and York, Winchester was a blend of English, Scotch-Irish, and German settlers. Along its main street stood buildings of English and Pennsylvania Dutch architecture, intermingled with shops of tanners, gunsmiths, and other artisans. In the fertile countryside around the town, planters grew wheat, tobacco, and corn. George Washington had begun his career in Winchester in 1748 as surveyor to Lord Fairfax, who lived at Greenway Court nearby. On another farm lived Daniel Morgan, who rose from wagoner in General Braddock's army to general in the Revolution.

Morgan put to use as artisans many of the Hessian mercenaries who had been taken as prisoners from the British and held in stockades near Winchester. He paid them the equivalent of $7.50 a month for their work as brick masons, carpenters, cabinetmakers, ironsmiths, and other craftsmen.

In Winchester, the Philadelphia Light Horse Guards delivered the Quakers to Colonel John Smith, county lieutenant of Frederick, who offered them the liberty of the town if they promised not to talk politics with townspeople. The Quakers agreed, assuring Smith that their principles precluded their engaging in party strife.

Winchester proved cruelly hostile, nevertheless. After a few local Quakers visited the prisoners, a gang of thirty armed men surrounded Bush's Tavern and demanded their removal. Smith, their bodyguard, persuaded the group that the Quakers should be permitted to remain pending further instructions from Governor Patrick Henry and the Continental Congress.

Smith hastened to write John Hancock, who was presiding over the Continental Congress in York:

> The inhabitants of this part of the country are, in general, much exasperated against the whole Society of Quakers [he explained]. The people were taught to suppose these people were Tories ... they determined not to permit them to remain in Winchester, for fear of holding a correspondence with the Friends of the adjoining counties.... I can assure you their lives will be endangered by their staying at Winchester.[4]

[149]

In a postscript Smith added: "In justice to the prisoners I can but inform you that their behaviour, since they have been at this place, has truly been inoffensive, and such as could give umbrage to no person whatever."

When Virginia's Council in Williamsburg learned of Winchester's hostility to the Philadelphians, it commended Smith for his fair-minded defense of them. Its members cautioned him that "any violence which may be offered the prisoners will be considered highly derogatory and dishonourable to the government." Apparently, the clamor gradually subsided.

Isaac Zane, Jr., and others welcomed the newcomers to Hopewell Meeting House, which Frederick County Quakers had built near Winchester in 1759. The homesick men were also befriended by the members of nearby Goose Creek Meeting House, near Leesburg. Many of these had emigrated from Bucks County, Pennsylvania, and built the village of Milltown, later renamed Waterford.

The internees were disturbed when they learned they were being charged ten shillings a day, Virginia currency, for their board at Philip Bush's Tavern. "This is twelve shillings and sixpence a day, Pennsylvania currency," one objected, "and we find our own beds, drink, and washing!" Bush reluctantly agreed to reduce the price.

New criticism arose when Owen Jones, Jr., was accused of trading gold for paper money with correspondents in Lancaster. Jones was ordered under guard to Staunton, fifty miles further down the Wagon Road, and jailed. Then George Gilpin, another internee, became seriously ill. He sent a deathbed message to his wife in Pennsylvania:

> Katy, I am going the way of all flesh, and I hope it is in mercy; thou has been a good girl, and my brothers will reward thee. There are many religions in the world, and a variety of forms, which have occasioned great persecutions, and the loss of many lives, each contending that they are right; but there is but one true religion, arising from faith in God and in his son Jesus Christ, and hope in his mercy. A monitor placed in every mind, which if we attend to, we cannot err...[5]

After repeated petitions to the Pennsylvania Council, the interned Quakers were told in April 1778 that they might return to Pennsylvania for a hearing. Gleefully they boarded their wagons, and the wagon train set out northward to Lancaster, where the Pennsylvania government was temporarily quartered. At length, after hearing their petitions, the Council on April 27 permitted the conscientious objectors to return home.

On April 30, the Quakers' wagons pulled into Philadelphia. At 3 P.M. the procession was admitted through the picket guard which stood at Sorrel Horse Tavern in Radnor.

> Although we were under pleasant feelings at our return [wrote one of the group], these were considerably abated by observing, as we approached to the city, the devastations committed by the English army in their excursions around it. The fences being generally destroyed, the fields of grass and corn left exposed, houses demolished and left desolate . . .[6]

The Quakers spent the remainder of the war unmolested. After peace had been declared and George Washington was inaugurated President of the United States, the Quakers of Pennsylvania, New Jersey, Maryland, and Virginia sent him an address of welcome from their 1789 yearly convocation. In it they pointed out again that "we can take no part in warlike measures on any occasion or under any power, but we are bound in conscience to lead quiet and peaceable lives, in godliness and honesty among men . . ."

Pointedly reminding the President that "we are a people whose principles and conduct have been misrepresented and traduced," they assured him of their loyalty to the new nation.

President Washington replied with his usual gravity.

> Your principles and conduct are well known to me [he wrote], and it is doing the people called Quakers no more than justice to say that (except their declining to share with others in the burthens of common defence) there is no denomination among us, who are more exemplary and useful citizens. I assure you very especially that in my opinion the conscientious scruples of all men should be treated with great delicacy and tenderness; and it is my wish and desire that the laws may always be as extensively accommodated to them, as a due regard to the protection and essential interest of of the nation may justify and permit.[7]

Thus ended the sad story of the Pennsylvania Quakers and their journey along the Wagon Road.

CHAPTER 17

"The Old Wagoner" against the King

In the five years of the American Revolution, wagon-drivers played a heroic part in supplying Continental forces with the arms needed to win. But none of the others gave so much toward victory as a rawboned veteran of the Wagon Road who led American forces in the Southern campaign of 1779–1781 and hastened Cornwallis' surrender at Yorktown.

He was Brigadier General Daniel Morgan, called by his troops "The Old Wagoner." Typical of his breed, he was a tavern brawler —easy to anger and quick to attack. Up and down the line, from Pennsylvania to the South, Dan Morgan had been famous along the Wagon Road as a tough man in a fight.

The tall outdoorsman had been born of Welsh extraction in Hunterdon County, New Jersey, in 1736. When he was seventeen he moved to Winchester, on the Wagon Road. From there in 1755 he had driven a supply wagon northward in Braddock's ill-fated expedition, and from Virginia and Maryland in 1776 he led a brawling company of frontier riflemen to Massachusetts and Canada, receiving a baptism of fire in early battles along the northern front.

Morgan was a natural leader. The bravery which had carried him through Indian attack and tavern brawl drew soldiers to him. He distinguished himself as a commander of riflemen in the battle of Quebec, and the Saratoga campaign, then angrily resigned his colonelcy in 1779, when the Continental Congress passed him over for promotion. His rough oaths and quick temper offended even military men!

The Old Wagoner might have sulked through the rest of the war if the British had not turned south for new conquests after seizing Philadelphia. That move, which was to spread the war to towns along the lower Wagon Road, brought Daniel Morgan bouncing back into service. He foresaw a British drive to sever South from North; if the British could cut off the vital flow of money and supplies into southern ports from French and Dutch islands in the Caribbean, they could end this colonial rebellion. Thus the campaign for the southern colonies began.

The red-coated invaders at first won several great victories. Landing on the South Carolina coast in the spring of 1780, they captured Charles Town, the South's major port, and pushed on inland, hoping the newly settled Scotsmen and Germans of the Carolinas would rally to Britain's support. Fanning out through the South Carolina piedmont, the troops of Lord Cornwallis seized Camden and pushed on westward, enveloping the Wagon Road and its heterogeneous population.

The Wagon Road determined the strategy of most of the fighting in the South, for it was the nervous system of the uplands. After cutting eastward through the Staunton River gap of the Blue Ridge Mountains, near Fort Chiswell, Virginia, the road turned south and crossed into North Carolina. Here it branched in several directions, like a river which streams and eddies around natural formations.

The principal route led past the Moravian settlements at Wachovia. Close to the road was Bethabara, while nearby were Bethania and Salem, which was destined to become a part of Winston-Salem many years later. Crossing the Yadkin River, it proceeded to Salisbury, which until the Revolution was one of the six largest boroughs in North Carolina. Made the seat of frontier Rowan County in 1753, Salisbury attracted Scotch-Irish and Germanic traders. Daniel Boone lived nearby in his youth, and Andrew Jackson was to receive his license to practice law there in 1787.

Thirty miles south of Salisbury was Charlotte, named for the young wife of George III. Like Salisbury, it was a hotbed of Presbyterianism. Designated as the seat of Mecklenburg County in 1768, it had grown large enough to be incorporated six years later. Anti-British feeling was strong there in the Revolution, fueled in 1773 by the English Privy Council's disallowance of a charter for Queen's College because of its Presbyterianism. In 1775, Mecklenburgers adopted resolutions which declared "all laws and commissions by authority of the king and parliament" to be void. They recognized instead the Continental Congress.

South of Charlotte, the Great Road branched in several directions. One course led southward to Georgia, while another followed the eastward flow of the Catawba River to Charleston via Camden, which was settled by Irish Quakers in 1758 as Pine Tree Hill and later renamed for the Earl of Camden, who won Americans' gratitude for opposing the Stamp Act in 1765.

As Cornwallis' forces moved inland to the Great Wagon Road, they won victories at Camden and Ninety Six, but they gathered few allies among the settlers. Besides, the cavalry forays of Colonel Banastre ("Bloody Ban") Tarleton and other invaders angered the frontiersmen. When Cornwallis led his army from Camden to Charlotte in September, he found it bitterly hostile. Food was hidden, and British troops were harassed. He called the village— then consisting of two streets and a dozen houses—"The Hornet's Nest."

The British forces gained the support of many Carolina merchants and Highland Scots, recently arrived via Charleston and Savannah, but most upland Carolinians opposed them. When frontier settlers along the Holston and Watauga rivers learned that British forces were looting and burning Patriots' houses along the Wagon Road, they formed a defense force of Virginians and Carolinians to cross the Blue Ridge and smite the invaders. More than 1,000 mounted men gathered at Sycamore Shoals on the Watauga on the night of September 15, 1780, to hear a Presbyterian minister preach them into battle, as their Covenanter ancestors had done in Scotland.

The frontiersmen knelt in the flickering light of burning pine knots as Samuel Doak, who had come west after a schooling at Augusta Academy and Princeton, asked God's blessing on their cause. From the Bible he read how an angel of the Lord had visited Gideon, son of Joash the Abiezrite, to demand that he make sacrifices for the Lord, while Gideon demanded miracles first, to be sure the angel spoke for the Lord.

As the Wataugans listened, Parson Doak told how the untried Gideon had been guided by his angel to winnow 32,000 Israelite soldiers down to 300, arming them with trumpets and lamps and leading them by night into triumphant battle against the Amalekites and Midianites. Not content with this victory, Doak told the frontiersmen, the faithful 300 then hacked off the heads of Oreb and Zeeb, the Midianite princes, and carried them in triumph.

In righteous wrath, Samuel Doak exhorted the frontiersmen to proclaim as their war cry: "The Sword of the Lord and of Gideon."

Crossing the Carolina mountains in snow, the horsemen hastened eastward to halt a raiding force from Cornwallis's army, led by a young Scottish lieutenant colonel, Patrick Ferguson. Commanding the Americans were four colonels: William Campbell of Western Virginia, John Sevier of the Watauga region, Isaac Shelby of the Kentucky territory, and Benjamin Cleveland of North Carolina. These four took turns as leader, with the understanding that Campbell, the most experienced, would command in battle.

The frontiersmen caught up with Ferguson's 1,100-man Loyalist force at Kings Mountain, a plateau at the end of a series of hills, just south of the North Carolina border. Unobserved by British outposts, they dismounted and tied their horses before marching in two columns almost to the plateau's base. When Patrick Ferguson learned of their arrival, he commanded his men to begin firing. Then, as successive waves of frontiersmen reached the plateau's top, Ferguson ordered his men to repel them with bayonets.

Three times the attackers were pushed from the mound, each time creeping back and picking away with their long squirrel guns at Ferguson's bloody forces. Screaming like Shawnees, the frontiersmen finally ascended the hillock while William Campbell egged them on: "Shout like hell, boys! Shout like hell!"

Ferguson, commanding his Loyalists on horseback, was killed by a shot in the midst of the bloody inferno. When it ended soon afterward, the Mountain Men had won a great victory. Only twenty-eight of them had been killed and sixty-two wounded. Of Ferguson's Loyalist forces, 157 had died in battle and an equal number were left on the field to die. Another 698 were taken prisoner.

Anticipating further British assaults on the Carolina back country, American defense of this area was turned over late in 1780 to that experienced Wagon Road veteran, Daniel Morgan. Five years had passed since Morgan's brave exploits at Quebec, and the Old Wagoner was now forty-five years old. His rangy body was stiffened with rheumatism, and he ached with sciatica and recurring malaria. Long years in the driver's seat had left him with hemorrhoids, he wrote a friend. But Morgan's victorious valor had become a legend, and the troops loved him for his very cussedness.

Learning of Daniel Morgan's arrival in South Carolina, Lord Cornwallis sent Tarleton dashing west of the Catawba River to pursue and destroy his army. Cornwallis emphasized the phrase "and destroy," for he feared another Kings Mountain disaster and its devastating effect on Loyalists in the Carolinas. Then, with Morgan's army out of the way and the Virginia–North Carolina supply line severed, the British would march northward to the Chesapeake Bay and complete the severance of the colonies.

It was an assignment made to order for the daring Tarleton and his green-coated dragoons. Since the British were riding close on Morgan's heels in upper South Carolina, the Old Wagoner was forced toward the waiting army of Cornwallis. Suddenly, at the Cowpens, a cattle-drivers' camp near the Broad River, Morgan decided to stand and fight. His officers opposed it, for the open field gave cavalrymen every advantage against foot troops, but Morgan was adamant.

As his men cooked supper and the next day's rations on the night before battle, Daniel Morgan strode through camp, teasing his soldiers and talking of the surprises he had in store for "Banny." Once or twice the Old Wagoner removed his shirt to show scars left by the cat-o'-nine-tails laid on by a British sergeant during Braddock's campaign. Fight bravely, he promised them, and the British would turn tail and run.

Shortly after dawn, Tarleton loosed his attack. Soon the two armies were in desperate battle, the field a blaze of blood and gunfire. The bagpipes of Tarleton's Highlanders added to the din. At that moment, to Tarleton's surprise, Morgan sent onto the battlefield Colonel William Washington's white-coated dragoons and Colonel James McCall's mounted Georgia infantrymen, their sabers unsheathed and ready to strike. Breaking the British force into small remnants, Morgan's troops soon overwhelmed it. Cornwallis' Southern campaign had suddenly gone sour.

Morgan had planned to go after Cornwallis' army when he finished off Tarleton's, but his superior officer, General Nathanael Greene, forbade it as too reckless. Disgruntled again, the Old Wagoner soon resigned and took his assorted ailments back to Winchester, where he used the labor of captive Hessian mercenaries to build himself a comfortable house. There he lived a gentlemanly plantation-owner's life at "Saratoga" until he died in 1802. By that time he had accumulated more than 250,000 acres on the Monongahela and Ohio rivers by buying up soldiers' grants. Few men knew the Great Wagon Road so well as he, either as wagoner or soldier.

After the battle of Cowpens, General Greene began to march the half-starved Patriot troops back up the Wagon Road to winter quarters in Virginia, where food was more plentiful.

Cornwallis, seeing his opportunity for a much-needed southern victory, set out in hot pursuit, hoping to annihilate Greene's army. After passing hastily through Charlotte and Salibury, Greene led his troops off to the east, through Guilford Courthouse, and then headed north in an effort to cross the Dan River, hoping to escape Cornwallis there.

The race to the Dan was a hairbreadth chase. For seventy miles, Nathanael Greene's troops sloshed through the Pine Barrens of Carolina in February rains. Most of the men were barefoot, and wagon wheels sank hub-deep in the red mud. At night they found what shelter they could, for they had no tents and only one blanket for every three men. The relentless drizzle slowed the weary marchers almost to a standstill. Occasionally Cornwallis' troops came so close that the men in Greene's rear lines could look back and see see them.

But Greene escaped. Reaching the south bank of the Dan on February 14, he moved his entire army across in boats a few hours before Cornwallis' panting troops reached the shore, frustrated and dismayed to see the Patriots safe on the other shore.

After gathering a new army in Virginia, Nathanael Greene returned to Guilford Courthouse in March 1781 and met Cornwallis' army in one of the bloodiest battles of the Revolution. When the Americans withdrew, they had lost 261 men. Although he held his ground, Cornwallis paid a heavy price for a questionable victory: 532 of his men were killed, wounded, or missing.

General Greene, who was probably the ablest of George Washington's Continental Army commanders, was impressed by the Wagon Road's people. Coastal dwellers "are sickly and but indifferent militia," he said, "but the back-country people are bold and daring in their makeup."

Looking back over his Southern campaign, Cornwallis had many regrets. The Frontiersmen had blasted Patrick Ferguson's raiders at Kings Mountain. Daniel Morgan had outmaneuvered Bloody Ban Tarleton at the Cowpens, and Nathanael Greene's army had got off too easily at Guilford Courthouse. Still, Cornwallis hoped, the Revolution in the South might yet die out if Virginia could be subjugated.

[158]

"I was most firmly persuaded," he mused later, "that until Virginia was reduced, we could not hold the more southern provinces, and that after its reduction, they could fall without more difficulty."

With this strategy still in mind, the courtly general led his Guilford survivors northward into coastal Virginia in the spring of 1781, still seeking the decisive victory that would "pinch the colonies in two." To England's grief, those brave hopes died at Yorktown, where a great French fleet under Admiral de Grasse joined with the armies of George Washington and Rochambeau to bottle up the British forces and to end at last Great Britain's dominance in North America.

When Cornwallis' army surrendered on October 19, 1781, an era ended in Great Britain's North American colonies. The good news was rushed by courier to the capitals of the thirteen colonies. Along the Great Philadephia Wagon Road, church bells pealed and taverns roared with toasts to "Liberty" and "Great George Washington." In Philadelphia, celebrating Patriots broke countless windowpanes in the house of Catherine Drinker, a leading Quaker and suspected Loyalist.

A new American age was a-borning. And nowhere was this felt more keenly than along the Wagon Road, which lay ready to lead thousands of Revolutionary War veterans to their promised land grants—a new beginning for many a poor man—beyond the towering Appalachians.

CHAPTER 18

Conestoga's Gift

A wagoner's life along the Road was a roistering career of daily crisis, enlivened by danger and ribald good humor. Over the 700 miles from Pennsylvania to Georgia, hundreds of these profane men drove in the years between the Lancaster Treaty of 1744 and the coming of the railroads a century later. They were a close brotherhood, linked by shared hardship. They made the Great Road a live and vital artery.

The backwoods wagoners were a rough lot, used to the harshest punishment of the weather. In winter, mud splattered their faces and mired their horses and wagons. In summer they were assailed by sunburn and May flies. Often they drove without stop through rain or snow, hastening to reach a house or inn before nightfall or the hostile elements overwhelmed them. In winter they were sometimes trapped in the mountains, unable to go forward or back. From the forests of the Alleghanies or the Blue Ridge, Indians might attack them and seize their goods.

Yet the fame of the wagoner spread afar, for his life embodied the adventure which drew hardy emigrants to the frontier. Raucous, uncouth, and ready to fight at the drop of a hat, he set the pattern for the stagecoach drivers and railroad builders who later moved America westward. He was the envy of the farmer and the livestock drover whom he passed on the road, cracking his whip and urging his horses onward.

"You, Beauty—what the hell's the matter thar?"

But his life had compensations. In spring, the greening of trees along the mountaintops made a ribbon of light against the blue sky. When mountain laurel and rhododendron brightened the mountain passes in May, they shone like pink clouds against the forest's green.

The best of all seasons was summer, when trees spread a gentle canopy over the road. Then the wagoner traveled most happily, singing to himself as he swatted May flies with his straw hat:

Come to me, my dear, and give to me your hand
And let us take a social ramble to some far and distant land,

Where the hawk shot the buzzard and the buzzard shot the crow,
And we all ride around the canebrake and shoot the buffalo.[1]

Sometimes the wagoner carried a guitar or banjo to amuse himself on the lonesome rides between settlements. A crack of his five-foot whip punctuated a verse's end. Whip-cracking drivers came to be known as "crackers." The jew's harp was popular, too, for it could be carried in a shirt pocket. Stores in Philadelphia, Lancaster, and other roadside towns stocked them by the dozen.

The road had many songs, and wagoners sang endlessly as they covered the miles between Big Link to Bethabara and southward to Salisbury:

> Tazewell County and Tazewell Town,
>   Lord have mercy and do look down.
> Poor and rocky and hilly, too,
>   Lord have mercy, what will these poor people do?[2]

An early chant revealed the rosy hopes of the pioneer:

> Droop not, brother, as we go
> Over the mountains, westward ho,
> Under boughs of mistletoe,
>   Log huts we'll rear,
> While herds of deer and buffalo
> Furnish the cheer;
> File over the mountains, steady, boys;
>   For game afar
> We have our rifles ready, boys,
> Aha-a-a-a-a-a!
>
> Cheer up, brothers, as we go
> Over the mountains, westward ho,
> When we've wood and prairie land,
>   Won by our toil,
> We'll reign like kings in fairyland,
>   Lords of the soil,
>   Then westward ho in legions, boys,
>   For freedom's star
> Points to her sunset regions, boys,
>   Aha-a-a-a-a-a![3]

Hymns were loudly sung, for the works of Isaac Watts and John Wesley were familiar to all who had heard the emotional calls to salvation from itinerant Methodist evangelists:

Since I can read my title clear
To mansions in the skies,
I'll bid farewell to every fear
And wipe my weeping eyes.[4]

Because of Pennsylvania's supremacy in early trade with the back country, many Germanic settlers in that colony built and drove wagons. In them the great Lutheran and Moravian hymns, usually sung in *hoch Deutsch,* were daily fare:

A mighty fortress is our God
A bulwark never failing
Our helper He amid the flood
Of mortal ills prevailing
For still our ancient foe
Doth seek to work us woe
His craft and power are great,
And armed with cruel hate,
On earth is not his equal.[5]

The camaraderie of the Wagon Road was real, for traffic was sporadic and news from home was hard to come by. Occasionally a wagoner had to pull aside to let a drover pass, shepherding his nervous sheep or herding his stolid cattle to the nearest butcher. Wagoners looked down on drovers, for the cattlemen were ill paid and smelled of the barnyard. They were not welcome at inns along the road where wagoners ate and drank and caroused after a long day on the road.

Once in awhile a wagoner passed a chaise bearing a well-to-do traveler, but these were few in the country. More common were farm wagons of the Mennonites and Amish in Pennsylvania or of the Scotch-Irish in Virginia and Carolina. The usual traveler went on foot, carrying provisions in a pack over his shoulder.

Trains of packhorses also traveled the road, sometimes linking a dozen or more riderless horses to the lead horse of the packman. Such trains often made a merry sound, for packhorses usually carried bridle bells to enable the packman to find them in case they were dispersed. Like Conestoga wagon horses, the pack animals were chosen for strength and docility, carrying loads up to 600 pounds.

Entire families sometimes rode horseback along the road to settle a new farm or to go to church. On the foremost horse rode father, a child seated on the horse's rump behind him, holding onto his waist. Other members of the family followed, the mother bringing up the rear with the smallest child in her arms.

On court days, courthouse squares from Pennsylvania to Georgia swarmed with countrymen in town to buy or sell goods. Auctions, political speeches, horse races, and cockfights often enlivened these occasions. (A Carolinian described "a certain peculiar shake of hand, called by farmers the electioneering shake.") Sometimes the head of a household was obliged to sit on a jury or to attend court as "viewer" or "overseer" for his segment of a country road. Occasionally the householder appeared as a principal or witness in a suit to recover a strayed or stolen horse or two. The feisty Scotch-Irish were especially litigious.

The wagon driver usually commanded a team of four or five horses, requiring constant attention and a firm hand on the "jerk line" which connected with the bit of the left wheel horse, or team leader. By this line the wagoner controlled his horses, walking alongside them or riding a seat behind the left front wagon wheel.

More important than the jerk line were the commands, which were those used by English countrymen from time immemorial. "Haw" meant turn left, while "gee" meant turn right. No other commands except "whoa" were needed. The large, strong wheel horses set the pace and provided braking power through their strong hindquarters on downhill grades. On steep plunges, the driver might insert a chain from the wheels to the coupling poles to provide a brake.

Wagons steadily increased in size and commercial importance in the early years of the American republic. Shopkeepers depended on them to bring manufactured goods from eastern seaport towns to the Great Wagon Road, while western farmers needed them to haul their produce "back east."

Most early American farmers made their own cart or wagon, fashioning it after the English county from which they had come. In this era the wagons made by German artisans in the Pennsylvania counties of Chester, Bucks, Lancaster, and York set the pattern for others throughout the east. Especially well-known after 1750 were those of the Conestoga Valley in Lancaster County.

These were the wagons which Benjamin Franklin obtained from German farmers for General Braddock's supplies on his ill-fated march to western Pennsylvania in 1758. From that time until the

Civil War, the Conestoga wagon carried America steadily westward in its progress across North America.

The chief virtue of the Conestoga was its large and well-balanced body. Built with its sides sloping inward like a well-made boat, it held its assorted cargo firmly in place, no matter how rough the terrain of the Great Wagon Road might be. As the road grew longer and wider, so did the Conestoga wagon, ultimately reaching a length of twenty-six feet and a height of eleven. Built of hickory, white oak, and poplar, it had hubs of black gum or sour gum and tires of iron. No wonder that it weighed 3,500 pounds at the height of its growth and required six horses to pull it!

To permit the wagon to be loaded easily, a hinged tailgate dropped downward at the rear. Feedboxes were attached to the sides for the horses, and tailgate fittings provided for a tether to horses or cows accompanying migrating families. The wagon was arched by a series of iron hoops, which were canopied with an awning of homespun or canvas. For its similarity to women's headgear, this was the "poke bonnet." The wagon's trim lines and billowed awning earned it the fanciful name, "ship of the desert."

> The capacious wagons which the Conestoga farmers then had in use [wrote a nineteenth-century Pennsylvanian], were the best means of land transportation which the times and circumstances of the country then afforded. These wagons and teams attracted attention and commanded admiration wherever they appeared; and hence the origin, as I conceive, of the horse and wagon to which the appellation of "conestoga" has been attached.... The harness was constructed of the best materials, with an eye to show as well as utility. In the harness and trimming of these teams the owners frequently indulged in expenses that approached to extravagance. It was, indeed, an animating sight to see five or six highly fed horses, half covered with heavy bear skins, or decorated with gaudily fringed housings, surmounted with a set of finely toned bells, their bridles adorned with loops of red trimmings ... as if half conscious of their superior appearance and participating in the pride that swelled the bosom of their master.[6]

In the wagon shops of the Conestoga Valley, German artisans fitted the wheels with four-inch-wide iron rims to uphold them on muddy roads. These were made of two pieces of iron, a half-inch thick, bent to the shape of the wheel and welded at both joints. A fire was built around the iron rim, and the heated metal was lifted by tongs and placed around the wooden wheel to be hammered into place. The wheel was then immersed in cold water to shrink the iron to a tight fit.

To give the wagoner relief from his seat astride the wheel horse, a "lazy board" was eventually built behind the left front wheel. From this developed the American practice of driving vehicles from the left.

By the time of the American Revolution, a Conestoga wagon sold for $250, while the six heavy wagon horses cost nearly $1,200. By then, use of the vehicles extended over a growing network of roads: to Pittsburgh, New York, Boston, Baltimore, and points south. Many of them traveled the so-called Post Road or King's Highway, which the colonies had linked together through their thirteen coastal capitals, from New Hampshire southward to Georgia. Like the Philadelphia Wagon Road which it paralleled, however, the coastal Post Road was rough and often muddy.

Winter driving challenged the wagoner's strength and skill. During the rainy season, ruts were hub deep. It was a common sight to see a wagon and team bogged down and unable to move. Occasionally a stalled wagon froze in the mud and was forced to remain until a thaw. Teamsters carried several days' forage for such emergency, together with a drag chain twelve feet long, an axe, shovel, clouts, a gallon keg of tar and oil (suspended from the rear axle), and extra horseshoes, nails, hames, strings, and lynchpins.

The wagoner also carried a straw mattress and emergency food, in case he failed to reach an inn or house by nightfall.

So bad was the Wagon Road that the first attempts to establish stagecoach service from Philadelphia failed. In 1784 and again in 1788, Pennsylvania newspapers advertised that regular "stage wagons" would carry passengers, mail, and freight to Lancaster and return. Not until 1796, however, after a turnpike company had hard-surfaced sixty-six miles of the road and renamed it the Lancaster Pike, was regular stagecoach service possible.

Wagons carried an endless variety of goods. An advertisement by two Tennessee-territory storekeepers in 1796 reported their wagons' arrival:

KING & CROZIER

In addition to their former assortment, have just come to hand, Irish Linens; Saddles and Bridles; Books and Stationery; Steel;

Nails, Window Glass; Queen's Ware; Glassware; Pipes; Lead; Gun powder; Coffee; Chocolate; Bohea, Green Sequin, and Hyson Teas; Loaf and Brown Sugars; Pepper; Allspice; Allum; Brimstone; Cooperas, etc.

They have also on sale as usual, Salt and Castings; and shortly expect a further supply of Bar Iron; All of which they will sell on reasonable terms, for cash, deer and bear skins, furs, hemp, bees' wax, keg butter, tallow, country linen, flax, &c, &c.[7]

About this same time, the French traveler André Michaux visited the Tennessee settlements and wrote that "the trades people get their provisions by land from Philadelphia, Baltimore, and Richmond in Virginia; and they send in return, by the same way, the produce of the country, which they buy of the cultivators, or take to barter for their goods . . ."

Until the advent of stagecoaches, after the Revolution, the wagons made at Conestoga and elsewhere offered the common transport over the Wagon Road and its offshoots. Besides those bought and driven west by immigrants, some were operated on a for-hire basis. These were numerous in Pennsylvania but diminished as the Wagon Road wended south, into the back country of Virginia and the Carolinas. Operators of such vehicles, called "sharpshooters," kept no schedule. They set out whenever they accumulated a load.

Wagons operated by a company were called "line teams," while those owned and driven regularly over the same route were "regulars."

Packhorse trains continued to serve the upcountry despite the increasing wagons. Packhorse drivers could be hired in most villages along the Road, especially in Pennsylvania. For a small price, they hauled the cities' manufactures to the frontier and brought back produce in return. To reach the deep backwoods settlements, packhorse trains followed steep and narrow horseways—sometimes called "tote roads" or "pack roads." Crossing streams, the packmen floated their cargo across on rafts and made the horses swim.

Necessities such as salt, sugar, rum, hardware, medicine, and gunpowder were commonly carried by packhorse caravans. Salt was especially needed, both to season food, to cure meat, and to dress furs which the frontier sent "back east" to coastal shippers. The packman rode at the head of his procession, a rope leading from the crown of his saddle back to the bridle of each succeeding packhorse. At the rear, a second horseman rode in readiness to reload a packsaddle or retrieve an errant horse.

Along the settled sections of the Great Road, rough log inns catered to packhorse drivers and provided overnight shelter for packsaddles and pens for horses.

The organization of a community pack train to haul the summer's produce to market was common along the Appalachian frontier in these years. The Reverend Joseph Doddridge thus described the process in his "Notes on the settlement and Indian Wars of the Western parts of Virginia and Pennsylvania":

> In the fall of the year, after seeding time, every family formed an association with some of their neighbors, for starting the little caravan. A master driver was to be selected from among them, who was to be assisted by one or more young men and sometimes a boy or two. The horses were fitted out with pack-saddles, to the latter part of which was fastened a pair of hobbles made of hickory withes—a bell and collar ornamented their necks. The bags provided for the conveyance of the salt were filled with feed for the horses; on the journey a part of this feed was left at convenient stages on the way down, to support the return of the caravan. Large wallets well filled with bread, jerk [smoked venison, bear, or other meat], boiled ham, and cheese furnished a provision for the drivers. At night, after feeding, the horses, whether put in pasture or turned out into the woods, were hobbled and the bells were opened.... Each horse carried two bushels of alum salt, weighing eighty-four pounds to the bushel. This, to be sure, was not a heavy load for the horses, but it was enough, considering the scanty subsistence allowed them on the journey. The common price of a bushel of alum salt, at an early period, was a good cow and a calf.[8]

When a frontier community sent out a pack train, it was essential that a leader be chosen who could trade his cargo profitably. As one chronicler wrote: "The whole amount of hide and peltries, ginseng, snake-root, and bears grease were exchanged or bartered for salt, nails, and other articles of iron, and occasionally for a few pewter plates and dishes for the table. The bartering for the settlement being finished, the caravan was ready for its retrograde march . . ."

Describing a horse path leading from the Wagon Road, a traveler wrote:

> The path, scarcely two feet wide, and traveled by horses in single file, roamed over hill and dale, through mountain defile, over

craggy steeps, beneath impending rocks, and around points of dizzy heights, where one false step might hurl horse and rider into the abyss below. To prevent such accidents, the bulky baggage was removed in passing the dangerous defiles, to secure the horse from being thrown from his scanty foothold. . . . The horses, with their packs, were marched along in single file, the foremost led by the leader of the caravan, while each successive horse was tethered to the pack-saddle of the horse before him. A driver followed behind, to keep an eye upon the proper adjustment of the packs, and to urge on any horse that was disposed to lag. In this way two men could manage a caravan of ten or fifteen horses. . . . When night came, a temporary camp and a camp-fire protected the weary travelers.[9]

Such was travel along the Wagon Road during the eighteenth century. It was the high noon of American individualism, for the bounty of the opening West offered opportunities which have never been equaled in American history. With the birth of the Constitution and the enactment of the Northwest Ordinance at Philadelphia in 1787, the call of the West grew ever stronger. Lands beyond the Ohio River were opened to settlement, and a host of Americans rushed forward to claim them.

In such an age, roads into the west were urgently needed. By the time Thomas Jefferson took office in 1801 as President, settlers along the Wagon and Wilderness roads were demanding better links with the east. To meet this demand, it was inevitable that Americans turned to the concept of the turnpike—a hard-surfaced road with adequate bridges, to be built as an investment by individuals and the states and to be liquidated by means of tolls paid by users. Such turnpikes, it was argued, would permit rapid communication by stage wagons, as was done in Great Britain.

Thus, as the new American republic emerged, the Wagon Road faced a new era which was to place the riches of Kentucky and Tennessee in easy distance from Augusta, Charlotte, Winchester, and the East. By the year 1800, the age of the turnpike was at hand.

CHAPTER 19

Hospitality, North and South

It stands all alone like a goblin in gray,
The old-fashioned inn of a pioneer day,
In a land so forlorn and forgotten, it seems
Like a wraith of the past rising into our dreams;
Its glories have vanished, and only the ghost
Of a sign-board now creaks on its desolate post,
Recalling a time when all hearts were akin
As they rested at night in that welcoming inn.[1]

Few hostelries in the American provinces boasted a better reputation in 1786 than did Casper Fahnestock's Admiral Warren Inn, near Lancaster. Here, on the Wagon Road from Philadelphia to the South, the plump German innkeeper played host to the stream of travelers who came over the road between Lancaster and Philadelphia. Many of them were emigrant Ulstermen or Palatinates, on their way south in search of cheap lands. Others were second-generation Americans, recently out of military service in the Revolution, headed west to claim their bounty lands.

Casper Fahnestock was a good innkeeper, known for miles around. He paid £2,000 in Pennsylvania money for his inn and 337 acres of surrounding land. He had brought the money in his saddle-bags when he rode from God's Acre, at Ephrata, where he had lived as a member of the Sabbatarian Baptists'[1] or "Sabbath-Keepers'," community, on the banks of Cocalico Creek. In German they were *sieben-tagers,* or "seventh-dayers."

Casper had been born in Germany in 1724, the son of Dietrich Fahnestock, founder of "the whole tribe of Fahnestocks in America," as one Pennsylvanian put it. He had come to New Jersey in 1726 with his father, mother, and two aunts. The family's only possessions then were an axe, a weaver's shuttle, a Bible, and a thaler—a silver German coin.

Dietrich Fahnestock lived for several years along the Raritan River in New Jersey, but one day he learned of the Sabbatarian colony at Ephrata, and he moved his family there. One aunt entered

[171]

the Sabbatarian convent as Sister Armilla. The whole family kept the strict mosaic laws of the sect, eating no pork and observing other dietary laws. Some people mistook them for Jews.

Fahnestock's Admiral Warren soon became a favored stopping place for wagoners, packhorse drivers, and emigrant families. In addition, it was popular with Lancaster County's Pennsylvania Dutch, as Teutonic peoples in America were then called, whether of Germanic, Swiss, Dutch, or Alsatian extraction. Among them were representatives of many cultures and religious denominations: Lutherans, Anabaptists, Sabbatarians, Reformed Calvinists, Moravians, and Dunkards. Especially distinctive in dress and austerity of life were the Mennonites (or Mennonists) and Amishmen.

Helping Casper run the inn was his wife, Maria. His good-natured mother-in-law, Elizabeth Gleim, ran the kitchen, while his son Charles poured drinks at the wooden bar. Two other sons, Dietrich and the crippled Daniel, looked after the horses and livestock tethered or corralled in the tavern yard. Casper's two daughters, Esther and Catherine, and Charles' wife, Susan, tended the tables and showed guests to their simple rooms.

Death visited Casper's happy household six months after he took over the inn: Elizabeth Gleim died in her seventy-fifth year. She was buried with Sabbatarian rites a few hundred yards from the tavern. First, the congregation sang and prayed to the north and south. Then Brother Jabez, the Ephrata prior, conducted the lengthy service.

In time, Casper Fahnestock's inn became the most popular stopping-place on the Wagon Road. In fact, he had difficulty finding room for guests, even though they sometimes slept three and four to a bed. Not only local "Deutscher" but also "Irischer," as the Pennsylvania Dutch called the Scotch-Irish, patronized Fahnestock's. So, too, did descendants of the old English and Welsh Quakers, who had first settled Pennsylvania and whom the Germans called "Gentlemen."

From "The Dutch Tavern," as it was called by the wagoners, Casper kept the corduroy causeway through the swamp adjoining his farm. As with everything, he did it conscientiously and thoroughly.

One of the many who stopped at Fahnestock's inn was Miss Marie Penrhy, who was one of the Moravian Sisterhood at Lititz and who stopped there in 1786 on her way from Philadelphia to Lancaster. Another guest was Governor Thomas Mifflin of Pennsylvania, who stopped there in 1794 when he came through Chester County recruiting men to quell the western Pennsylvania Whisky Insurrection, at the behest of President Washington. Although the pacifistic Fahnestock made objections to having his inn used for military purposes, a recruiting office was opened in his tavern and a whole company was signed up.

When the Lancaster Turnpike was built from Philadelphia in 1795 and stagecoach service was inaugurated, Casper Fahnestock saw need for a larger inn. Accordingly, he moved his establishment to the other side of the road and there built a handsome new Admiral Warren Inn. With Germanic thrift, he and his sons led a few hired hands in felling the trees, hewing and sawing the timbers, burning the lime, hauling the sand, and quarrying the stone for their new hostelry.

Working his men late one night in the stone quarry, Casper Fahnestock almost brought on an insurrection. Several mischievous young employees dressed themselves in blankets and accosted him in the moonlight with yells and horn-blowing. Casper was momentarily startled, but he almost immediately went back to his sledge. "I bees not afrait von yous if you bees der teufel [devil]," he said over his shoulder. "*Wer auf Gott vertraut kan weder tod nicht teufel schaden.*" ("Whover trusts in God neither death nor Satan can harm.")

The traffic which moved over the new Lancaster Turnpike trebled Fahnestock's business, but he would not relinquish control of his inn to his sons. He believed in the old German maxim "No father should give the reins of his hands to his child as long as he lives." However, when he reached the age of seventy-seven in 1799, he was forced to pass on the heavy responsibility to his son Charles. But he insisted that the inn continue to close its bar Sunday, posting a large sign in the lobby:

> No Liquor
> Sold on the
> Sabbath

A frequent visitor to the Admiral Warren was the Reverend Andrew Fahnestock, a nephew of Casper and a cousin of Charles.

[173]

He was a staunch Sabbatarian and traveled on foot from one preaching mission to another, dressed in long coat, broadbrimmed hat, and carrying his *Pilgerstab,* or pilgrim staff, in his hand. He gave his wealth to the poor, saying, "The Lord will never suffer me to want." He refused pay for his preaching, trusting to the Lord for his support. He never ceased to upbraid Charles Fahnestock for deserting the Sabbatarians to join the Presbyterians.

One night at the Admiral Warren a wagoner asked Andrew Fahnestock if he believed in the devil. The minister replied stoutly that he read about him in the Bible. The wagoner then inquired if Andrew had ever seen the devil.

"I never want to see him plainer than I do just now," the old Sabbatarian replied.

Inns and ordinaries along the Wagon Road varied in quality, but for many years most of them charged each guest three shillings a day. For this the traveler got his lodgings, three meals, beer between meals, and a hearthfire if the weather required it. So important were such inns to the traveler that distances along the Road were printed and quoted from one tavern to the next.

With newspapers and postal deliveries few, frontiersmen along the Road avidly received strangers arriving from north or south. No sooner had a traveler dismounted at the inn but news of his arrival circulated and neighbors gathered to welcome the visitors and learn what news they brought from the outside world. Inns were favorite locations for legal notices and proclamations. Advertisements of runaway slaves were frequently posted there, and notices of sales, wagon and packhorse train departures, and forthcoming religious revivals were common.

Larger inns in Pennsylvania like Casper Fahnestock's, usually contained a public assembly room with adjoining bar, dining room, and kitchen. Liquor was stocked in barrels, jugs, and bottles, which were locked in the semipartitioned barroom. Upstairs, two or three bedrooms contained three or four beds each.

Patrons willing to pay the price could sleep singly, but if the inn were crowded travelers were accommodated three or four to a bed. In such case, the few women guests were placed in one room and the men in others. As males outnumbered females five to one in most of the American colonies in the seventeenth and early eighteenth centuries, the patronage of inns was largely masculine.

Landlords considered it their duty to give hospitality to all who came, expecially in bad weather. If beds were unavailable, a traveler was permitted to spread blankets on the floor or to sleep on the hay in the barn. Often, in winter, late arrivals rolled themselves in blankets and slept with their feet toward the hearthfire in the main public room.

Travelers frequently complained of the rustic accommodations in the Valley of Virginia and southward in the Carolinas. Some of these had neither bed curtains, washbasins, water jugs, coat racks, mirrors, towels, or even tablecloths. The traveler washed at a wooden tub at the rear of the inn or at the watering trough in the stable yard. A towel was passed from one patron to the next. Sometimes visitors encountered fleas or bedbugs.

At the Fahnestocks' Admiral Warren Inn, the host proclaimed breakfast at five or six in the morning with a blast on a cow's horn. This was the signal for the late riser to jump into his clothes and rush to the table. Meals were bountiful, but few rural inns outside the Pennsylvania German belt received praise for their food. Everything was heaped in platters on the table, and these were passed from guest to guest until food—or diners—were exhausted.

South of Maryland on the Wagon Road, most stopping places were farmers' households which afforded a few extra beds and meals for passers-by. Those which declared themselves to be "publick houses" were restricted by county law to charge no more than the standard permitted price for food, drink, and lodging. In a private residence, the householder could charge a guest nothing unless guest and host had agreed upon a price on arrival.

Even so, travelers along the Wagon Road found most hosts hospitable. Wrote one early visitor in the South:

> The inhabitants are very courteous to travelers, who need no other recommendation than being human creatures. A stranger has no more to do but to inquire upon the road where any gentleman or good housekeeper lives, and then he may depend upon being received with hospitality. This good-nature is so general among their people that the gentry, when they go abroad, order their principal servants to entertain all visitors with everything the plantation affords; and the poor planters who have but one bed will often sit up, or lie upon a form, or couch all night, to make room for a weary traveler to repose himself after his journey.[2]

[175]

On a lesser scale, this was true of the log-cabin dwellers of the uplands, who shared their hospitality at such towns as Augusta, Charlotte, Bethabara, Harrisonburg, and Strasburg.

Illustrative of regulations of inn prices was the North Carolina law, passed in 1779, requiring that "the justices in each county shall once a year . . . rate the prices of liquors, diet, lodging, fodder, etc., and every ordinary keeper shall . . . obtain . . . a fair copy of such rates, which copy shall be openly set up in the common entertainment room of such ordinary, and there kept until the rates are again altered . . ." or subject himself to a fine of £100.

A Tennessee county of North Carolina promulgated the following rate schedule in 1793:

For Diett	16 cents
Corn per gallon	10 cents
Oats per ditto	10 cents
Fodder per bundle	3 cents
Whiskey per half pint	8 cents
Brandy per ditto	12 cents
For rum per half pint	16 cents
Wine per ditto	16 cents
Beer per quart	8 cents
Cyder per ditto	8 cents
Lodging per night	6 cents
Pasturage per day	8 cents[3]

Another Tennessee rate card, published two years later, carried a wider variety of refreshments:

For breakfast	20 cents
Dinner	25 cents
Supper	16⅔ cents
Lodging for night	8 cents
Keeping a horse with a sufficiency of hay, Fodder, or Sheaf Oats, 24 hours . . .	33⅓ cents
Pasturage, 24 hours	8 cents
Corn or Oats per gallon	8 cents
Common Rum, per half pint	25 cents
Jamaica Spirits, per half pint	33⅓ cents
Brandy, per half pint	12½ cents
Whiskey, per half pint	8 cents
Teneriffe Wine per quart	$1.00

Lisbon Wine, per quart $1.25
Madeira, per quart $1.50
Beer, per quart . . . . 8 cents
Cider, per quart . . . . 12½ cents
Metheglin, per quart . . . . 12½ cents
Meal of Cold Victuals, half price of other meals[4]

Of all inns in the colonies, those operated by Germans were generally the best. The Germanic respect for good food and cleanliness showed up in such establishments as the Admiral Warren, the General Paoli, the King of Prussia, and other area hostelries. In addition, the Pennsylvania government made an effort to properly regulate such inns. As early as 1763 it required

that only one [inn] should be in such a defined distance, or in proportion to so many inhabitants, that the bar rooms should be closed upon the Sabbath day, as it would tend to prevent youth from committing excesses to their own ruin and injury of their masters and the affliction of their parents and friends.[5]

But even in Pennsylvania, there were poor inns. One European visitor wrote:

I set out from Philadelphia on horseback, and arrived at Lancaster at the end of the second day's journey. The road between Philadelphia and Lancaster has lately undergone a thorough repair, and tolls are levied upon it to keep it in order.... This is the first attempt to have a turnpike road in Pennsylvania, and it is by no means relished by the people at large, particularly the wagoners, who go in great numbers by this route to Philadelphia from the back parts of the State. On the whole road from Philadelphia to Lancaster, there are not any two dwellings standing together excepting at a small place called Downing's Town, which lies about midway. The taverns along this turnpike are kept by farmers, and they are all very indifferent. If the traveller can procure a few eggs with a little bacon, he ought to rest satisfied; it is twenty to one that not a bit of fresh meat is to be had, or any salted meat except pork. Vegetables seem also to be very scarce, and when you do get any, they generally consist of turnips, or turnip tops boiled by way of greens.
The bread is heavy and sour, though they have as fine flour as any in the world; this is owing to their method of making of it; they raise it with what they call sots: hops and water boiled together.

The traveller on his arrival is shown into a room which is common to every person in the house, and which is generally the one set apart for breakfast, dinner and supper. All the strangers that happen to be in the house sit down to these meals promiscuously, and the family of the house forms a part of the company. It is seldom that a single bed room can be procured, but it is not always that even this is to be had, and those who travel through the country must often submit to be crammed into rooms where there is scarcely space to walk between the beds. No dependence is to be placed upon getting a man at these taverns to rub down your horse, or even to give him his food; frequently, therefore, you will have to do everything of the kind for yourself if you do not travel with a servant; and indeed even where men are kept for the purpose of attending to travelers, which at some of the taverns is the case, they are so sullen and disobliging that you feel inclined to do everything with your own hands rather than be indebted to them for their assistance; they always appear doubtful whether they should do anything for you or not, nor will money make them alter their conduct.

It is scarcely possible to go one mile on this road without meeting numbers of wagons passing and repassing between the back parts of the State and Philadelphia. These wagons are commonly drawn by four or five horses, four of which are yoked in pairs. The wagons are heavy, the horses small, and the driver unmerciful; the consequence of which is that, in every team, nearly, there is a horse either lame or blind. The Pennsylvanians are notorious for the bad care which they take of their horses. Except the night be tempestuous, the wagoners never put their horses under shelter, and then it is only under a shed. Each tavern is usually provided for this purpose. Food for the horses is always carried in the wagon, and the moment they stop they are unyoked and fed whilst they are warm. By this treatment half the poor animals are foundered. Most people travel on horseback with pistols or swords and a large blanket folded up under their saddle which they use for sleeping on.[6]

Another European who disdained the Wagon Road's inns was the French botanist André Michaux, who traversed it frequently in the years 1785–1801, obtaining specimens for his book on North American botany, *Flora Boreali-Americana,* published in 1803. (His son, François André Michaux, also rode the Wagon Road a few years later to study the forest trees of the new continent, described in his *The North American Sylva,* published in 1818.) Wrote the elder Michaux:

> The taverns along the road are almost everywhere very bad; nevertheless, rum, brandy, and whiskey are always to be had, these articles of provision being considered as being of the first necessity, and the profits of those who keep taverns arise principally from the liquors, of which there is a very great consumption. At breakfast they serve up bad tea, worse coffee, and small slices of fried ham, to which are sometimes added eggs and boiled fowl. Dinner—a piece of salt beef and roast fowls, with rum and water for drink; at night coffee, tea and ham. There are always several beds in the rooms in which they sleep, while sheets are seldom met with; happy the traveller who arrives on the day they are changed.[7]

Tea and coffee served in inns were universally criticized. A Virginia traveler, Congressman John Randolph of Roanoke, spat out the tea he was served in one rural ordinary. "Sir," he commanded the tavern-keeper, "if this be tea, bring me coffee. And if this be coffee, bring me tea!"

The table manners of wagoners and other travelers were also deplorable. When food was placed on the table in platters, country style, it was every man for himself and the devil take the hindermost. "It was the custom for guests to reach across table or across three or four persons sitting next to them when they wanted some dish," an observer wrote.

Politicians came to regard the friendly inn along their route as a second home. James G. Blaine, who served as Secretary of State under President Garfield, recalled in old age:

> We did not use the high sounding "hotel" but the good old Anglo-Saxon "tavern," with its wide open fire in the cheerful bar room, and the bountiful spread in the dining room, and the long porch for summer loafers, and the immense stabling with its wealth of horse-flesh, and the great open yard for the road wagons. How real and vivid it all seems to me this moment![8]

In good weather, travelers sometimes slept in their wagon or on a straw pallet under the stars. Effort was made to stop near a spring or creek, where the driver would build a fire and his companion prepared the meal. Meanwhile, the horses were tethered so they might forage. Care had to be taken to keep them from eating mountain laurel, which was poisonous to livestock.

An account of the traveler's vexations was written by a Philadelphian headed for Lancaster during a winter snow. Wrote he:

> I remained a fortnight waiting for a change of weather, but it never came; the roads, however, had become quite practicable for traveling and I at length determined on departure. At 5 o'clock in the morning I accordingly drove to Market Street, where I took possession of a place in a sleigh shaped like an omnibus. The snow lay deep on the ground, and the weather was cold in the extreme. After some delay the vehicle got in motion.
>
> The mail sleigh in which I found myself was one of the most wretched vehicles imaginable. The wind—a northwester—penetrated the curtains of the machine at a thousand crevices and, charged with particles of snow so fine as to be almost impalpable, communicated to the faces of the passengers the sensation of suffering under a hurricane of needles. We breakfasted at a wretched cabaret, and the pretensions of the dinner house were not much greater. The fare, though coarse, was abundant; still, a traveler, to get on comfortable, must take things as he finds them.

After many hardships, the sleigh driver found he could go no further:

> When the existing circumstance rendered it impossible to proceed further with the stage, he unloosed the horses and endeavored to take them to the nearest inn, a distance of about a mile and a half. He rode about half a mile when his four horses became imbedded in a snowbank. They were so perfectly chilled that they were almost incapable even of walking, much less of extricating themselves. . . . he procured a rail from an adjoining fence and dug out of the snow. Then with one horse, he delivered the mail. He arrived with eyelashes cemented together with ice and himself so benumbed that he could scarcely articulate.[9]

Weary travelers often complained of the noisy singing, card-playing, and fisticuffs at wayside inns. Unless the host were a forceful peace-keeper, like Casper Fahnestock or General Joshua Evans of the General Paoli, barroom brawls endangered anyone dining or loitering in the tavern room. Travelers along the Great Road occasionally found a whole tavern in an alcoholic uproar with rooms, stairs, and innyard filled with drunks. Such hazards were greatest at drovers' and wagoners' inns, which the gentry avoided.

Traveling over the Wagon Road to the nearest town after summer crops had been harvested, Appalachian farmers brought wagonloads of flour, grain, and tobacco, which they had collected to barter for manufactured products needed on the frontier. Many traders were Scotch-Irishmen, who were known for their shrewd trading and frugal living. Other wagon-drivers were farmers who took to the road after harvesting their crops in autumn and "hired out" as wagoners until planting time in spring.

To save money, the wagoner often arranged with a tavern-keeper to let him sleep on his blanket or pallet on the barroom floor. After a quick jigger of rum, he would return to the innyard to unhitch his horses and tether them on each side of the wagon tongue, on which he placed a trough of hay and oats. Then, smelling of the road, he would help himself to a mountainous meal. After supper he lost himself in drinking and card playing, to the light of candles and a hearthfire. When the bar closed, the wagon-driver would make his bed on the floor until the breakfast horn sounded next morning.

Despite his addiction to whiskey, the wagoner was generally an honest and conscientious man, known throughout the frontier for his strength and endurance. Rising early to feed and clean his horses, he would eat a quick breakfast and take to the road in order to travel the thirty miles or more which wagoners tried to traverse in a good day's work. If the wagoner were employed by a storekeeper, the usual allowance for his meals was twenty-two cents apiece, and this was for breakfast and supper only; lunch was a snack to be eaten on the road or during a midday stop to water the horses.

In addition to Casper Fahnestock, another well-known resident of the Wagon Road countryside was Joshua Evans, who operated the General Paoli. In 1769, Evans petitioned the August session of the Court of General Quarter Sessions at Chester, Pennsylvania, as follows:

> That whereas there is no house of public entertainment between the Yellow Springs and the Square in Newton, on the road leading through a large body of the upper part of this country by the Valley Church to Chester, Darby, &c., which is too great a distance for one stage, being 14 miles apart, and of consequence must be attended with great disadvantage to the large concourse of people passing that way; and as your petitioner has a very commodious house situated in the township of Tredyffrin, on Lancaster road,

where the aforesaid road meets with the same, . . . your petitioner humbly requests your Honors to recommend him to his Honor, the Governor, for a license to keep a public house of entertainment in the aforesaid place . . .

Joshua Evans[10]

The tavern was named for Pasquale di Paoli, a Corsican general and patriot admired by Americans for leading his people in rebellion against the Genoese in 1755. Appropriately enough, it became a gathering place for Revolutionary-minded Chester County men in the years leading to the Revolution. In that conflict, Joshua Evans briefly deserted his hostly duties to serve as a general in the Pennsylvania forces.

The General Paoli Inn long survived, being remodeled as late as 1881 to serve as a resort. It gave the name Paoli to the township which became a suburb of Philadelphia.

Another well-known stop between Philadelphia and Lancaster was the Green Tree Inn, which was patronized chiefly by wagoners. Like the General Paoli, it was known as a "Whig house" because of the pro-Revolutionary sentiments of its operator, one Coffman. Its meals were celebrated. When customers arrived in unexpected numbers, the tavern-keeper would go into the tavern yard with a handful of corn, call his chickens to eat it, then knock them out with a cane and deliver them to the waiting cook.

Both innkeepers and patrons suffered hardships, but the camaraderie of the road united them. Such men as Casper Fahnestock and Joshua Evans became an important part of the life of their time. Not only were they hosts but they filled many other functions: as arbiters of quarrels, physicians to the ill, counselors to migrating Europeans, dispensers of news, postmen, military recruiters, and politicians. With their help, America moved forward.

> Oh, the songs they would sing, and the tales they would spin,
> As they lounged in the light of the old country inn.
> But a day came at last when the stage brought no load
> To the gate, as it rolled up the long, dusty road.
> And lo! at the sunrise a shrill whistle blew
> O'er the hills—and the old yielded place to the new—
> And a merciless age with its discord and din
> Made wreck, as it passed, of the pioneer inn.[11]

CHAPTER 20

The Spirit of Luther

To the "German Tract" which developed in the Valley of Virginia a few years before the Revolution there came a new minister from Pennsylvania. He was Peter Muhlenberg. Tall and of a commanding presence, he became pastor of a small flock of Lutherans at Woodstock, in the foothills of the Massanutten Mountains south of Winchester.

Most Germanic settlers shied away from the politics of the frontier, but not Peter Muhlenburg. Well-educated and fluent in both English and German, he became a leader among emigrants from the Palatinate and Switzerland who had begun to farm along the Appalachians beginning in the 1730s. By the time the American colonies won their independence in 1783, Muhlenberg was a household name.

Peter Muhlenberg enjoyed a great advantage, for he was known to many Virginia Lutherans before he came south from Pennsylvania in 1771. His father, the venerable Pastor Heinrich Melchior Muhlenberg, had come to Pennsylvania in 1742, straight out of the German universities of Halle and Göttingen. Old Heinrich was not only a strong preacher but an organizer. In 1748, he succeeded in bringing together representatives of all the Lutheran congregations in Pennsylvania, Delaware, New Jersey, and Maryland. Thus had been born the first Lutheran Synod in the New World.

On his farm at Trappe, Pennsylvania, Pastor Heinrich Muhlenberg and his wife reared a large family. Each Sunday he rode his horse to preach to one of the scattered congregations of his faith in the vicinity. At night he taught his daughters and sons. Of these, two were to enter the ministry and to become leaders of men. One was John Peter Gabriel Muhlenberg, who was born at Trappe four years after his parents reached Pennsylvania from the Old World. The other was Frederick Augustus Conrad Muhlenberg, who came along four years later.

The Muhlenberg brothers had the dignified presence of their father. Furthermore, they grew up at a time when Germanic emigrants to Pennsylvania needed spokesmen to represent their views

[183]

to English-speaking county officials and tradesmen—and to explain the confusing maze of Pennsylvania's laws and customs to them in their native tongue. For, unlike the unworldly Mennonites and Amishmen, Lutherans wanted to be part of the new world into which they had come.

By the 1760s, when young Peter Muhlenberg returned to his native Pennsylvania from the University of Halle, he found that Germans were moving in large numbers from the Pennsylvania frontier to the Valley of Virginia. There they clustered in farm villages between the mountain ranges of the Blue Ridge, the Massanutten, and the Shenandoah.

Although the Germans spread over a dozen upland counties, they favored the Massanutten area. They named one village Strasburg for the Alsatian capital from which many had come. Such towns as New Market, Dayton, Harrisonburg, and Bridgewater had a strong Germanic flavor. In 1740, the Lutherans among these settlers built Hebron Church, their first, supporting a pastor as best they could. At nearby Upper Peaked Mountain Church, for example, members paid two shillings sixpence for each child the minister baptized, five shillings for confirmation, and similar sums for each burial and eucharist.

True to their founder's precept, Lutherans made their pastors teach as well as preach. To aid them, Martin Luther had written two catechisms setting forth his faith. He also enjoined that all adherents be instructed to read so that they could absorb the scriptures, which he believed to be the foundation of Christian faith. Old Heinrich Muhlenberg and his two sons, Peter and Frederick, were teachers as well as ministers.

As did the Moravians, Martin Luther and his followers emphasized music as a form of religious worship. Like Count Zinzendorf in the *Fratres Unitas,* Luther wrote many hymns which ultimately became familiar throughout Christendom. Such was

> A mighty fortress is our God
> A bulwark never failing
> Our helper He amid the flood
> Of mortal ills prevailing
> For still our ancient foe
> Doth seek to work us woe
> His craft and power are great,

> And armed with cruel hate,
> On earth is not his equal.[1]

Peter Muhlenberg came to the Valley of Virginia in 1771 through the efforts of James Wood, a far-sighted English settler. Wood first founded the town of Frederick as county seat of Frederick County in 1744, later renaming it Winchester for his native city in England. A few years later he established Woodstock about twenty miles further south on the Wagon Road, naming it for himself.

Under Virginia law, the Anglican Church was the established church of the colony. When a new county was established and new settlements made, houses of worship were built with taxes extracted from residents. To minister to the Germanic people settling around Woodstock in 1771, James Wood was concerned as clerk of Frederick County to find a minister who could preach to them in German. Learning that Pastor Heinrich Muhlenberg had a minister son serving Lutheran churches in New Jersey, Wood persuaded the Woodstock parish vestry to offer young Peter Muhlenberg the position.

Accordingly, James Wood wrote to him on May 4, 1771:

Rev. Sir:

I have been requested by the vestry of a vacant charge in Virginia to use my endeavours to find a person of unexceptionable character, either ordained or desirous of obtaining ordination in the Church of England, who is capable of preaching both in the English and the German languages. The Living as established by the Laws of the Land, with Perquisites, is of the value of Two hundred and Fifty Pounds, Pennsylvania currency, with a Parsonage House and a Farm of at least Two Hundred Acres of Extremely Good Land, with every other convenient Out House belonging to the same, which will render it very convenient for a Gentlemen's Seat.

And having just now received a Character and Information of you from Mr. John Vanorden of Brunswick, New Jersey, I am very inclinable to believe you would fully answer the expectations of the people of that Parish: the Gentleman of whom I have had information does not know whether You are ordained by the Bishop of London or not. However, be that as it will, if you can come well recommended to the Vestry they will recommend you in such a manner as to make your ordination certain.

If you should think those proposals worth your acceptance, I shall be glad. You could write me an Answer, to be left Philadelphia at the Sign of the Cross Keys, where I shall stay a few days on my return home, when, if I find You inclined to accept of this Living, you may expect to hear from me . . .

I am, tho' unacquainted, Rev. Sir, Yr Obt Servt.

New York, 4th May, 1771   James Wood

P.S. If you should determine to go to London, I make no Doubt of the Vestry advancing sufficient sum to defray the expenses.[2]

Peter Muhlenberg, then twenty-five years old, accepted the offer. He went to London in 1772, and was ordained by the Bishop of London as a minister of the Church of England. Then, coming to Virginia, he presented himself to his new parishioners, who greeted him warmly.

Like his father, Peter was not only a forceful minister but an excellent organizer. He was soon busy ministering to the Anglican congregation at Woodstock and to Lutherans there and at Rude's Hill nearby.

The Valley folk found Peter sympathetic to their complaints against British rule. The minister was elected to the Frederick County Committee of Safety, created to mobilize local militia in case of war with England. In 1775, he was sent as a representative to the Virginia Convention in Williamsburg, where he was appointed a colonel in the Virginia militia and authorized to enlist a regiment to defend the Great Road, if war should come.

Unlike most of their fellow Germanic emigrants, the Lutherans were not pacifistic. By 1771, many had learned some English and had involved themselves in the business and politics of the frontier. Along the Great Road, German immigrants kept taverns, made wagons, smelted iron, tanned leather, and ground wheat and corn into flour and meal. Along with other Germans and Swiss, they had built numerous log cabins since they first arrived in the 1730s, fitting squared logs onto one another and filling the chinks with mud to keep out the cold.

When Peter Muhlenberg arrived in Woodstock, he found prosperous Germans living in Pennsylvania-type houses of fieldstone and hewn limestone. They built barns of wood, painting them dark red and decorating them with traditional hex signs to ward off evil. For escape from Indians, they dug stone-walled cellars, reached through trap doors when the alarm bell was rung.

Like the Germans of Pennsylvania and Maryland, Woodstock's parishioners lived well. They grew good crops, rotating their plantings and carefully fertilizing them with manure from the cow barn. By banding together to harvest crops, they made efficient use of their labor. Only Sunday was a day of rest.

As in Pennsylvania, a few skilled gunsmiths lived in the Valley and supplied their customers with the long barrels which the Indians feared. Henry Spitzer in New Market, Adam Haymaker in Winchester, the Sheetz family near Luray, and several others were producers of these *jaeger* rifles, which Virginians called "squirrel guns" or "Virginia rifles."

Henry Spitzer, who had come from Pennsylvania, produced a rifle each week at his home workshop, charging about £4 apiece. These he decorated with brasswork hex designs, inlaid into their wooden stocks, to give the hunter luck. Following the practice in Germany, the earliest Germanic rifles in America were of large caliber to kill bear or deer. However, the size was soon reduced for greater utility and lighter weight. Virginia and Kentucky rifles by the time of the Revolution were usually of .36 caliber. Each local militiaman was required to own such a rifle plus a bayonet or tomahawk for hand-to-hand fighting.

In the German Tract around Woodstock, travelers encountered the same Old World foods they had enjoyed at taverns around Lancaster, York, and Frederick. The *hausfrau* kept a spotless house and treasured the cuisine of the Rhine Valley and the Palatinate: yeast breads, sauerkraut, liverwurst, scrapple, pig's knuckles, apple butter, and other Teutonic specialties.

The Germanic houses of the region were simply provided with homemade furniture. Occasionally a treasured family chest or chair was brought with a family from Europe and then overland from Pennsylvania. A few Germans were proficient cabinetmakers, but most of these centered in Philadelphia. Homemade furniture was painted in bright Bavarian colors and decorated with stylized tulips, birds, and symbolic designs.

To record births and marriages, *fraktur* drawings were made by loving hands, embodying the names of children and parents and the important dates in their lives. These stylized pictures resembled medieval illuminated manuscripts and were decorated with figures of Adam and Eve, Moses, and other biblical figures.

To grind the wheat which abounded in the German settlements, many mills were built by German pioneers. These were turned by the plunging torrents of narrow mountain streams which descended from the Blue Ridge and Massanutten Mountains to form the upper headwaters of rivers which flowed eastward to Chesapeake Bay.

Building a mill was a difficult process. To turn the heavy mill wheel—which resembled the paddle wheel of later river steamers —a heavy volume of water had to be forcefully channeled between retaining walls of rock. The resultant turning of the water wheel provided power to rotate the heavy stone mill wheels, which slowly ground the wheat or corn.

Some millers "bolted" their flour by sifting it through a sieve to remove the coarser fragments, known as bran. Bolted flour or meal was sold at a premium. For his service, the miller traditionally retained a specified percentage of the flour or meal which he ground. The usual "toll" was one-tenth.

The cutting of millstones was a specialized craft in the settlements. A hard porphyritic granite with a clean crystal face was needed in order to provide a sharp cutting surface.

To the mills around Woodstock farmers brought their crop of wheat or corn each fall. On the appointed day, the countryman unloaded his crop from his farm wagon and helped the miller feed it into the mill wheels. One hour was required to grind a bushel of corn. Some mills had a second set of coarse-surfaced millstones to grind the "chop" or chaff, from which a mash or coarse bran was made to feed cattle, poultry, and hogs after snow covered the ground.

As the millwheels turned, the miller carefully controlled the flow of grain. Now and again he felt the flour with fingers to be sure it was ground to the desired texture. Overheating of the milled grain was to be avoided, for this affected the flour's taste. "Waterground" flour or meal—an assurance of quality—was cherished as the best to be had.

Music played a large part in the life of Peter Muhlenberg's parish, as it did in Lutheran and Moravian churches everywhere. For these people shared the rich musical heritage of the medieval German *minnesingers* as well as of the composers Johann Sebastian Bach, Dietrich Buxtehude, Heinrich Schutz, and countless anonymous hymnists of the Reformation. Martin Luther himself—Peter

Muhlenberg's great predecessor—spoke to these Germanic pioneers as perhaps no other voice spoke in these dangerous years:

> Did we in our own strength confide,
>   Our striving would be losing
> Were not the right man on our side,
>   The man of God's own choosing.
> Dost ask who that may be?
>   Christ Jesus, it is he.
> Lord Sabaoth his Name,
>   From age to age the same
> And He must win the battle.[3]

Close to the parish which Peter Muhlenberg served, riding through winter's snow or on many a moonless night to minister to the ill or comfort the bereaved, a pioneer school of Germanic religious music soon arose in the little village of Singer's Glen. And nearby, at New Market, a German printer named Solomon Henkel set up the first printing press in the Valley of Virginia to produce Lutheran religious tracts and hymnals of Germanic music.

During the life of the Great Wagon Road, the Henkel press published more Lutheran theological works in English than any other publisher in the world.

By the year 1776, the peaceful Valley into which Pastor Muhlenberg had come was visibly stirred by the alarms of war. In Philadelphia, the Continental Congress on July 4 of that year declared the thirteen colonies independent of Great Britain and prepared to go to war. In New York City, Peter Muhlenberg's younger brother resigned his pastorate of Christ Lutheran Church and hurried to Pennsylvania to join forces with the American patriots. The cry of "Liberty or death!" inflamed all America.

Not long after independence had been declared, Peter Muhlenberg made his fateful choice. At the end of one Sunday-morning worship service at his Woodstock church, the tall preacher cast off his black clerical gown as he stood in the pulpit of Beckford Parish Church. Beneath it he wore the uniform of the Virginia militia.

"I am a clergyman, it is true," he told his surprised congregation. "But I am a member of society, as well as the poorest layman. My liberty is as dear to me as any man.

"Shall I, then, sit still and enjoy myself at home when the best blood of the continent is spilling? Heaven forbid it!"

[189]

With that, Peter Muhlenberg handed his resignation to the parish vestry and went to war as a brigadier general of Virginia's forces.

He served well and in many sectors, culminating in a series of battles which ended in the great victory at Yorktown in 1781. When the war ended in 1783 the towering soldier had risen to the rank of brevet major general. Returning to Pennsylvania, he was elected three times to the House of Representatives of the young United States of America.

Peter Muhlenberg was one of the few Germanic emigrants along the Great Philadelphia Wagon Road who played so conspicuous a part in the Revolution. Many others served as soldiers of the line or drove army wagons to carry ammunition and provisions for the troops.

Yet they all made a contribution to the growing ethnic amalgam called America. They wove into the fabric of a new nation a mutual tolerance, a belief in religious freedom, and a devotion to a system of government which protected them against kings or feudal landlords.

The idealism of Martin Luther became an inseparable quality of America.

> And though this world, with devils filled
> Should threaten to undo us;
> We will not fear, for God hath willed
> His truth to triumph through us;
> The prince of darkness grim
> We tremble not for him;
> His rage we can endure,
> For lo! his doom is sure.
> One little word shall fell him.[4]

CHAPTER 21

In the Cabins along the Road

The frontiersman was a familiar character in American life from the time of Jamestown until the West was subdued in the 1849 Gold Rush. He existed in a particularly vigorous form along the eighteenth-century Appalachian frontier, when the great westward expansion of the seacoast colonies got under way.

The uplands attracted fugitives from the law, and they gave it a reputation for lawlessness which stuck with it. The hillbillies of the twentieth century, living in crude mountain cabins and making corn whiskey beyond the reach of the "revenooers," were offshoots of earlier fugitives from the more effete coastal settlements.

Some of these were descendants of English felons, transported to the colonies to clean out England's jails. (Jefferson wrote that "2,000 felons came to Virginia from the earliest settlement until 1787 . . .") Some were indentured servants who fled their masters, or Negro slaves who had fled west to freedom. Others were reputed to be Hessian soldiers who served as mercenaries for the British in the Revolution and stayed on in the new Land of Opportunity.

Many South Carolina hill-dwellers were English debtors, who had been encouraged by Governor Oglethorpe after 1733 to find a new life in the young Georgia colony. However, when they were faced with military service to avert threatened Spanish attack from Florida, many of these made their way to the South Carolina up-country, where they became "poor whites."

Here and there along the Wagon Road, colonies of intermixed whites and Indians took root. Near Lexington, in the Valley of Virginia, a hybrid group called "the brown people" clustered on the hillsides. In Amherst County, Virginia, a similar group called "the issues" lived. Nearby were other self-contained colonies called "melungeons" and others called "ramps." Similar mixed-breed groups were found along the Carolina and Georgia frontier.

"The frontier draws both the very best and the very worst," it was said, and this was true. An English traveler, Nicholas Cresswell, who visited upland Virginia before the Revolution, reported "nothing but whores and rogues in this country." Isaac Zane, Jr., a leading Quaker of early Winchester, Virginia, openly kept a mistress. Along the Appalachian frontier, where men outnumbered women five to one, illegitimacy was commonplace.

Others complained of the shrewd business practices of frontier dwellers. One such critic was Charles Lee, an English-born professional soldier who served as a general under George Washington in the Revolution and retired to upland Virginia to spend his last years. "We in Virginia live (if it can be called living)," he wrote, "neither under Monarchy, Aristocracy, nor Democracy—if it deserved any name it is a Macocracy, that is, a Banditti of Scotch-Irish Servants or their immediate descendants (whose names generally begin with Mac) are our Lords and Rulers." Lee specified in his will that he not be buried "within a mile of any Presbyterian or Anabaptist meeting house; for since I have resided in this country, I have kept so much bad company when living that I do not chuse to continue it when dead."

But the frontiersmen had their admirers, too. G. P. R. James wrote glowingly of Valley of Virginia settlers:

A valley farmer is a noble specimen of the yeoman. He has little Latin and less Greek, having derived his education in an "old field school-house," from a stern Scotch school master.... The Valley farmer is shrewd, sensible and refined, with just views of human affairs, generous to others, but frugal to himself; industrious and attentive to business, but full of fun in his hours of leisure; a Democrat in politics, a Presbyterian in religion, and a colonel in the militia.[1]

The earliest Appalachian settler, the hunter or fur-buyer, lived in a tent or log lean-to. He slept on a bed of dried leaves or rushes, close to the embers of his campfire. Leaving some Wagon Road village in the fall, after the leaves had fallen and the rattlesnakes had disappeared, he walked or rode his horse along the notched hunters' trail. Underfoot was the summer's undergrowth, killed by frost. His deerskin hunting shirt was fringed with bright cording, worn over breeches and leggings. A cap of beaver or otter kept off the rain, and Indian moccasins protected his feet.

The belt at his waist held his hatchet, and a sling over his shoulder held his sheath knife and his shot pouch or powder horn. Rolled in the pack on his back were an extra shirt, a blanket, flints, and a few standbys: brandy for medicine and disinfectant, salt to cure hides, and jerked beef or pemmican.

"W-a-a-l-l-l now," one bearded Long Hunter was heard to exclaim to the stars as the brandy warmed his entrails, "ef I just had the ol' woman and babbies here, I should be fixed for fair."

Such sharpshooters made up the county militia who protected the frontier in the French and Indian Wars and the Revolution. "Colonels" and "captains" abounded. Wrote a frontier visitor who signed himself Porte Crayon, "There is not a tavern-keeper or stage-owner in all western Virginia, or a great wood chopper, who has not some military title. And anyone who kills a rattlesnake is made a major on the spot."

The lowlanders who first reached the uplands built in rustic American style: walls of adzed timbers or of woven rushes, or wattle covered with heavy mud or daub. The early houses were small, usually about sixteen by twenty feet. Roofs were covered with wide boards, chinked with clay or covered with skins. Swedes who had settled along the Delaware River beginning in 1638 first built the log huts which became the favorite abode of the frontiersman. Its stout walls, pierced with small gunports, offered better protection against Indians.

Seventy to eighty trees were felled to build a log house. Working steadily, a half-dozen men could erect one in a week or two.

The advantage of the Delaware log house was that it could be built with no tools except an axe and an adze. The log walls, built over an earth flooring, were chinked with clay against the wind. The few small window openings were covered with greased paper, which admitted a little light. For lack of metal fittings, shutters and doors swung on wooden pegs.

Roofs were often shingled with white oak or chestnut shingles, painstakingly rived, one by one, with mallet and froe.

To "chink" against bad weather, moss and mud were stuffed into the cracks. Slabs of rough-sawn wood made the floor, and a ladder led up to an unventilated sleeping room. Mattresses were cotton bed ticking, stuffed with chaff, pine needles, or moss.

Metals for houses and wagons was rare in Wagon Road country until the Germans came through, bringing skillful blacksmiths and ironworkers. Iron in bars, rods, and sheets was brought by wagon from ironworks in eastern towns. Because of iron's rarity and expense, builders learned to work without nails or screws. Houses were framed and joined with mortises, tenons, and pegs. Masonry foundations and chimneys were mortared with clay. Metal was valued; when a wagon rim was no longer serviceable on the wheel, the farmer heated it red hot and beat it into shape for a strap hinge, an iron pin, or a cleat for a plow or harrow.

The log houses of Daniel Boone's day were poor protection against rain or snow. Rough-hewn flat wooden slabs formed the roof, and the chimney was built of fieldstone or rocks, mortared in clay. Furniture was homemade: a trestle table and benches, a high bed with a trundle bed for the children beneath it, and a few three-legged stools. The fireplace was the heart of the house, affording warmth and cheer. On iron pots hung over the flames, meats and vegetables were cooked. In Germanic houses, a Dutch oven was built into the fireplace for baking and roasting.

Log houses were built larger and better as the years passed. Often the logs were adzed square for better fit. Sometimes they were covered with plaster. Such a structure in the Great Valley was called a Virginia-style house.

The food of the Wagon Road was simple. Ashcake, made of cornmeal and water, was wrapped in green cornhusks or cabbage leaves and cooked on the hearth in wood ash. Meats were sometimes speared on a spit, suspended over live coals. A thick porridge called "mush," made of cornmeal boiled with milk or water, was eaten with molasses, boar's oil, or gravy. Smoked pork was a common meat, for hogs grew to maturity in eight months on the beechnuts, acorns, and chestnuts on the forest floor.

The housewife depended on this staple, as one of them testified in James Fenimore Cooper's *The Chainbearer:* "I hold a family to be in a desperate way when the mother can see the bottom of the pork barrel. Give me the children that's raised on good sound pork afore all the game in the country. Game's good as a relish and so's bread; but pork is the staff of life."

The fare of Germanic families in the lower Pennsylvania counties of Lancaster, York, Berks, and Chester was especially famous. Here a rich limestone plain produced abundant grain and vegetables. Until the railway era, Lancaster's produce made Philadelphia's markets the cheapest and best in the world. Travelers along the Wagon Road noted that the small farmhouses were dwarfed by barns 100 to 150 feet long and 50 feet high, marked with hex signs. It was a profuse land of wheat, rye, corn, potatoes, tobacco, and cattle.

The simple life of the upcountry householder was praised by Andrew Burnaby, an archdeacon of the Church of England who visited Germanic farms in Virginia in 1759. "I could not but reflect with pleasure on the situation of these people," he wrote home to England, "and think, if there is such a thing as happiness in life, that they enjoy it. They are subject to few diseases; are generally robust; and live in perfect liberty; they are ignorant of want, and acquainted with but few vices. Their inexperience with the elegancies of life precludes any regret that they possess not the means of enjoying them."

This was a fair assessment of life along the Wagon Road until the arrival of the industrial twentieth century.

Life in the mountain cabins was compounded of piety, pleasure, and frequent danger. Most of the mountain settlers "laid by" a few goods which they sent by passing wagoners to market: skins, furs, hemp, ginseng, grain, cheese, and butter among them. In return, the wagoner brought them patent medicines, shoes, iron, and hardware which he had bought or bartered for them. Salt was always in demand, and the family salt gourd was guarded. A few pioneers made their living selling salt from salt licks which had once attracted buffalo and Indians.

The dress of the cabin-dweller was as simple as his house. Homespun garments of linsey-woolsey—a blend of cotton and wool— were usual in the early years. Later, when cloth was brought in by wagon, women wore everyday ginghams and calicoes, saving their one dress of silk, velvet, satin, or shalloon for "Sunday-go-to-meeting" best. Pioneer men favored the hunter's garb of coonskin cap and fringed hunting shirt, which they considered a symbol of masculinity. In villages and religious colonies, men usually wore broadcloth in summer and serge or linsey-woolsey in winter. Men wore caps and women bonnets to keep sun and May flies away.

Among the Amish, Moravians, Sabbatarians, and Mennonites, a monastic plainness reminiscent of the Roman Catholic orders continued to prevail. In these pietistic sects, simplicity and self-denial extended even to periods of celibacy among married couples. Men sometimes shaved their heads and substituted wigs or white caps. Men's breeches were short, fastened at the knee, and worn with long stockings. The broadbrimmed hats they wore to church harked back to John Calvin and his Geneva reformers. Elders and children shunned the outside world. Then as now, the horse-drawn wagons of the Amish were conspicuous on county roads as church-time neared. To them, to be "plain" was to be undefiled by worldly society.

Little Moravian girls wore a net cap tied under the chin with pink ribbon. Older girls wore white linen caps with red ribbons after they became church members. Married sisters wore caps tied with light blue, while widows' ribbons were white.

Boys and girls on the frontier matured and married young. In a world fraught with danger and epidemic disease, life must be lived fast. Boys often married at sixteen and girls at fourteen. As soon as a mother weaned one child, she expected another. Frontier midwives were busy delivering babies, for physicians were few.

Occasionally a husband long absent at war or in Indian territory was presumed dead, leading a lonely wife to remarry. In such cases of unintentional bigamy, the wife was permitted to choose between spouses.

Frontiersmen taught their children to read from a hornbook, a vellum sheet imprinted with the alphabet and Lord's Prayer and covered with a thin sheet of transparent horn. Scotch-Irish and Lutheran ministers usually instructed a few diligent older lads who were preparing to enter the ministry or the law. From such beginnings arose academies and log colleges like those at Neshaminy and Fagg's Manor, in Pennsylvania, and at Timber Ridge in Virginia.

To take advantage of daylight, the frontiersman arose at dawn and went to bed not long after dark. The principal meal at midday was proclaimed by ringing a farm bell or beating a pan. After supper, the family sat before the hearth, the mother spinning or weaving. Sometimes she sang as she spun, or "trapezied" in, mincingly, letting the yarn flow from her hand into the spinning wheel.

While the men of a community plowed, planted, tended livestock, and brought in the harvest, the women sewed, knit, cooked, made soap, and put up food for winter. Many early households supplied all their own necessities but salt, lead, and iron. Wild honey served for sugar.

Plows were usually pulled by oxen, which were stronger and more patient than horses. Mules did not come into use until the nineteenth century.

Church on Sunday was a relief from work, parents and children riding there together on horseback or wagon. Weddings brought out young and old, dinner often being served on the church grounds before the ride home. An amorous young Scotsman was described as "brigady" and a truculent one as "feisty." At nightfall, after the bride and bridegroom had nervously entered the sleeping loft, friends serenaded them with a "shivaree" (from "charivari"), beating on kettles to proclaim the glad tidings. It was an unsophisticated age.

In Germanic households, a bride was subjected to the prankish theft of her shoe, despite the defense of her giggling bridesmaids.

"Court day" was another family occasion. Then rural neighbors bartered produce and sat as jurymen, or met as viewers or overseers to provide for the upkeep of their portion of the Wagon Road.

Recalling the arrival of his mother and father in Kentucky in 1779, Chief Justice George Robertson of that state wrote in 1843:

> Behold the men on foot with their trusty guns on their shoulders, driving stock and leading packhorses; and the women, some walking with pails on their heads, others riding with children in their laps, and other children swung in baskets on horses, fastened to the tails of others going before; see them encamped at night, expecting to be massacred by Indians; behold them in the month of December, in that ever-memorable season of unprecedented cold called the "hard winter," traveling two or three miles a day, frequently in danger of being frozen or killed by the falling of horses on the icy and almost impassable trace, and subsisting on stinted allowances of stale bread and meat; but now lastly look at them at the destined fort, perhaps on the eve of merry Christmas, when met by the hearty welcome of friends who had come before, and cheered by fresh buffalo meat and parched corn, they rejoice at their deliverance, and resolve to be content with their lot.[2]

Like rural people everywhere, the Appalachian pioneers found pleasure in simple things. Mothers sang to babies as they rocked:

> Hush, little baby, don't say a word
> Mama's gonna buy you a mocking bird.
> If that mocking bird don't sing,
> Mama's gonna buy you a diamond ring.
> If that diamond ring turns brass,
> Mama's gonna buy you a looking glass.
> If that looking glass gets broke,

Mama's gonna buy you a nanny goat.
If that nanny goat don't pull,
Mama's gonna buy you a cart and bull.[3]

Churning butter or kneading bread, the housewife worked her hands to the rhythm of a song. So did her husband as he planted corn in the field outside:

One for the blackbird,
One for the crow,
One for the cutworm
And one to grow.[4]

Men made light work of building a log house by cutting timbers and handling heavy logs together. Neighbors pitched in, the host supplying food and grog. When the roof-pole went up, he passed the brandy bottle around, and the sweating workmen cheered and drank lustily, for the job was nearly done. The owner could hew the rest himself: puncheons for flooring, wall pegs for hanging clothes, a ladder leading to the attic, and the crude hickory furniture, made from leftover lumber.

While neighboring farmers were raising a barn or helping each other kill hogs, wives shucked corn or sewed around the fire at a quilting bee. Quilt covers were pieced from scraps of leftover cloth —wool, silk, or cotton—and lined for warmth with goose down or layers of homespun. A feather mattress, a quilt, and bed linen formed the proud dowry of many a Wagon Road bride.

Music lightened the load of the Appalachian pioneer. The fiddle gave a lift to wedding parties, and the jew's-harp twanged incessantly on wagons plying the road. A few households boasted a dulcimer, a stringed instrument struck with padded hammers.

Plaintive ballads, learned in childhood in England or Scotland, were cherished by emigrants and passed down "by ear" to children and grandchildren.

It was in and about the Martinmas time,
When the green leaves were a-falling,
That Sir John Graeme, in the West Country,
Fell in love with Barbara Allan.[5]

To the meter and the doleful minor mode of English and Scottish balladry, frontiersmen developed songs of their own. In the pine-covered mountains of Virginia and the Carolinas, many a local Homer contributed to the lore of the misty hills and valleys. Isolated from outside influences by mountain fastnesses, Elizabethan ballads and their Appalachian offspring continued to resound into the twentieth century. They were the basis for the "country music" which later emerged in Kentucky and Tennessee.

Akin to the Appalachian's plaintive ballads were folk hymns, sung to popular early European tunes and handed down to the Great Road's settlers by generations past. Some of these went back as far as the Norman Conquest, when an Archbishop of York was described as writing verses to fit the melody of the minstrels' bawdy songs. Sixteenth-century Scotsmen added to these folk hymns.

In the Wesleyan revival of eighteenth-century England, hymn-writers Isaac Watts and John Wesley contributed their singable hymns to those of the Presbyterians and Quakers. Though at first disclaimed by old school Anglicans, their music came into great popularity in nineteenth-century America and England.

Folk spirituals sung in the early Appalachians ranged from ballads like "The Romish Lady," who was martyred for espousing Protestantism, to such naive hymns as:

> Alas! and did my Savior bleed,
> And did my Sov'reign die?
> Would He devote that sacred head
> For such a worm as I?
> I yield, I yield, I yield.
> I can hold out no more.
> I sink by dying love compell'd
> And own Thee conqueror.[6]

Many colloquial hymns later adopted throughout Christendom entered America over the Great Road. Others originated during the great Methodist revivals, stirred by Francis Asbury and his associates, which converted thousands of Appalachian dwellers after the Revolution. Many of these were published in the 1800s in English and German-language songbooks—several of them in Scotch-Irish and Germanic centers like Philadelphia, Hagerstown, and Singer's Glen, Virginia.

In Germanic "shaped note" songbooks—so-called because of their simplified system of musical notation—are primitive versions of later hymns, together with anonymous melodies like "Turkey in the Straw" and "Home, Sweet Home." There too are pioneers' songs which were absorbed or adapted by Negro slaves in their spirituals and jubilee songs.

Humor was often crude. Among the Scotch-Irish, a nightshirt was called an "ebenezer," from the Hebrew for shrine or place of worship. When Presbyterian worshippers sang their hymn, "When I Lift My Ebenezer," an embarrassed smile was sometimes seen.

Along with ballads, the Appalachian pioneers enjoyed country dances, which were akin to the morris dances of medieval England. These included the lively nineteenth-century innovation, the Virginia Reel, in which a fiddler scratched out a melody like "Turkey in the Straw" while a caller set the rhythm and put the dancers through their steps:

> Bow to your partner,
> Dosey-do,
> Chicken in the bread pan,
> Kickin' out dough.[7]

From such country dances came the rural hoedown of later years. Similar was the barn dance, which derived from the "bran" dance performed at a house warming. For such occasion, corn chaff called "bran" was spread on the new flooring so that the oily kernel could be pressed into the wood to polish it.

Such was the life of the Wagon Road—a life which demanded faith and hardihood, leavened with humor and entertainment. The spirit which animated these people was the humor of a Daniel Boone, an Andy Jackson, or an Abe Lincoln. It was to become a vital part of the exuberant American tradition.

Recalling the days of the Wagon Road, a chronicler of early Tennessee asked:

> Could there be happiness or comfort in such dwellings and such a state of society? To those who are accustomed to modern refinements, the truth appears like fable. The early occupants of log cabins were among the most happy of mankind. Exercise and excitement gave them health; they were practically equal; common danger made them mutually dependent; brilliant hopes of future wealth and distinction led them on; and as there was ample room for all, and as each newcomer increased individual and general security, there was little room for that envy, jealousy, and hatred which constitute a large portion of human misery in older societies.
>
> Never were the story, the song and the laugh better enjoyed than upon the hewed blocks, or puncheon stools, around the roaring log fire of the early western settler.[8]

Such was life in the cabins along the frontier trail.

CHAPTER 22

Tuckahoe versus Cohee

The colonies were buzzing with indignation against the Stamp Act in the autumn of 1766 when the Reverend Charles Woodmason rode out of Charles Town and headed inland toward the back country of South Carolina.

Ambling uphill astride his saddle horse and followed by his English servant on another, the newly ordained minister pondered his mission. He had volunteered to the Bishop of London, who directed the Church of England in the colonies, to establish a parish along the Great Wagon Road and spread the Anglican gospel among the thousands of Cohees (so-called for their Scottish locution, "Quoth he") scattered through the uplands. He would set up a church at Pine Tree Hill and try to instill the fear of God in the rowdy settlements of the frontier.

He was to find it an impossible job. For the next six years, the zealous missionary worked feverishly, riding more than 3,000 miles annually to preach throughout his circuit. He organized thirty scattered congregations, and he baptized and married hundreds of people. But he found it impossible to keep up with the growing upland population and its problems. He was forced to give up his arduous labors in 1772, in the face of the oncoming Revolution, and return in two years to England. At fifty-two he was worn out.

Woodmason's experience along the Great Road reveals the chasm which had developed by 1766 between Mother England and her backwoods American colonists. Though he was strongly pro-Tory when he went there, his experiences at Pine Tree (soon renamed Camden) and along the settlements of the Wateree, Catawba, and Saluda rivers gave him sympathy for the unchurched and neglected backwoodsmen. When the upcountry "Regulator" movement came to a head in 1772, Charles Woodmason championed its demands upon His Majesty's representatives at Charles Town.

The energetic Englishman was well-qualified to judge the Great Road settlements. He had been born about 1720 of genteel English parents and had emigrated to South Carolina as a young man and acquired plantations and a store. However, after a kick from a horse disqualified him for "nuptial" rites, his wife refused to come to

America, and he spent his years in South Carolina as a bachelor. In his journals, Woodmason describes several attempts by back country women to lure him to bed. However, he pictured marriage as

> a Circumstance I am wholly unfit for, as being both Old and Impotent for many Years past, thro a fall received from a Horse, and a Kick received in the Scrotum. And this Incapacity for Nuptial Rites, was the Reason, that a Wife I had in England refus'd coming to America, to live with the Man, who sacrificed all he had in Life, for her Benefit. I told our Vestry my Unfitness, which they laughed at as a Joke—and I courted two Ladies, and fairly told my Case—who declared they choose not to live as married Nuns.[1]

Woodmason left his political offices and his Carolina lands in 1762 to return to England for a year, apparently to settle the estate of his deceased wife and provide for his son. When he returned to Charles Town, he decided to remain in that comfortable capital as an officeholder. He prospered until 1765, when he applied for the post of stamp distributor under the unpopular Stamp Act. The bitter reaction of Charlestonians, who suddenly regarded him as "a private Spy and Correspondent of the Ministry," evidently persuaded him to apply for the position of itinerant Anglican minister in the upper part of St. Mark's Parish, which included the Great Wagon Road and the Catawba and Cherokee paths.

Anglican ministers were few in South Carolina, and the devout Woodmason was accepted for the new parish provided he would go to England for theological examination and ordination to the priesthood. He did so, and on September 12, 1766, set out from Charles Town through intermittent thunderstorms for Pine Tree Hill.

Like most coast-dwelling Tuckahoes (so-called for the fibrous plant root which early coastal settlers had eaten), Woodmason failed to understand or sympathize with the upcountry settlers, even while depending on them to hold off Indian incursions from the west. Many of these were lured by a grant of 100 acres, free of quitrents for ten years, which Governor Boone of South Carolina was authorized to make after 1761. Woodmason was incensed that evangelistic New Light Baptists were coming into South Carolina in the wake of the French and Indian Wars, and wrote the Bishop of London that he would "disperse these Wretches" and cause them to "fly before Him as Chaff."

Like many Anglican clergymen of his day, Woodmason failed to understand the need for a simple and direct ministry to reach the masses of uneducated people who thronged the frontier. To fill this great need, the New Side Presbyterians, Baptists, and Methodists were spreading religious heterodoxy along the Great Wagon Road. It was the demands of these people which would lead to the separation of Church and State after the Revolution.

The new minister realized none of this when he set out for the back country. He was anxious to convert the raw frontier into a peaceable English landscape. He wished to "New Model and form the Carriage and Manners, as well as Morals of these wild Peoples" and "bring about a Reformation" in their lives.

Arriving at Pine Tree Hill, Woodmason preached in the Presbyterian meeting house.

> The People around [he wrote], of abandon'd Morals, and profligate Principles—Rude—Ignorant—Void of Manners, Education or Good Breeding—No genteel or Polite Person among them—save Mr. Kershaw an English Merchant settled here. The people are of all Sects and Denominations—a mix'd Medley from all Countries and the Off Scouring of America. Baptized 20 Children this Week and rode about 40 Miles.[2]

While continuing to use the Presbyterian meeting house, Woodmason sent a petition to the South Carolina Assembly to build a chapel for the Established Church's use. He was forced to reside in the local tavern for lack of a house he could rent "fit to put my Head or Goods in." He found his parishioners all new settlers, pitifully poor, and living in log cabins "like Hogs." But Woodmason was unexpectedly befriended by Samuel Wyly, one of the Irish Quakers who had settled Pine Tree Hill in 1752.

Woodmason's English servant was soon hired away from him, but the minister was not discouraged. Though some communities ignored his services, others turned out in great numbers. At the Cheraws in January 1767, he preached for nearly six hours to 500 people and baptized 60 children. The next day he addressed a similar multitude at Lynch's Creek, where some of his hearers complained of having been "eaten up" by itinerant ministers from New England and Pennsylvania—"Baptists, New Lights, Presbyterians, Independents, and an hundred other Sects."

The anticeremonialism of the Scotch-Irish Presbyterians offended Woodmason especially. Visiting their church at the Waxhaws (where the family of young Andrew Jackson worshipped), Woodmason listened sympathetically to the outpourings of the Reverend William Richardson, who had been ordained by the New Side Presbyterians of Pennsylvania. "They will not suffer him to use the Lords Prayer," Woodmason fumed. "He wants to introduce [Isaac] Watts' Psalms in place of the barbarous Scotch Version, but they will not admit it."

Wherever he went, Woodmason read the proclamation by King George III *for the encouragement of piety and virtue, and the preventing and punishing of vice, prophaneness, and immorality.* "I therefore made Public Notice ev'ry where be given," he recounted, "that whoever did not attend to be legally married, I would prosecute them at the Sessions—and that all who had liv'd in a State of Concubinage on application to me, I would marry Gratis." He noted with regret that, for lack of Anglican clergy in North Carolina, judges in that colony were permitted to conduct weddings, attracting some couples from South Carolina.

During the rainy Carolina February, Woodmason continued to make his rounds. He observed with pity the settlers living in log lean-tos with hardly a blanket to cover them. So scarce was food that he could hardly obtain any for himself or his horse.

Woodmason encountered outright hostility in some Scotch-Irish settlements, where the memory of religious persecution by erstwhile Irish Anglican landlords still lingered. Such a congregation awaited him at Hanging Rock Creek:

> Found the Houses filled with debauch'd licentious fellows, and Scot Presbyterians who had hir'd these lawless Ruffians to insult me, which they did with Impunity—Telling me, they wanted no D—d Black Gown Sons of Bitches among them—and threatening to lay me behind the fire, which they assuredly would have done had not some Travellers alighted very opportunely, and taken me under Protection—These Men sat up with, and guarded me all the Night— In the Morning the lawless Rabble moved off on seeing the Church People appear, of whom had a large Congregation. But the Service was greatly interrupted by a Gang of Presbyterians who kept hallooing and whooping without Door like Indians.[3]

Even bitterer hostility awaited him at the home of a well-to-do Presbyterian tavern-keeper in the Waxhaws, where he went seeking food for himself and his horse:

> When I told him my Necessity—how sick I was with long fasting—Horse jaded and tir'd—My Self Weary and faint thro' fatigue and Cold, and took out Money to desire Refreshments He would not comply nor sell me a Blade of fodder, a Glass of Liquor (tho' he own'd he had 2 Barrel of Rum in House) nor permit me to sit down nor kindle up a Fire—All my arguments were in vain. He looked on me as an Wolf strayed into Christs fold to devour the Lambs of Grace. Thus did this rigid Presbyterian treat me. At length I got a little Indian Corn for my Horse, paying treble Price. Such was the Honesty of the Saint.[4]

But the worst indignity Woodmason received from the Presbyterians was the invasion of his worship service by a pack of dogs:

> They hir'd a Band of rude fellows to come to Service who brought with them 57 Dogs (for I counted them) which in Time of Service they set fighting, and I was obliged to stop. In Time of Sermon they repeated it—and I was oblig'd to desist and dismiss the People.[5]

Woodmason also encountered objection to the Anglican practice of reading the sermon, instead of preaching extemporaneously as the New Light Presbyterians and New Side Baptists did. "I . . . give an Extempore Prayer before Sermon," he concluded, "but cannot yet venture to give Extempore Discourses, tho' certainly could perform beyond any of these Poor Fools. I shall make Trial in a short time."

Summing up the results of his ministry in 1767 (40 couples married, 782 people baptized, 20 congregations formed), Woodmason wrote:

> Thus You have the Travels of a Minister in the Wild Woods of America—Destitute often of the very Necessaries of Life—Sometimes starved—Often famished—Exposed to the burning Sun and scorching Sands—Obliged to fight his way thro' Banditti, profligates, Reprobates, and the lowest vilest Scum of Mankind on the one hand, and of numerous Sectaries pregnant in these Countries, on the other—with few Friends, and fewer Assistants—and surmounting Difficulties, and braving Dangers, that ev'ry Clergyman that ever entered this Province shrinked even at the thoughts of—

Which none, not even the meanest of the Scotch Clergy that have
been sent here, would undertake, and for which he subjected himself to the Laughter of Fools and Ridicule of the Licentiousness for
undertaking.[6]

The moral laxity of the frontiersmen disturbed Woodmason, who
frequently commented on the nakedness of the young people. "How
would the Polite People of London stare," he observed in 1768,

> to see the Females (many very pretty) come to Service in their
> Shifts and a short petticoat only barefooted and Bare legged—with-
> out Caps or Handkerchiefs—dress'd only in their Hair, Quite in a
> State of Nature for Nakedness is counted as Nothing—as they sleep
> altogether in Common in one Room, and shift and dress openly
> without ceremony . . ."[7]

The revealing dress and loose behavior of frontiersmen shocked
the decorous Woodmason. He wrote indignantly of

> the Men with only a thin Shirt and pair of Breeches or Trousers on
> —barelegged and barefooted—The Women bareheaded, barelegged
> and barefoot with only a thin Shift and under Petticoat—Yet I can-
> not [break] them of this—for the heat of the Weather admits not
> of any [but] thin Cloathing—I can hardly bear the Weight of my
> Whig and Gown, during Service. The Young Women have a most
> uncommon Practise, which I cannot break them off. They draw their
> Shift as tight as possible to the Body, and pin it close, to show the
> roundness of their Breasts, and slender Waists (for they are gen-
> erally finely shaped) and draw their Petticoat close to their Hips to
> shew the fineness of their Limbs—so that they might as well be
> in Puri Naturalibus—Indeed Nakedness is not censurable or in-
> decent here, and they expose themselves often quite Naked, without
> Ceremony—Rubbing themselves and their Hair with Bears Oil and
> tying it up behind in a Bunch like the Indians—[8]

Such laxity led to promiscuity and early marriage—either legally
or by common law. Woodmason observed:

> When the Boys are 18 and Girls 14 they marry—so that in many
> Cabbins You will see 10 or 15 Children. Children and Grand Chil-
> dren of one Size—and the mother looking as Young as her Daughter.
> Yet these Poor People enjoy good Health; and are generally cut off
> by Endemic or Epidemic Disorders, which when they happen,
> makes Great Havock among them.[9]

[206]

Though Woodmason was only forty-six years old when he began his ministry in the Great Wagon Road region, its hardships and privations bore heavily on him. He severely indicted the Church of England for neglecting the American frontier and thus encouraging other sects to come in. So few Church of England clergymen were attracted to the provinces that all of South Carolina had only ten or twelve in 1768, "so that my Duty grows heavier and more weighty ev're Day, While I am wearing away, and almost destroyed by the Great Burden on my Shoulders," he wrote.

Though he was permitted by South Carolina law to receive 12 shillings 6 pence for every baptism, Woodmason refused to accept it. He also declined payment for most of the marriages he performed. "Their Poverty is so Great," he observed, "that were they to offer me a fee, My Heart would not let me take it." On the other hand, he asserted that the itinerant Presbyterian and Baptist ministers returned to Pennsylvania and New England with pockets full. "I find them a Sett of Rhapsodists—Enthusiasts—Bigots— Pedantic, illiterate, impudent Hypocrites—Straining at Gnats, and swallowing Camels, and making Religion a Cloak for Covetousness, Detraction, Guile, Impostures and their particular Fabric of Things." He particularly deplored the zealous Presbyterians' "persecution" of persons of other religious view.

He accused Presbyterian zealots of altering church-door announcements of the place and date of his services, causing congregations to gather fruitlessly. On another occasion, he said that some ill-wishers had posted a paper announcing that the King had discovered the "Popish Designs" of Woodmason and other Anglicans and had sent orders to South Carolina to suspend them and order them returned to England, thus forestalling further Anglican services.

In a list of the "Insolencies and Audacity" of Scotch-Irish Presbyterians and New Light Baptists, Woodman set down these:

At the Congaree Chapel, they enter'd and partly tore down the Pulpit—At St Marks a Sett of Waggoners got round the Church with their Whips, and oblig'd the Minister to quit the Service. On Whitsunday following after the Communion was ended, they got into the Church and left their Excrements on the Communion Table, and at Lynchs Creek they oblig'd the People to desist from building a Chapel. At Congarees, the Baptist Teacher entered at head of his Gang and began preaching when the minister had ended . . .[10]

After repeated urging by frontiersmen to preach extemporaneously, Woodmason nervously attempted it in 1769. Some of his own denomination urged him to do so in order to discredit his detractors. The Englishman preached and prayed for an hour and a quarter, and his congregation was overwhelmed with his eloquence. "The Dissenters were confounded and astonished and the Church People, pleas'd and delighted," he recorded.

An Old Gentleman (a Capital Person among them) took me home to his House—treated me very genteely (in their Way) introduc'd me to his Daughter (an agreeable Girl) and offer'd her in Marriage —But I declin'd the offer—she being too Young for me . . .[11]

Many of the severities of Scottish Calvinism were relaxed along the frontier. The Scotch-Irish were foremost among all settlers in their proficiency in making whiskey and brandy, as Woodmason and others observed. "The Stills will be soon at Work to make Whiskey and Peach Brandy," the minister wrote in August 1769. "In this Article, both Presbyterians and Episcopals very charitably agree (Viz.) That of getting Drunk."

Despite his inbred Anglican disdain for the ignorance and uncouthness of the frontier, Charles Woodmason soon recognized the unfair treatment which the back country received from South Carolina's colonial government. He especially disliked the General Assembly's unwillingness to create frontier parishes of the Established Church, since such parishes, entitled to representation in the General Assembly, would threaten the dominance of the low-country legislators.

Residents of the Great Wagon Road area were aroused anew when a new influx of lawless men from the North poured into piedmont South Carolina in 1765 and committed robberies and murders along their frontier. Although inhabitants of the uplands petitioned the Assembly for better protection and communications, they received no tangible help from Charles Town. By 1767, residents of the upcountry, calling themselves Regulators, took matters in their own hands and went after a band of men suspected of stealing horses.

In support of the Regulators, Charles Woodmason drew up a

protest, which was signed in the name of 4,000 back countrymen and submitted on November 7, 1767, to the South Carolina Assembly. Persuading them to "lay aside desperate Resolutions," the minister carefully prepared an account of back-country grievances and demanded just treatment for the frontier.

Woodmason's remonstrance, asserting that "We are Free-Men—British Subjects—not Born Slaves," was backed by threat of a frontier invasion of Charles Town unless reforms were assured. Within four days of its presentation, legislation was initiated and the Governor asked to raise two companies of soldiers to protect the back country. Long overdue help was on its way to the back country.

Writing to England in 1771 about the Regulator movement, Charles Woodmason admitted that

> you may think that I am out of my Proper Sphere. But Sir, if acting for the Good of Mankind in General The Right and Liberty of the Subject—the Relief of the Poor, the Needy, the distress'd—the Stranger—the Traveller—the Sick and the Orphan—If the Advancement of Religion—Good of the Church, Suppression of Idleness, beggary, prophaneness, Lewdness and Villany—If banishing of Ignorance Vice and Immorality, promoting Virtue and Industry, Arts and Sciences, Commerce and Manufactures, and ev'ry Public Work, be Characteristic of a Christian I hope that I have not . . . deviated from what my Great Master came into this World to establish—Glory to God Peace on Earth—and Good Will among Men.[12]

Ill and exhausted by his constant trials, Charles Woodmason in 1773 went northward over the Great Wagon Road into Virginia and Maryland, preaching as far north as York, Pennsylvania. Sensing the oncoming conflict between his native Britain and the American colonies, he sailed in 1774 for England and spent his declining years in the vicinity of Bristol.

In him, the growing back-country demands for justice found a voice. And by 1776, "Justice" to most Americans meant independence from England.

BOOK FIVE

Division and Reunion

1789–1877

CHAPTER 23

Stagecoaches and Turnpikes

When George Washington took the oath as President of the United States on April 30, 1789, in New York, the colonial era of America had come to its end. It had been 182 years since three ships had brought the first Virginians to Jamestown. Now thirteen states stretched from Georgia to New Hampshire, and the tide of settlement was flooding through the Appalachians into the West.

The energy which Americans had spent in war against Britain was channeled now into westward expansion. Into the lands along the Great Road poured thousands of war veterans, headed west to the velvet green valleys beyond the mountains.

It was an age of farmers. New York, the largest town in North America, had only 33,000 residents. Philadelphia had grown into a metropolis of 28,000 when President Washington and the Congress moved there in 1790, pending the choice of a permanent capital city. Otherwise, the United States was open land, dotted only occasionally with small towns like Boston, Albany, Baltimore, and Charleston.

It was a time of vigorous movement, as traffic over the Wagon Road showed. Besides the pack train and the wagon, a fast-moving vehicle called the stage began to rumble over the rough dirt thoroughfare. Pulled by four or six horses, these scheduled carriers began after 1750 to replace the express riders and "for hire" wagons which had carried mail and passengers. Starting in New York and Philadelphia, stage wagons and stagecoaches were soon operating on major roads.

A northern newspaper about 1750 began advertising John Butler's Philadelphia stage wagon. By 1780, a more comfortable coach with five passenger places and a "boot" for mail had replaced the canvas-covered wagon.

Horses were changed at "stages" along the way—usually taverns, but occasionally a newspaper office where mail was exchanged with the printer, who doubled as postmaster.

The new stagecoaches were far faster than wagon travel. Embarking from Philadelphia at 2 A.M., the Lancaster stage traveled thirty-three miles to reach Downing Mill (later Downingtown) by night-fall. The second night brought the traveler to Lancaster, another thirty-three miles away. By traveling twelve to eighteen hours a day, the stagecoach covered from twenty-five to forty miles, depending chiefly on the muddiness of the road.

To a world unaccustomed to speed, the stagecoach was a romantic carrier of news and excitement. Charles Dickens, who bumped over the Great Wagon Road on several speaking tours, wrote sentimentally of

the numbers of people to whom once, those crazy, mouldering vehicles had borne, night after night, for many years, and through all weathers the anxiously expected intelligence, the eagerly looked for remittance, the promised assurances of health and safety, the sudden announcement of sickness and death. The merchant, the lover, the wife, the widow, the mother, the school boy, the very child who tottered to the door at the postman's knock—how had they all looked forward to the arrival of the old coach.[1]

Mail coaches moved so briskly that they sacrificed the comfort of passengers to the demands of the postal service. In winter they offered "no other protection against the weather than a curtain of leather, often fastened in a negligent manner to the posts which support the roof." One traveler complained that "they troubled themselves little about the passengers' comfort."

By order of the Post Office Department, mail coaches after 1799 presented a gala appearance on the Great Road and other highways:

The body painted green, colors formed of Prussian blue and yellow ochre; carriage and wheels red, lead mixed to approach vermilion as near as may be; octagon panel in the back, black; octagon blinds green; elbow piece on rail, front rail and back, red as above; on all doors, Roman capitals in patent yellow, "United States Mail Stage" and over these words a spread eagle of size and color to suit.[2]

The U.S. Mail Stage, known as the "Good Intent Line," advertised in the *Pennsylvania Gazette* that its stage left 284 Market Street in Philadelphia in the morning at two o'clock for Lancaster and Pittsburgh, carrying six passengers plus mail and cargo. Other lines advertised services to New York and Baltimore.

Taverns from Philadelphia to Lancaster provided stopping places for the stage lines which early developed beyond those towns. An early Pennsylvania almanac listed these taverns and mileages:

PHILADELPHIA TO	MILES
Colters Ferry	1
Black Horse	6
Merion Meeting	7
Three Tuns	9
The Buck	11
The Plough	13
Radnor Meeting	14
Mills Tavern	16
The Ball	19
Signe of Adr'l Warren	23
White Horse	26
Downing Mill	33
The Ship	34
The Wagon	41
John Miller at the Tun	47
Pequa Bridge	48
Douglas's Mill	49
Widdow Caldwells "Hat"	53
John Vernon's	60
Conistoga Creek	64
Lancaster Court House	66[3]

By 1800, stage traffic between Philadelphia and Lancaster had encouraged so many taverns that they averaged one every mile. The best of them were operated by Germanic settlers, by this time known as Pennsylvania Dutch because of the *hoch Deutsch* or Palatinate German dialect which they spoke. To such patrons the Brown Horse Tavern was known as *Braunes Pfed* and the Fox Tavern as *Der Fuchs*.

Traffic along the Great Wagon Road was swelled by daily mail and passenger service to Lancaster and west to Pittsburgh in 1804. The first of these stagecoaches departed John Tomlinson's Spread Eagle Tavern on Market Street, Philadelphia, on July 4. A large crowd gathered to drink to the success of the venture, cheering the passengers loudly as they took off behind four handsome, beribboned coach horses and a whip-cracking driver.

As the stage crossed the new bridge over the Schuylkill, the crowd roared a welcome. So it went as the stagecoach drew up before the Buck, the Eagle, the General Paoli, and other inns. About 2 P.M., as the equipage approached the Admiral Warren, the keeper of the tollgate blew six loud blasts on his bugle to signal the number of passengers for midday dinner. Host Charles Fahnestock, son of the great Casper, warmly greeted the arrivals and fed them bountifully while fresh horses were harnessed up. Then, with a patriotic volley to speed it, the mail stage rolled on toward Lancaster.

Many travelers from Philadelphia were on their way west to Pittsburgh or Wheeling, to board Ohio riverboats for new lands in the Northwest Territory. Others after 1818 came over the Great Road to Hagerstown, where they turned west to Cumberland and the National Road to Wheeling, built over the route which George Washington and General Braddock's wagon train had traversed in the French and Indian Wars.

Passengers paid approximately five cents a mile for stagecoach service. The fare from Philadelphia to Pittsburgh was twenty dollars, each passenger being allowed twenty pounds of baggage. Beyond that, the baggage rate was twelve dollars per hundred pounds, "if the packages are of such dimensions as to be admissable for conveyance."

Faster travel required better roads, for horses and wagons were frequently mired in deep mud. Drivers were hard put to thread their way around bogs which might tear the wheels from their axles. A mudhole grew so cavernous in front of one Virginia tavern that a permanent detour developed around it. Of the road in winter, one traveler wrote:

> I say it's not passable,
> Not even jack-assable,
> And those who would travel it
> Should get out and gravel it.[4]

Summer droughts made the road a dust bowl and covered passengers with grime. "It was so dusty in Summer," one old-timer said, "that when Mrs. Spencer's rooster chased Mrs. Filbates' hen across the road, it raised such a cloud of dust you couldn't see the other side for 30 minutes."

Traveling from Philadelphia in 1789, Miss Marie Penrhy experienced the difficulties common to the road. A member of the Moravian Sisterhood at Lititz, she had with her a former English army officer, his wife, and children, who were en route to Lancaster to visit relatives. Arriving at the Fahnestocks' inn, they met a marooned Scotch-Irish emigrant and his wife, who were headed west over the Great Road.

Miss Penrhy and her companions agreed to let the "Irish Gentlewoman" ride with them, after her driver had refused to proceed over the rough road; but her English husband was compelled to walk for lack of carriage space. After a hectic mile, Miss Penrhy's overloaded vehicle broke an axle, and the passengers had to walk two miles to the Sheaf of Wheat, the nearest inn. There a compassionate farmer offered to transport them in his open wagon to Downingtown.

The thirty-three-mile trip consumed thirteen hours, but Miss Penrhy sighed that "politeness and good nature had lessened every difficulty."

Another uncomfortable Great Road traveler was Bernhardt, Duke of Saxe-Weimar-Eisenach, who in 1825 traveled south from Maryland to see the famous Natural Bridge of Virginia, near Lexington. He complained of the uncomfortable coaches and "rugged road." However, he was luckier than an Italian, Count Castiglioni, who had attempted to visit Natural Bridge a few years earlier. After waiting six days to ford a nearby river which was flooded by a six-day downpour, he was finally told that he could safely cross. However, when Castiglioni's servant attempted to ride the coachhorse across, he was swept away and nearly drowned. The unhappy count finally crossed next morning.

To combat mud and dust, corduroy coverings were laid by Charles Fahnestock and other Great Road dwellers. They placed poles close together across the road, covering the mudholes but forming a corrugated surface which shook passengers until their teeth chattered and their senses were addled. To smooth the washboard road, lumber was planed into planks. Parts of the Great Road were planked after 1850, but the lumber gradually rotted and the mud triumphed again.

The driving of cattle and hogs over the Great Road continued in these years. About 120 cattle formed a drove, with the "manager" directing the movement from horseback. Two "footmen" assisted him, one leading a steer in advance of the group. The herd grazed along the way, but even so the animals lost almost fifteen percent of their weight. Pigs were moved in droves numbering as many as 5,000, creating a nuisance for travelers on foot or horse. A swine-herd could drive his squealing animals only eight miles daily.

In response to the demand for better roads, the states after 1790 began to charter private turnpike companies. Impoverished by the Revolution, states were unable to build highways, though a few public improvements were made with funds raised by lottery. In this emergency, the states permitted investors to incorporate and improve sections of road in return for fares received from travelers.

The first stone-surfaced turnpike undertaken was from Phila-delphia to Lancaster in 1792. This sixty-six-mile project was com-pleted in two years, at a cost of $465,000, and it became the pattern for many others. One enthusiast called it "a masterpiece of its kind . . . paved with stone the whole way, and overlaid with gravel, so that it is never obstructed during the most severe season." Nine tollgates (called *Schlagbaume* by the Pennsylvania Dutch) col-lected fares from passers-by.

In the next hundred years Pennsylvania chartered 428 toll-road companies, largely financed by the investment of farmers and businessmen.

The growth of stagecoach lines and turnpikes brought into use the macadam road, which was introduced by John Macadam in England about 1815 and soon adopted in the United States. Sec-tions of the Great Road were soon covered with a macadam surface of compacted layers of small stones, cemented together by stone dust and water. The cost of such surfacing limited its use at first to a few heavily traveled segments of the Great Road. Many lesser turnpikes were of corduroy or plank.

Travel on the Philadelphia-Lancaster Turnpike reached its height before 1834, when the Philadelphia & Columbia Railroad went into operation. In the heyday of horsedrawn wagons, before the advent of steam, "it was a frequent sight to see long lines of Conestoga wagons going towards the city, loaded with the products of the West or going in the opposite direction, freighted with the produc-tions of Eastern mills or foreign merchandise," wrote a Pennsyl-vania observer.

These wagons were usually drawn by five stout horses, each horse having on its collar a set of bells consisting of different tones, which made very singular music as the team trudged along at the rate of about four miles an hour. Emigrants could also frequently be seen on their way, generally in companies for mutual assistance, going with their families and worldly possessions towards the new West— there to settle and found homes for their posterity. Large herds and flocks also furnished their quota to this ever-moving living panorama.[5]

The success of the Lancaster Turnpike encouraged the building of many other toll roads, including the Valley Turnpike through much of Virginia in the 1830s. Lacking state funds to modernize the road, the Governor and General Assembly of Virginia in 1834 chartered a corporation of upcountry investors and authorized them to hard-surface "the old stage road" from Winchester westward through Staunton as a toll turnpike. Describing the efforts of Bushrod Taylor, president of the turnpike company, to improve the Great Road, his great-niece wrote:

Up to 1825 Virginia had been the most populous state in the Union, but the opening of the Erie Canal, connecting the Hudson River with the Great Lakes, made central New York a highway for the movement of population westward. Large cities grew up there, capital was attracted, and manufacturing began on a large scale; the result was that the population soon went beyond that of any other state.

Uncle Bushrod craved a similar prosperity for his own state, and thought it entirely attainable. Already, in his eager imagination, he saw trains of white-covered wagons carrying hardy emigrants through and onward to the forests & mines of the Piedmont Country, or heard the sweet, tinkling music of the "bell-teams," the loud and jocund laughter of the trusted Negro teamsters, as in large companies they conveyed their precious freight of grain and flour to the fast clipper ships lying in the Baltimore harbor waiting to carry it to the markets of the distant world.

Uncle Bushrod had been busy forming plans for pushing the construction of the road he had set his heart upon making through the Valley. To do this had necessitated many and long absences from home. He met with many disappointments, but he did not allow them long to discourage him. When the National Government would not favor the scheme, he turned hopefully to the power of the state of Virginia.

In the rapid growth and expansion of our country the question of

"Internal Improvements" had sprung into such importance as to constitute a political issue in the campaigns of 1825 and 1830, and had brought about a new division of parties. The Democrats denied any constitutional authority to the government to build roads, canals, etc. The States' Rights Whigs likewise denied to the National Government the authority to build such works, but conceded it to the state. Uncle Bushrod had been a steady Whig from the formation of the party; so, pocketing his documents, credentials, etc., and accompanied by his valet, Billy Button, he posted down to Richmond [from Winchester] to urge his project by special legislation.

There he found no lobbying could make a breach in the wall of Democratic opposition to the use of state aid for internal improvements, and he could obtain no concession beyond a charter permitting the road to be made by private enterprise, were that possible. Having secured this much, Uncle Bushrod then proceeded to engage engineers, contractors, labourers, etc. and in a short time the work was well under way.[6]

Taylor at last persuaded Virginia's conservative Board of Public Works to subscribe to two-fifths of the stock as soon as three-fifths had been bought by the public. The turnpike company then proceeded to macadamize the ninety-three miles of the Great Road from Winchester through Harrisonburg to Staunton. The improved road plus bridges cost $425,000. As each five miles was completed, a tollgate was installed and the section opened to the public.

Like most turnpikes, the Valley Road hardly repaid more than its maintenance cost, but it increased the tempo of the expanding nation.

Under common law, farmers taking grain to mill could pass a turnpike free. As a consequence, shrewd travelers sometimes defrauded toll-takers by carrying grain bags full of bran. Resentment frequently arose against toll-takers to the point that tollgates were torn down. Local travelers also developed backwoods "shun-pikes" to avoid paying tolls. In one country this notice was posted:

NOTICE TO GATEKEEPER

We ast you not to collect no more tole, you must Not collect one cent if you do we are Going to Destroy your House with fire are Denamite So you must Not collect No more tole at all. We don't want to do this but we want a Free Road and are agoing to have it, if we have to kill and burn up everything. Collect no more tole we mean what we say, so Fair warning to you.[7]

The farther one went south over the Wagon Road, the worse it grew, for the population of the Carolinas and Georgia was too small and scattered to support many turnpikes. "As poor as a Georgian" was a common measure of poverty.

> The roads are bad [wrote John James Audubon of the South], and now and then all hands are called to push on the waggon, or prevent it from upsetting. Yet at sunset, they have proceeded perhaps twenty miles. . . . Days and weeks pass before they gain the end of their journey. They have crossed both the Carolinas, Georgia, and Alabama. They have been traveling from the beginning of May to that of September.[8]

As an outgrowth of Savannah, which in the Revolutionary years was the southern terminus of the Wagon Road, rapid settlement of the Savannah River area took place. Many Virginians and Carolinians came down the road to claim farmlands and to create for a few years a tobacco economy like that they had left behind. Thus grew the towns of Petersburg, Lisbon, Edinburgh, and Alexandria in Georgia and Vienna in South Carolina. Here, along the "tobacco road," developed a society which produced many of early Georgia's leaders.

The Wagon Road strongly influenced Georgia's early years. The whip-cracking wagoners of the region earned the name "crackers" for the state. John Lambert, an Englishman who visited the area, wrote of it in 1814:

> These waggoners are familiarly called *crackers* (from the smacking of their whips, I suppose). They are said to be often very rude and insolent to strangers and people of the towns whom they meet on the road, particularly if they happen to be genteel persons. . . . The waggoner constantly rides on one of the shaft horses, and with a long whip guides the leaders. . . .

Southern population expanded rapidly after the War of 1812 and the acquisition of Florida. A hopeful note was sounded by Governor William W. Bibb of the Alabama territory in 1818. "Permit me to recommend to the attention of the legislature the subject of roads, ferries, and bridges," he said. "The strength of the country consists in its population, and it is peculiarly the interest of this territory to invite emigrants hither, by furnishing every possible facility of communication."

Though the Great Road area was still thinly settled in the Deep

South, the threat of Spain in Florida and of France in Louisiana made it strategically important. When Florida was acquired by the United States in 1819, a new frontier was opened to migrating Americans. Ex-President Thomas Jefferson wrote to Albert Gallatin that "emigration to the West and South is going on beyond anything imaginable," and Secretary of War John C. Calhoun told Congress that "it only remains to consider the system of roads and canals connected with the defense of our Southern frontier, or that of the Gulf of Mexico."

Even so, travel in the South was still hard going. A traveler headed overland from Augusta, Georgia, to New Orleans was urged "to bid adieu to all comforts" and to

> make the necessary preparations for a hard and rough campaign. If he has a wife and children unprovided for, and to whom he has not the means of leaving a suitable legacy, let him by all means be careful to insure his life to the highest amount the office will take; for the chances of perishing on the road are at the rate of ten to one.

The Louisiana Purchase also encouraged emigration over the Great Wagon Road into Texas. Sharing a common border with Louisiana, this Spanish province began to lure Southerners further south in 1821, after Moses Austin had sold his Fort Chiswell lead mines in Virginia and obtained a Mexican grant. Austin's son Stephen, who had been born near Fort Chiswell in 1793, began settling his fellow Southerners below the Rio Grande in 1822. Sam Houston, who had migrated as a boy from Rockbridge County, Virginia, to Tennessee, freed Texas from Spanish rule and became its president in 1836. Other easterners found similar opportunity at the southern end of the Great Road.

One traveler who followed the Road southward was surprised to see how much poorer South Carolina was than was the busy Pennsylvania he had viewed from the Lancaster Turnpike.

> The appearance of things in the Slave States [wrote Robert Sutcliffe], is quite the reverse. . . . We sometimes meet a ragged black boy or girl driving a team consisting of a lean cow and a mule, sometimes a lean bull or an ox, and I have seen a bull and a cow, each miserable in its appearance, composing a team. . . . The carriage or wagon appeared in as wretched a condition as the team and its driver.[9]

[222]

A traveler wrote in the *Augusta Chronicle* that he had seen one pioneer pulling the shafts of his cart while his wife walked alongside with a rifle and driving a cow.

So the Great Road from Philadelphia grew, and America grew with it. To a large section of the United States, it remained the nerve center: a channel of communication, a center of commerce, and means of emigration and population growth. Nevertheless, its primacy was about to be challenged by the iron horses which, in a few decades, were to link the east coast with the Mississippi River and the West.

That new era was foreshadowed in April 1834, when the first steam locomotive of the Philadelphia and Columbia Railway rode over the rails paralleling the Lancaster Turnpike.

"Within a month after the first train went down the road, drawn by the Black Hawk, matters changed," a Pennsylvanian wrote. "It was the twentieth of May, a dark rainy day, when the last regular stage passed the Warren on its way eastward. . . . The various local stages still ran, so did the Pitt teams, but neither were accustomed to stop at the Warren, nor could the old tavern keeper bring himself to cater to that class of custom . . ."[10]

Soon the lament was heard:

> Come all ye wagoners, who have got good wives,
> Go home to your farms and there spend your lives.
> When the corn is all cribbed and the small grain is good,
> You'll have nothing to do but curse the railroad.[11]

In spite of the advent of the locomotive, the Great Road was by no means dead. The railroad soon revolutionized transportation as no other invention had since the discovery of the wheel, but it too would be superseded in another century.

Meanwhile the Great Road continued to pump new blood into the expanding states.

CHAPTER 24

Great Days of the Horse

In the life of the Great Wagon Road, the frontiersman's constant friend was his horse. In a peculiar degree the history of the southern Appalachians is intertwined with the development of the American horse, which was bred to its highest form in early Virginia, Maryland, and the Carolinas. After the Wilderness Road came into being, "horse fever" spread to Kentucky and Tennessee.

The story of the Wagon Road is the story of men and horses: of fiery Virginia's mounts with a precious trace of the Byerly Turk or of the Darley Arabian or Godolphin Barb in their veins; of heavy Conestoga drays, which pulled the red-and-blue Pennsylvania wagons; of sturdy Choctaw and Chickasaw ponies from the Deep South which gave speed and stamina to the quarterhorse.

The annals of the Great Road are laden with allusions to the sturdy mounts which carried the pioneers. We see Nolichucky Jack Sevier, spurring on his charger to lead the Wataugans up the heights of Kings Mountain. Or we glimpse young Andrew Jackson, jogging toward Salisbury on his grass pony. Often fine horses pulled a chair or chaise, like the one which bore young James Madison— "poor, withered little Jeemy Madison"—and his bride Dolley up the Great Road in 1794 for their honeymoon at Isaac Hite's Belle Grove plantation.

"Light, stranger. Hitch your horse and come in," was the greeting at lonesome farms and plantations in the South. "Dismount! Dismount!" a host would enjoin any stranger, coming forward to take the reins and offer the hospitality of the road. (A far cry, some said, from New England, where the first question was "Who are you?" and the second, "What's your business here?")

Horses and horsemanship were indispensable in the rural states, where tobacco, corn, wheat, and later cotton required draft oxen— usually castrated Hereford bulls—or plow horses. The first English settlers had brought horses to Virginia before 1610, developing a small "Virginia horse" which visiting officials of His Majesty's government admired for its fleetness and flowing mane.

An eighteenth-century Englishman expressed amazement at the

planters' passion for horses. "Virginians, of all ranks and denominations are excessively fond of horses," wrote the English visitor J. F. D. Smyth. "Even the most indigent person has his saddle-horse, which he rides to every place, and when hunting; indeed, a man will frequently go five miles to catch a horse, to ride only one mile . . ."[1]

An early master at the College of William and Mary, the Reverend Hugh Jones, thought them "such lovers of horses that almost every ordinary person keeps a horse."

How did Virginia horses differ from their English progenitors? Some said it was because an English trader in 1651 went south from Virginia and brought Choctaw ponies up from the Indians of the Gulf Coast—probably descendants of Spanish mounts which Hernando de Soto had introduced to America a hundred years earlier—and bred them with the English horses of Virginia.

Whatever the case, Virginians soon bred fleet quarterhorses, whose strong hind legs gave them the thunderous power needed for the quarter-mile straight races which enlivened court days at southern county seats for 200 years to come.

As tobacco prosperity grew, infusions of English Thoroughbred stock were introduced by Virginia and Maryland grandees. In 1756, the great English stallion Janus was brought to Virginia to sire the famous line called the Januses in the next decade. In the same era, planters imported from England such proven Thoroughbreds as Fearnought and Diomede, which had acquired unusual size, speed, and stamina through the crossbreeding of English horses with Arabian and Turkish stock. Horse racing became a consuming passion among well-to-do seaboard planters, with jockey clubs springing up at Williamsburg, Charles Town, and other villages to sponsor annual stake races.

In this virile world of hunting and cockfighting, such men as Daniel Boone and Davy Crockett, Wade Hampton and John Sevier, Andrew Jackson and Henry Clay grew to vigorous manhood. "It's a great life for dogs and men," said one Great Road resident, "but it's hell on women and steers."

Horse racing embraced the upcountry farmer in a camaraderie which extended from rural Georgia to the fashionable racecourses of England. The small piedmont North Carolina farmer with three or four brood mares was a kindred spirit with the irascible aristocrat,

John Randolph of Roanoke, who left 130 horses at his death or of Sir Peyton Skipwith of Mecklenburg County, Virginia, who sold 80 brood mares and colts at one fell swoop in 1782. Except in wars or financial panic which frequently shook the nineteenth-century world, a brisk trade in "bred" horses went on.

Numerous ads in post-Revolutionary gazettes offered the services of Thoroughbred studs at farms over Virginia, Maryland, and the Carolinas. Illustrated with a line-cut of a racing or ramping stallion, its nostrils aquiver with nervous energy, each proclaimed the unsurpassed merit of its imported Thoroughbred sire.

As breeding season approached each winter, owners brought their mares to such stud farms to be serviced. Accompanied by her trusted Negro groom, each nervous filly awaited her turn.

An ad for the Thoroughbred stallion Sir Archie proclaimed in 1817 that he "will stand the ensuing season" at William Amis's stable in Northampton County, North Carolina. "He will cover mares at fifty dollars the season," it promised. In addition, the mare's owner must pay a dollar to Sir Archie's breeding groom plus twenty-five cents daily for his mare's feed to Amis. In his twenty-one years at stud Sir Archie brought in the unheard-of profit of $76,000 in stud fees, not including his track earnings. From Sir Archie's line sprang such legendary champions as Boston, Lexington, Man o' War, Gallant Fox, Native Dancer, and War Admiral.

With the decline of tobacco exports after the Revolution, many low-country families moved west to new land near the Great Road. From coastal Virginia, an outpouring of younger sons of planters went into piedmont Virginia and the Carolinas as well as to Tennessee and Kentucky. Several brothers of John Marshall settled in Kentucky. Wherever they went, planters like the Burwells, Nelsons, Blands, Willises, and Claibornes took with them their love for racing.

The westward movement in Virginia led over two principal routes. The first was the prehistoric Occonneechee Trading Path, which went from Bermuda Hundred on the James River to Occonneechee Island in the Roanoke River and thence into North Carolina by way of Hillsborough and Guilford Courthouse to the early crossroads town of Salisbury on the Great Road. (West of Charlotte, the "Cherokee Path" plunged through the highlands by way of Kings Mountain, the Cowpens, and early Spartanburg to the mountainous Cherokee villages.) The second route from Tidewater Virginia, known as the Green Path, went west from Isle of Wight County to Weldon in North Carolina and on to Pine Tree Hill (later Camden) and Augusta.

In the land along these paths settled many expatriate Virginians. They spread their love for horse breeding and quarter-racing inland, thus consuming the energies—and some of the wealth—of the upcountry men.

"The soil still had plenty of lime to build big bones among the colts," explained Nat G. Hutcheson, a chronicler of past racing in the piedmont. "The land hadn't been overworked, and it was ideal for horse-breeding and cattle-raising." But the golden age of piedmont Virginia and North Carolina horsemanship was short-lived. Before the Civil War, heavy-feeding crops had begun to deplete piedmont's soil as they had earlier in Tidewater. After Appomattox, the center of American horse breeding moved west again, this time to Kentucky and Tennessee.

Horsemanship came naturally to descendants of the rural Englishmen who settled the coastal South. Farmers had new grazing land, and Negro stable-help was cheap. A blooded horse or two lent style to a household. Furthermore, "there is nothing so good for the inside of a man as the outside of a horse," as one planter emblazoned over the entrance to his land. In the piedmont South, every nineteenth-century politico kept a fine horse to ride over his acres and to the courthouse. "In the good old days," one recalled, "almost every farmer had a blooded mare, who was looked upon as too good for any kind of work, but occasionally to take her master on a short jaunt."

Quarter-races run at Camden, Salisbury, Charlotte, Staunton, and elsewhere along the Road were the favored entertainment of all ages until the Baptists and Methodists gained influence. Even though Virginia yielded to them in 1792 and imposed a seven dollar ceiling on bets, these headlong charges continued to attract throngs. As the crowd lined the narrow course, the snorting and ramping horses, ridden by Negro jockeys, went to the post. Then, to the bang of a big drum, the racers were off.

"Come on, Janus!" or "Come on, Mercury!" the crowd would roar.

Straw hats and bandanna handkerchiefs were waved violently as the foaming chargers pounded down the short stretch. Then came the finish and screams of mingled delight and dismay.

Race meets brought swarms of people—white and black, old and young, rich and poor. Congressman John Randolph bred and raced horses at many a county seat. He viewed people, like horses, in terms of their blood lines, describing one Secretary of War as "like a half-bred horse: too slow for the track and too weak for the plow." Leading politicians followed the horses: John Marshall, Andrew Jackson, John C. Calhoun, Henry Clay, and Nathaniel Macon among them. Politics and racing seemed to go together.

An Englishman who traveled the Great Road thought quarter-racing "the most animated sport" he had ever known. He described the finish as a "tornado of applause from the winner's party, the niggers in particular halooing, jumping, and clapping their hands in a frenzy of delight, more especially if the horses had happened to jostle and one of the riders had been thrown off with a broken leg . . ."

The names of piedmont horses like Sir Archie, Timoleon, Flori-zelle, and Potomac became bywords in the years 1823 to 1834, when the top Thoroughbreds of North and South ran a series of thirty heavily bet races at the Union Race Course on Long Island. Horses from the South won seventeen of these, giving comfort to the region which regarded its people as inheritors of the knightly valor and gallantry portrayed by Sir Walter Scott in *Ivanhoe* and *Kenilworth.*

The dominance of Southern Thoroughbreds was such that in 1827 the Washington Jockey Club's races discouraged entries from below the York and Pamunkey rivers in Virginia. When a North Carolina weekly objected, the editor of *The National Intelligencer* in Washington gracefully conceded:

> We are afraid that our friends in North Carolina are *displeased* at our Jockey Club's having excluded the Roanoke racers, but surely without reason. Do they not perceive that, in so doing, our Clubs pay them the compliment of considering them invincible? Our breeders acknowledge themselves beaten to their heart's content—they give up: What more would our friends in the South ask of them? Whenever we can produce animals that are able to compete, with any chance of success, with those south of the Pamunkey, our friends may be assured that they will be welcome. Of late, the associations here and at Baltimore have had all the pleasure of making up purses, for the Roanokers to come and take for asking. This was not only an expensive amusement, but it also defeated the object of these "trials of speed," as our friends at Boston call them, which is, to hold out

inducements to emulations in the improvement of the breed of horses.[2]

At the same time, North Carolina breeders protested the overweening repute of Virginia horses despite the fact that some so-called "Virginia" champions had been bred in the Old North State. "The best Virginia racers have been for many years raised in North Carolina, and a few counties of Virginia lying between the James River and Roanoke," a Tarheel asserted in the Warrenton, North Carolina, *Reporter* in 1825. "Most of the capital race horses which within the last thirty years figured on the turf as Virginia racers, were actually foaled and raised in North Carolina . . ."

The writer then listed thirty-nine horses which he felt erroneously credited to Virginia. He concluded: "*Our* cotton, *our* tobacco, and *our* race horses are called by the name of Virginia; while our *ague and fever,* our *bad roads,* and our *bars and shoals* are admitted, even by the Virginians themselves, to belong to North Carolina."[3]

Another area which bred fine horses was the northern Virginia segment of the Great Road, from Watkins' Ferry on the Potomac south to Winchester. A wave of Tidewater planters who had been lured by its rich soil after the Revolution—Burwells, Pages, Byrds, Randolphs, Wormeleys, and Carters—took with them their imported stock. Centering in the rolling counties of Frederick, Clarke, Warren, Berkeley, and Jefferson—the latter two to become part of West Virginia in 1864—these grandees perpetuated until the 1840s the high life which was disappearing around Chesapeake Bay. Rich purses were offered at Jockey Club meets in Winchester, Martinsburg, and Charleston, and winners raced in Washington and Baltimore.

Southern horses may have been supreme on the track, but Pennsylvania's were supreme on the road. Just as Pennsylvanians had developed the Conestoga wagon, so they bred heavy Conestoga horses, which were hitched four or more at a time to pull the heavy loads between Philadelphia, Lancaster, York, Gettysburg, and nearby towns. Known also as Lancaster or Pennsylvania horses, they were the largest in America, sometimes exceeding seventeen hands in height.

It was not unusual to see a hundred Conestoga wagons in one day carrying produce from Great Road towns to Philadelphia, wrote Dr.

Benjamin Rush in 1789. And each wagon, he observed, was drawn by four or five large horses of "a peculiar breed" developed in Pennsylvania.

Actually the Conestoga was a hybrid of English and Flemish draft horse and of saddle horse. Originated by farmers of the Conestoga Valley, these patient plodders developed greater size and strength over the years. This was partly due to the good feeding and care provided by the "just, humane, and generous" Germans of the valley. As one farmer put it, "being well fed, protected from the cold and inclemency of the weather when not actually in service, and never overworked or abused, this horse, under this kind treatment, attained the full development of his natural powers."

Weaned at three months, a Conestoga colt was turned out to pasture until two and a half years old, when it was broken to the bridle. Thereafter it was accustomed gradually to pull its load while growing to mammoth size.

Pennsylvania Dutchmen did not humor horses as Southerners did. Neither their brood mares nor stallions were exempt from pulling plow or wagon as needed. Occasionally a prized stud horse was absolved from labor in mating season, but thrifty Germans exacted hard service of all who worked for them. Mares were worked until a few weeks before foaling. They returned to work usually a week afterward, their colts tagging along at their side.

When pioneers threaded the Wilderness Road to Kentucky and Tennessee, they took the beginnings of horse racing with them. As early as 1788, *The Kentucky Gazette* in Lexington advertised that Pilgarlick, son of the great sprinter Janus, was standing at stud in Mercer County. Soon other ads offered other sires. The first Kentucky racecourse was built in 1789 at Lexington. Then and there Kentucky's long love affair with racing began.

Horse breeding also had an early beginning in Tennessee. A weekly there advertised in 1799 that Spotted Medley, "got by Gimrack, got by Imported Medley, a beautiful dapple gray, rising six years, full 15 hands high," was at stud at Flowery Spring plantation. The fee was "three dollars the leap."

The bluegrass of mid-Kentucky and Tennessee proved ideal for the horses which had carried early horsemen through Cumberland Gap. There the settlers found lustrous meadows of thick, matted turf enclosed in the dense virgin forest of the Ohio Valley. There the wild pea vine grew luxuriantly, attracting hosts of deer and buffalo. In these fields, burned clear of trees by the Indians, colts could browse the year round and absorb the lime to build strong legs and long bodies.

The primacy of Virginia horses was soon to be challenged by the new West!

Old-school horsemen of the East at first pooh-poohed the brash claims of Kentucky and Tennessee breeders. They questioned the pedigrees of western challengers and disparaged their claimed speeds as the figment of erring "Kentucky watches." Diehards like John Randolph thought the area a dumping ground for inferior stock.

However, the emergence of Andrew Jackson's Thoroughbred Truxton, which outran the previously undefeated Ploughboy in a celebrated race at Clover Bottom, Tennessee, in 1806 forced Easterners to look again. After the Civil War, mid-Kentucky became the horse-breeding capital of America, abetted by the sporting tastes and fortunes of planters and distillers.

Proposing Jackson for the Presidency in 1822, *The Nashville Whig* saw politics as a horse race:

GREAT RACING ! ! ! ... The prize to be run for is the Presidential *Chair.* . . . There have already four states sent their nags in. . . . Why not Tenneessee put in her stud? and if so, let it be called *Old Hickory.*[4]

Just as English colonies along the Chesapeake had inherited England's horsemanship after 1610, so in turn the new West fell heir to that legacy. Kentucky's Thoroughbreds raced around the globe. Tennessee's walking horses and quarterhorses moved westward with the pioneers, serving on farms and ranches. The agile quarterhorse became known in the west as the "cow pony," so useful did it prove to herdsmen.

Thus, for more than two centuries, the horses of the Wagon Road were almost as much a part of its moving history as were men, women, and children.

CHAPTER 25

The Cherokees Go West

As the towns and farms of the Appalachians increased after the Revolution, Indians who had frequented these lands were slowly forced out. Within a few decades after the colonies gained their independence, the Iroquois tribes which had created the Great Warriors' Path down the early Appalachians were to find themselves without a homeland.

The dilemma of America's Indians began when Virginia settlers first set foot on Chief Powhatan's lands in 1607. It grew and increased as the wave of white settlement moved westward across the continent. In these two centuries, tribe after tribe sadly ceded its primeval hunting lands and moved westward—ultimately onto government reservations.

From the viewpoint of the American pioneers, displacement of the aborigines was essential to the expansion of a nation. To the proud warriors of the Appalachians, however, it was a bitter betrayal by the white pioneers who had killed their wild game, taken over their paths, and enlisted them to fight against the French.

The naive red man was no match for the settler in bargaining. By their treaties at Albany, at Lancaster, and in a half-dozen villages along the Appalachians, the Indians of the region by 1784 had ceded all their lands from Pennsylvania south to Georgia except for the western fringes of Georgia, the Carolinas, and Tennessee. Seduced by whiskey and soothing words, countless trusting chiefs had sold their tribal birthrights for a little gold and a paltry collection of guns, clothing, and trinkets.

Unified by Revolution, the states in 1784 adopted a united policy of negotiation with the Indians. To the newly created War Department they gave responsibility for the conduct of diplomacy with the tribes. Fearing possible conspiracy between the Indians and Spain along the Mississippi River, many residents of the new West urged that the remaining tribes be encouraged to move to reservations beyond it.

Except for the Cherokees and Creeks, plus a few small remnants of other tribes, most of the Indians had already disappeared from

[233]

the Appalachians by 1784. Many had succumbed to the white men's diseases—chiefly tuberculosis and smallpox—or to chronic drunkenness. The Tuscarora tribe of North Carolina had gone north to the Great Lakes in 1713, thereby increasing the Five Nations to six. Other Iroquois had fled north from Virginia and Pennsylvania in the Revolution, some settling with the Cayuga in New York State and others around Lake Erie in Canada.

President James Monroe stated the basis for the policy of forced removal of the remaining eastern Indians when he said in 1817: "The hunter or savage state requires a greater extent of territory to sustain it than is compatible with the progress and just claims of civilized life, and must yield to it." In other words, the Indian did not fit into an America of private enterprise.

On its face, the policy of forced removal was a humane one. Yet in more than one case it was used to force a peaceful and inoffensive tribe from its lands in order that white profiteers might be enriched by them.

A wise and eloquent Shawnee chieftain, Tecumseh, attempted with his brother, the Prophet, to organize Indian opposition to the plan for forced removal. They urged Indians of all tribes to refuse to sell any more land, arguing that they had no right to convey a legacy intended for endless generations. Tecumseh also proposed that the nation's Indians become an active part in the Federal union by creating an Indian state, to be admitted to the union on the same basis as others.

Eloquent though Tecumseh was, he and his followers discredited their cause when they joined forces with the British in the War of 1812.

Among the sufferers under the "forced removal" program were the Cherokees, who were the most numerous and widespread tribe of the Appalachian region. The frontier demand for Indian removal was heightened after 1828, when gold was found on Cherokee land in Georgia. Soon thereafter, a bill supported by President Jackson was enacted by Congress to displace the remaining eastern tribal groups—Cherokees, Creeks, Chickasaws, Choctaws, and Seminoles —to the Federal Indian reservation lands west of the Mississippi.

Led by its chief, John Ross, known as "Kooweskoowe," the 16,500 members of the Cherokee nation in Georgia, the Carolinas, and Tennessee desperately contested the removal order. Well-organized and governed, the nation included many responsible businessmen and landholders among its members. Its 2,700 families held 7,200,000 acres, many of them profitably planted in cotton and other crops.

Ross, the principal chief, was the son of a Scottish trader father and a mother who was one-eighth Cherokee. He presided over an American-style legislature of thirty-two members which convened to make laws for the Cherokees at New Echota, Georgia. The Cherokee nation had by this time achieved its own constitution and law code, written in a language system which had been developed in 1821 by Sequoyah, who was also the son of a white trader and an Indian mother.

Opposing their removal, Ross and his fellow chiefs reminded Georgians of Congress' assurances that Indian rights would be respected in the newly formed United States. From the Northwest Ordinance of 1787, he quoted the statement: "The utmost good faith shall always be observed toward the Indians; their land and property shall never be taken from them without their consent; and in their property, rights, and liberty, they shall never be invaded or disturbed unless in just and lawful wars authorized by Congress . . ."[1]

In the nation's desire to avert foreign invasion, however, such promises were disregarded. The Cherokees seemed a threat to internal security. Therefore, they must move.

To legitimize the removal, a treaty was drafted which would exchange the tribe's Appalachian empire for new land beyond the Mississippi in what was to be the Oklahoma territory, plus an indemnity of only $5,000,000. In opposition to this proposal, 16,000 Cherokees signed a protest and sent it to the United States Senate in objection to the treaty.

Missionaries who befriended the Cherokees were arrested and convicted of violating Georgia law, but the United States Supreme Court held Georgia's acts unconstitutional. Chief Justice John Marshall ruled that the rights of the Cherokees under their treaty with the United States had been abridged. However, President Jackson scoffed at the decision. "John Marshall has rendered his decision," Jackson said. "Now let him enforce it."

When Chief John Ross and other Cherokees refused to sign the removal treaty, its advocates persuaded a minority of the tribe to hold a rump meeting and do so. Ignoring the irregularity of these proceedings, the Senate approved the Treaty of New Echota by a majority of one, and Jackson signed it into law.

The Cherokees were now deeply angered. Armed warfare was feared. To prevent Ross from going to Washington to protest, he was arrested by the Georgia State Guard, under orders of the Governor, and held without charge. The Cherokee newspaper, *The Phoenix*, was suppressed and seized to prevent word from reaching tribesmen.

To enforce the removal, General John E. Wool of the Army was dispatched by the Secretary of War to the Cherokee country. When Ross wrote the President in protest, Jackson reprimanded Wool for transmitting the letter and ordered that no more Cherokee objections be received.

The Senate treaty allowed the Cherokees several years to move to Oklahoma, but few complied by the deadline. To force them, Georgia decreed that any Cherokee who influenced another not to emigrate should be imprisoned. The few civil rights remaining to Cherokees were abolished, and they were disqualified from testifying in court against a white person.

When most Cherokees ignored the departure deadline, their property was seized under false pretenses. One Cherokee planter, Joseph Vann, lost his $10,000 house and 800 acres of farmland on the specious charge that he had violated the law by hiring a white man to oversee his farm in his absence. Vann and his family were then driven from their house and escorted in the snow across the state line into Tennessee.

The estate of Chief John Ross was also seized and given to the holder of the winning ticket in a Georgia land lottery.

Despite threats and cajolery, only 2,000 of the 16,500 Cherokee had obeyed the edict to move from the Appalachians by May 22, 1838. To remove the other 14,500, General Winfield Scott was ordered from Washington to replace General Wool. A contingent of 7,000 Federal and Georgia troops patrolled Cherokee lands and prepared to carry out Federal orders.

General Scott established headquarters at New Echota and issued a direful proclamation. "My troops already occupy many positions," he warned, "and thousands and thousands are approaching from every quarter to render assistance and escape alike hopeless.... Will you, then, by resistance compel us to resort to arms ... or will you by flight seek to hide yourself in mountains and forests and thus oblige us to hunt you down?"[2]

When the Cherokee failed to move, Scott's troops rounded them up and herded them into stockades. In their haste, the Indians left behind almost everything except what they wore. Divided into small knots under guard, they were then loaded on flatboats and embarked under tow of paddle-wheelers on their 800-mile journey. It was a trip to go down in Cherokee annals as "The Trail of Tears."

Lieutenant Joseph Harris, an army officer assigned to direct the movement, was deeply moved by the Indians' grief. He wrote:

> The parting scene was more moving than I was prepared for; when this hour of leave-taking arrived I saw many a manly cheek suffused with tears. Parents were turning with sick hearts from children who were about to seek other homes in a far off and stranger land, and brothers and sisters with heaving bosoms & brimful eyes were wringing each others' hands for the last time. And often I observed some young man whom the spirit of roving or adventure had tempted to forsake all that was dear to him here, to seek alone an uncertain future in other climes; or some young wife who was tearing herself from father and mother, "kith & kin," to follow the fortunes of her husband whithersoever they should lead, turn again & again to the embrace of those they loved and were leaving, in seeming forgetfulness that they had already rec'd their adieux . . ."[3]

The overloaded flatboats were dogged by smallpox, cholera, and mishaps. One vessel carrying sixty-seven people sank in the night, barely allowing its passengers to escape. Illness spread rapidly. "At one time I saw stretched around me and within a few feet of each other, eight of these afflicted creatures dead or dying," Harris wrote. "Yet no loud lamentations went up from the bereaved ones here. They were of the true Indian blood; they looked upon the departed ones with a manly sorrow and silently digged graves for their dead and as quietly they laid them out in their narrow beds. . . . There is a dignity in their grief which is sublime; and which, poor and destitute, ignorant and unbefriended as they were, made me respect them."

Of those who embarked on the enforced journey, nearly a fourth died of illness and hardships. The pitiful remainder reached Oklahoma in March 1839, after a six-month journey. It was the darkest moment in the history of the Cherokee nation.

Senator Daniel Webster of Massachusetts, stunned by accounts of the Cherokees' treatment, expressed public indignation when the facts finally emerged. "There is a strong and growing feeling in the country," he said, "that great wrong has been done the Cherokees by the Treaty of New Echota." But it was too late to undo the sins committed in the name of national security.

Not all the Cherokees followed the "Trail of Tears," however. When General Scott's troops attempted to round up all Cherokees, nearly a thousand managed to hide out in the Appalachians. A few of these later colonized near Augusta. The greater number, deprived of the leadership of John Ross and the other deported chiefs, turned helplessly to an Indian trader, Colonel William Holland Thomas, for guidance.

Sympathizing with their plight, Thomas bought lands for them in his own name, for North Carolina law did not then permit Indians to own property. He divided the area into the communities of Bird Town, Paint Town, Wolf Town, Yellow Hill, and Big Cove, and assisted the demoralized tribesmen in establishing a new tribe.

Thus, hidden in the dark pine uplands of the Great Smoky Mountains, the eastern Cherokee came to roam again through the forests their forefathers had known. There they killed deer and bear, fished the cascading streams, and cultivated the dark earth. There they also perpetuated their familiar skills, carving ceremonial masks and weaving baskets.

When William Thomas died, his creditors sued the eastern Cherokees for their dearly bought land, but Federal policies, now more enlightened, came to the Cherokees' aid. In 1876, the tribesmen were granted possession of 43,000 acres, called the Qualla Reservation, and this was later enlarged. There, after many sorrows, the descendants of Dragging Canoe, Sequoyah, and other Cherokee warriors regained part of the mountaintops which were once theirs.

Less fortunate than the Cherokees were the Catawba, whose braves in colonial times had spread terror through the North Carolina settlements and threatened to unman the northern Iroquois. Granted a reservation on South Carolina's upper border in 1763, the tribe had great difficulty holding it after Scotch-Irish immigrants came flooding south over the Great Wagon Road into the area.

Their numbers reduced by smallpox and other ills, the Catawbas gradually sold off all but one acre of their original tract. Thus reduced, the Catawbas lived in indolence and poverty until the Federal government and the state of South Carolina came to their aid. The reservation was finally divided between the few surviving tribesmen. Both the Catawbas and their reservation dwindled almost to nothing.

Thus, by the mid-nineteenth century, the Appalachian nomads who had stirred the admiration of Franklin and Jefferson were reduced to a few remnants of once-mighty tribes: Cherokees and Creeks in Georgia and North Carolina, Catawbas in South Carolina, Nanticokes in Maryland, and Senecas in Pennsylvania. A few mixed-blood descendants dwelt in Virginia and Maryland.

Moved westward to Oklahoma about the same time as the Cherokees were the Delawares of Pennsylvania and Maryland and the Creeks, Choctaws, and Chickasaws of the Georgia region. Several other tribes which once traversed the Great Warriors' Path disappeared completely.

The chief cause of Indian difficulties in the Appalachians was not emigration but illness and demoralization. Smallpox epidemics wiped out thousands; half of the Cherokees died in an epidemic in 1738. Lacking immunity to European diseases, they were easy prey to tuberculosis and venereal infection.

Equally important, the tribal mentality of the Indian was unable to deal with the complex life which European ways fixed upon him. Dazed and demoralized, he took to drink and lawlessness. The drunken Indian became a cliché in American literature.

As early as 1700, the Indians of Virginia, who had numbered more than 18,000 when the English incursion of America began, were reduced to a mere 2,000. Similar declines occurred in the other colonies.

Belatedly in the nineteenth century, the United States began to see that it had wronged a vulnerable people. With the support of President Monroe, Congress in 1824 established the Bureau of Indian Affairs and created reservations in the West for tribes whose existence was imperiled. It was in the misguided fulfillment of this program that Georgia's Cherokees were uprooted.

Thus, as towns and turnpikes grew along the Great Road in America's third century, the primeval America of Daniel Boone was left in the past. No longer were the Appalachians the impassable wall they had been to the first primitive wanderers of these hills and valleys—wanderers from man's primordial past who left their indistinct trace over the region, thousands of years before the Europeans came.

> Some of these people, [one archeologist has surmised] lived here in the age in which the long extinct mammoths and mastodons roamed the earth, and the glaciers reached down their icy fingers from the Arctic pole. Some think that they retreated into this valley before the advancing glaciers of the Ice Age. Others lived here when Moses led his people from Egyptian bondage to the Promised Land, and others when Imperial Rome was mistress of the then known world . . .[4]

Like other romantic features of rural America—the buffalo, the bald eagle, the endless flocks of wood pigeons—the Appalachian Indian fell victim to a rising American population and a rising American greed. It was to be a nation's lasting shame.

CHAPTER 26

The Day Doctor Junkin
Drove North

Spring filled the air of Lexington, Virginia, but the hearts of students and townspeople were heavy with dread. For this was no ordinary spring. It was April of 1861, and President Lincoln had just issued a call for troops to put down the insurrection of South Carolinians, who on April 13 had fired on the Union garrison at Fort Sumter and forced its surrender.

On the green hillside where Washington College stood, the news arrived by dispatch-bearer over the Great Wagon Road from the South. To students at the Presbyterian school, the news was a bitter relief, for a divided Virginia had stood at the brink of secession for two months. But to Dr. George Junkin, the college's Unionist president, the dispatch sounded a death knell to all his hopes.

When Virginia's Convention voted next day to secede, Dr. Junkin's dread was confirmed. Students quickly climbed to the roof of the white-pillared college, pulled down the American flag which flew above the statue of Washington, and replaced it with the banner of secession.

Against the blue haze of the Valley, the disunionists' flag stood out like a dagger at the heart of the school. Created as a one-room academy in 1749, it had been expanded by hard-working Scotch-Irish farmers into the first college beyond the mountains. Strengthened by $50,000 from George Washington in 1796 it now drew students from throughout the Scotch-Irish countryside which followed the Great Road from Pennsylvania and crossed the Appalachians into Kentucky and Tennessee.

"This thing must be stopped," Junkin roared as he spied the alien flag. Several times in the tense past days, students had climbed Washington Hall and hoisted the direful flag of disunion. Each time the clergyman president had ordered it removed.

Now that Virginia had seceded, things were different. This time the students accompanied their defiance with a petition to the faculty. President Junkin, somber in his black pigeon-tail coat, scowled as he read it beneath the new-leafed maples:

It being our unanimous opinion that we, as a portion of the young men of Virginia, should signify our approbation of the recent action of our State Convention, and our willingness, if need be, to sustain the same in the trying scenes that may ensue, we have hoisted a Southern flag over the College, as the best exponent of our views. It is now our unanimous desire, that the flag should continue to float; and we, therefore, respectfully request, that you will not suffer it to be taken down. There can be no opposition to it from any quarter *now*, save from the enemies of Virginia, and we know that the people of this vicinity are loyal to the old Mother State, and that they have no desire to interfere with it.[1]

As a Pennsylvanian who had opposed secession, Junkin was of course suspect in this sectional conflict. Yet he had many adherents. Called to Virginia in 1848 from the presidency of Lafayette College, which he had founded, he had been well received by the stern Covenanters of Rockbridge, a county formed in 1778 from part of Augusta and named for its famous Natural Bridge—one of the "seven wonders of the modern world." He had preached their stern Calvinism from the pulpits of Valley churches, and he had defended their moral right to hold slaves—a right which his unpopular predecessor in the presidency had denied.

Beyond this, Dr. Junkin had become a part of the life of his adopted state. Two of his sons held Presbyterian pastorates in Virginia, and a daughter—the well-known poet, Margaret Junkin— had married Colonel John Thomas Lewis Preston of Virginia Military Institute, whose campus adjoined his own. Another, Eleanor, had been briefly married until her death to another V.M.I instructor, Thomas J. Jackson, later to be known as Stonewall.

On the fateful morning in April 1861, President Junkin faced a decision which many other borderers along the Great Road would face in the great tragedy of 1861–1865: whether to follow the dictates of conscience or act in loyalty to family and kin. To be true to himself, George Junkin knew he had only one course. Time after time he had upheld the glorious idealism of the American union, darkly painting the alternative: civil war. He could not now accept secession.

Lecturing to the college seniors on the Constitution, he had tried to convince them that "Union preceded *Independence,* and even the *Articles of Confederation;* much more the present *Constitution;*

that neither the Continental Congress nor the Articles of Confederation created and constituted a Government." He tried to show them "that *Union* was always the master thought in the minds of American patriots; that Union was the basis of all their actions; that without *Union* there could be no *freedom*, no *nation*, no independence."

Secession, he concluded, "is the essence of all immorality; it neutralizes the highest obligations."

The union of the states was the source of American strength, character, and greatness, he had said. "In 1790 we became one people," wedded to a government which was the "fruit of the Divine skill . . ." In union were "enshrined the hopes of bleeding, groaning humanity," he had urged. "The master idea of every American head and heart is union—and it was never deeper seated than in this distracted hour. Who wants to dissolve the Union?"[2]

But Dr. Junkin fought a losing fight. Deep passions had been aroused by President Lincoln's call to arms. Junkin heard himself called "Lincoln Junkin" and a "Pennsylvania Abolitionist."

Despite the students' attempt to explain in their petition, Dr. Junkin regarded the secession flag as an affront. A professor who had talked with the students assured him that it was intended merely to voice approval of Virginia's action, but the president was unswayed. If the faculty supported the students' action,

> he would never give another Lecture or hear another recitation . . . until the flag was taken down; and, if the Faculty did not have it removed at once, he would . . . hand in his resignation . . .[2]

Though Rockbridge County was divided in its sympathies, as were most of the mixed English-Scottish-Germanic communities of the Great Road in Virginia, the faculty of Washington College was clearly Southern in sympathy. The professors denied that the students intended to violate college laws or insult their president. For "the present," the faculty resolved to allow the secession flag to fly.

When Dr. Junkin met his class in Moral and Mental Philosophy that morning at eleven, he learned from his students that the objectionable flag was still aloft. "Then, gentlemen," he said, "I am under the necessity of assuring you that I cannot submit to this kind of coercion," and he dismissed them. One student rushed out, shouting, "Thank God for that! Thank God for that!"

When the flag still flew when he met his next class, Dr. Junkin dismissed the students with the explanation, "I never will hear a recitation or deliver a lecture under a rebel flag."

Other events in Lexington revealed to President Junkin that he and his friends—even his own family—were hopelessly divided in the face of the great conflict to come. A "Union pole" flying a flag bearing the American Eagle was raised by Unionist sympathizers one day and cut down by those who had raised it several days later, after Lincoln had issued his call for troops. On Lexington's Main Street, students from Washington College and V.M.I. clashed with a group of workmen. Only the timely arrival of Colonel Francis H. Smith, Superintendent of V.M.I., dispersed the students and averted bloodshed.

In the blaze of emotions aroused by Fort Sumter, the stoic Junkin realized that if he was to continue to live in Rockbridge County, "absolute silence, or a voice in favor of secession," must be the price of his personal safety. The price was too great for him to pay.

With the help of his daughter and sons-in-law, the seventy-one-year-old educator disposed of his property and paid his debts. In the president's house of the college, surrounded by the April bloom of dogwood and redbud, he left his furniture and his books, abandoned, he said ironically, to the mercies of "Mr. [Judah P.] Benjamin's confiscation law, as expounded by himself." Then he bade good-bye to his family and friends.

A day after the faculty had hoisted the disunion flag, the seventh president of Washington College handed his resignation to the trustees. Profoundly touched, they thanked him for his services and grasped his hand in appreciation. As he parted from them, several "were overpowered with tender emotions." Wise and experienced in the hardships of life, some sensed the futher grief that they would have to bear.

Unwilling to wait for a seat on the next stagecoach, Dr. Junkin bought a carriage and, with a daughter and a niece, headed back toward Pennsylvania, up the Great Road. Driving out of Lexington, he passed the home of his old friend and fellow member of the Franklin Literary Society—"Honest John" Letcher, who as Governor of Virginia since 1860 had worked feverishly to compose sectional differences and avoid secession, all to no avail.

Perhaps he remembered, too, some other blasted hopes: his efforts, while a young minister in Pennsylvania, to dispel the bitterness of abolitionists; his urgings to Pennsylvania to enforce Federal laws compelling the return of fugitive slaves, to remove one pretext from Southern extremists' arguments for secession. Most of all, perhaps he remembered his work for the Colonization Society, which sought to have Congress appropriate $5,000,000 a year to transport to Africa all Negroes willing to go. Such a plan, he had preached in the 1850s, "would free a half million Negroes from real bondage—would civilize untold millions in the forests of Africa—would save the Union."

But none of this was to be.

Crossing the North River on the covered bridge leading out of town, he headed north through Timber Ridge, where the Reverend John Brown had conducted his early log college academy—the seed of hope which George Washington's gift and the work of Scotch-Irish schoolmasters had nurtured into Washington College. On through the "Irish Tract" he drove, past the green farms of Houstons, McDowells, McCormicks, and other ruling elders of Rockbridge and Augusta. Then up the Valley Turnpike to the Potomac at Williamsport, Maryland, "having driven the last thirty-five miles from Winchester," he testified, "without stopping to feed horses."

After a pause in Maryland, according to a report which came back to Lexington, to "shake the dust of Virginia forever," he followed the Wagon Road into antislavery Pennsylvania, where he settled in Chester County, suffering in every nerve for the Union he had sought to save.

A day or two after Junkin left Lexington, on Sunday, April 21, Captain Thomas J. Jackson began to march a group of V.M.I. cadets over the Wagon Road, on Junkin's heels to Staunton, where they entrained for Richmond to become drill sergeants.

It had been a long time coming, but the prospect of civil war had consumed men like Junkin. Though secession was the immediate issue, beneath it lay more profound causes: the South's insistence on slavery and the North's growing dominance through the power of industrial wealth.

Thoughtful men—Northern and Southern alike—had tried to avoid war. "Surely," Junkin's neighbor, Governor Letcher, had told the Virginia Convention, "no people have been blessed as we have been, and it is melancholy to think that all is now about to be sacrificed on the altar of passion."[4]

But eloquence was not enough.

The roots of the conflict ran back to the Constitutional debates of

1787, when wise men felt forced to accept slavery in order to create the Union. Even then, however, farseeing slaveholders like Jefferson saw and warned of the ills which slaveholding bred. Listing the distinctions between Northerners and Southerners for a foreign friend, the Virginian then wrote:

IN THE NORTH THEY ARE	IN THE SOUTH THEY ARE
cool	fiery
sober	voluptuary
laborious	indolent
independent	unsteady
jealous of their own liber- ties, and just to those of others	zealous for their own liber- ties, but trampling on those of others
interested	generous
chicaning	candid
superstitious and hypo- critical in their religion	without attachment or pre- tensions to any religion but that of the heart

To this, Jefferson added:

These characteristics become weaker and weaker by graduation from North to South and South to North, insomuch that an observing traveler without the aid of any quadrant may always know his latitude by the character of the people among whom he finds himself. It is in Pennsylvania that the two characters seem to meet and blend and to form a people free from the extremes both of vice and virtue.[5]

It was a conclusion which Junkin could accept.

The rise of Northern industry and the decline of Southern fortunes by 1861 had exacerbated the early differences Jefferson described. Back in Pennsylvania, George Junkin found a very different atmosphere from that of Virginia. In Pennsylvania, Negroes formed less than three percent of the population, while in Virginia and North Carolina, slaves made up a third of the population. In South Carolina and Georgia they even outnumbered whites.

Like many a Unionist prophet in the border states, Junkin lived to see his dire forecast of Southern disaster come true. Many of his old students died in the early exchange of gunfire. The young rebel who had run from his last class shouting "Thank God for that!" fell at Bull Run. Newspapers brought names of other casualties.

From all I have heard [the minister wrote to a Lexington friend], I am painfully impressed with the belief that more than fifty per cent of all those misguided youth who were active in rebelling against me have paid the forfeit of their folly by the sacrifice of their lives. It is the cause of unfeigned sorrow; for a very large proportion of them were youth of remarkable promise for talents, diligence in study, purity of moral and religious character; who, but for those bloody fallacies would have lived long and adorned the higher walks of professional life.[6]

After the bloodbath at Gettysburg in 1863 (when Lee's second attempted invasion of the North was repulsed), George Junkin went to the battlefield to seek out Southern prisoners. In the hospital he met a handful of his Washington College students and preached to them.

As they gathered around him, apparently most glad to meet him again [a witness wrote], he took from his pocket the old class-book, and commenced to call the roll, and rehearsed the history of each member, showing how all had suffered more or less in consequence of their resistance to the best government which God had ever given to man.[7]

Though he was elected again to his former position as president of Lafayette College, Junkin declined it. In 1868, he died and was buried in Pennsylvania.

Years later, when the bitterness of war had ebbed, the body of the unreconciled president was brought back down the Valley Pike through the "Irish Tract" to the limestone hills of Rockbridge County. There in a mute symbol of the triumph of the Union he loved, the old Covenanter was buried in the Lexington cemetery next to the body of his son-in-law—like Junkin, a victim of the war: Stonewall Jackson.

As George Junkin had foreseen, the news from Fort Sumter which had reached Lexington that April day in 1861 had set off a sequence of violence which had run its course. Though peaceful commerce along the Great Road was resumed in 1865, it was many years before Rockbridge and the Valley Pike regained the serenity they had known in the golden days of the young republic.

The Great Philadelphia Wagon Road would never be quite the same again.

CHAPTER 27

Hot Heads and Cold Bodies

When Major Thomas J. Jackson led the V.M.I. cadets up the Great Road from Lexington to Staunton on April 21, 1861, the emerging shape of the Civil War was already evident to his military mind. Union armies would throw their weight against the Confederacy's capital at Richmond and attempt to neutralize Virginia, the most powerful of the seceded states. The Confederates would bar the approaches to Richmond to gain the time needed to form and train their army. Then the Confederacy could take the offensive.

Much of this came true—some of it through the efforts of Thomas J. Jackson. In this strategy the Valley of Virginia became a major battleground. There, on the limestone hills of his Calvinist forebears, Jackson won the name "Stonewall," and fame forever. Guarding the border against Maryland and the District of Columbia, this mystic Celt fought with such inspired skill that he triumphed repeatedly over forces larger than his own. At his death in 1863, he was idolized as was no Confederate other than his commander in chief, Robert E. Lee.

The two men embodied the contrast between the Tuckahoes and Cohees, who had built up the South: Lee the aristocratic scion of Tidewater, Jackson the devout Presbyterian elder, as rugged as the seamy mountains which had produced him.

Commissioned a colonel in Virginia's forces, Jackson was rushed to command at Harper's Ferry on the Maryland border, to defend the Valley against attack from the north. Here, at the Potomac, the Great Road was cut in two for the next four years, closed to the wagoners and emigrants who had built it. The soldiers assigned him were an ill-trained lot, but the methodical West Pointer soon had them in shape. Jackson's brigade became a disciplined machine, made up of rugged youths with the same background as his own.

But the earnest colonel chafed at his defensive role. "I would suggest that a force destined for the northwest be assembled," he wrote Lee, "ostensibly for the defense of this part of the State, at Winchester, or some point near here, and that the moment that the governor's proclamation announces the ratification by the people of the ordinance of secession, such troops ... be immediately thrown into the northwest, and at once crush out opposition."

Jackson was warned about the large number of pro-Union Virginians living west of the Alleghanies, whose opposition to secession placed their loyalty in doubt. Within a year these western counties, constituting a third of Virginia's great expanse, seceded from Virginia and formed West Virginia.

When Brigadier General Joseph E. Johnston took command for the Confederacy at Harper's Ferry, he named Jackson one of his brigade commanders. Now at last the dark-eyed zealot would see the action he cherished. Confidently he led his troops in the battle of First Manassas, where he won the name "Stonewall" and established the fame which grew to worldwide proportions in the remaining months of his brief career.

Throughout it all, the mystic and introverted Jackson remained the devout man of God he had grown up to be in Clarksburg, in northwestern Virginia. To his troops, he soon became "Old Blue Light" for the flaming intensity of his belief. To him, death meant little; he cherished the Bible's assurance, "For we know that if our earthly house of this tabernacle be dissolved, we have a building of God, a house not made with hands, eternal in the heavens."

A day after the battle of First Manassas he wrote the Reverend W. S. White, minister of Lexington Presbyterian Church, where he served as elder and Sunday-school teacher:

> My dear pastor, in my tent last night, after a fatiguing day's service, I remembered that I had failed to send you my contribution for our colored Sunday-school. Enclosed you will find my check for that object, which please acknowledge at your earliest convenience, and oblige yours faithfully,
>
> T. J. Jackson.[1]

To divert Federal pressure from Tidewater Virginia to the Shenandoah Valley, Stonewall was soon placed in charge of the defense of the uplands. He chafed at his remoteness from the Potomac theatre, but the Confederate Secretary of War assured him that "your intimate knowledge of the country, of its population and resources, rendered you peculiarly fitted to assume this command" and that "the people of that District with one voice have made constant and urgent appeals that to you, in whom they have confidence, should their defense be assigned."

Placing his headquarters at Winchester, Jackson soon had the Valley of Virginia under his surveillance. "If this Valley is lost," he warned, "Virginia is lost." Meanwhile he ceaselessly trained his "foot cavalry" for the attacks he expected from the north.

Besides having to deal with Unionist sympathizers in Virginia's northwest, Stonewall also met wth resistance from Dunkard pacifists who lived along the Great Road near Harrisonburg. He agreed to exempt these conscientious objectors from combat but compelled them to do supply and staff work and to drill, "so that in case circumstances should justify it, arms may be given them."

Like earlier Germans in the Revolution, many served as wagoners, driving Confederate war-trains down the Great Road in a harrowing effort to keep up with the lightning movements of Jackson's troops.

Much of the bitterest fighting of the Civil War took place in the Virginia mountains in 1862–1863, when Jackson unleashed his Valley campaign to draw Federal forces from the approaches to Richmond. At Lee's suggestion, he began this series of attacks in May 1862, to draw the Federal army of General Irvin McDowell from its intended support of General George B. McClellan's Peninsula campaign. Jackson's success gave heart to the Confederacy and contributed to McClellan's eventual replacement.

After his first victory of the Valley campaign, Jackson sent these typical orders to his army:

> I congratulate you on your victory at McDowell, I request you to unite with me, this morning, in thanksgiving to Almighty God, for thus having crowned your arms with success, and in prayer that He will continue to lead you on, from victory to victory, until our independence shall be established, and make you that people whose God is the Lord. The Chaplains will hold Divine service at 10 o'clock, A.M., this day, in their respective Regiments.

After Jackson's further victories at Front Royal and Winchester, Lee's strategy produced its effect. President Lincoln now feared for Washington's safety. On May 24, 1862, the President telegraphed McClellan:

> In consequence of Gen. Banks' critical position I have been compelled to suspend Gen. McDowell's movement to join you. The enemy are making a desperate push upon Harper's ferry, and we

are trying to throw Fremont's force & part of McDowell's in their rear.[3]

After Jackson's victories in the Valley towns of Cross Keys and Port Republic, the Confederate high command considered letting him cross the Potomac, as he had proposed, and pressing the war against the North. However, Lee's crucial immediate need for Jackson caused his diversion to eastern Virginia, where Stonewall proved an able lieutenant in the Seven Days' Battles.

When Jackson achieved his wish and crossed the Potomac into Maryland in September 1863, it proved a disappointingly peaceful invasion. Preparing to move further north into Pennsylvania, Lee dispatched Jackson on a lightning mission to capture the Federal garrison at Harper's Ferry, which he accomplished brilliantly.

At Harper's Ferry, General Jackson was sought out by his friend, the Reverend David X. Junkin, son of the resigned president of Washington College and brother to Jackson's beloved first wife, Eleanor Junkin Jackson. Like his father, Junkin opposed secession and urged Stonewall to recant. Despairing at last of changing Jackson's course, the minister took leave. "Farewell, General," he said. "May we meet under happier circumstances; if not in this troubled world, may we meet in . . ." He choked with emotion.

After one battle with Federal troops beyond the Potomac, at Sharpsburg in Maryland, Lee and Jackson and their forces withdrew across the Potomac again into Virginia. There, at the battle of Chancellorsville, a decisive Confederate victory seemed to open the way for a successful invasion of the North. As the fighting approached a victory for the South, Jackson was accidentally wounded at dusk by fire from his own men.

Lee, receiving the dread news, grieved for the loss of his right arm. "Such an executive officer the sun never shone on," he said. "I have but to show him my design, and I know that if it *can* be done it *will* be done. No need for me to send or watch him. Straight as the needle to the pole he advances to the execution of my purpose."

Still seeking a successful invasion of the North to bring the war home to the Unionists, Lee advanced up the Great Road from Winchester and moved again over the Potomac into Maryland. By July 1, the massed armies of North and South had come together at Gettysburg, in the lush Germanic farm country of southern Penn-

[252]

sylvania. There, in one of the bloodiest battles of history, they fought to a stalemate.

The Confederacy had reached the apogee of its power. Now its fortunes began to decline rapidly.

The spring of 1864 brought a new threat to the Valley of Virginia, whose vast wheatfields were the granary of the Confederacy. General Ulysses Grant, the new commander of Union forces, had ordered a concerted drive against Confederate supplies on all fronts. To the Valley he sent General Franz Sigel to cut off essential supplies of flour, beef, baggage wagons, and rifles which had been reaching Lee's armies by way of Staunton.

This was the precarious situation of the Valley on May 10, 1864, when the cadets and townspeople of Lexington gathered at Stonewall Jackson's grave there for a memorial service on the first anniversary of his death. Studying in their barracks after supper, the cadets were disturbed by the clattering arrival of a Confederate dispatch rider in the courtyard of their quadrangle. He brought to the superintendent, General Francis H. Smith, a request from Major General John C. Breckenridge, the Kentuckian who had assumed Confederate command in the Valley, for V.M.I.'s help.

Breckenridge's dispatch had been written at Staunton earlier that day:

> Sigel is moving up the Valley—was at Strasburg last night. I cannot tell you whether this is his destination. I would be glad to have your assistance at once with the cadets and the section of artillery. Bring all the forage and rations you can.
>
> Have the reserves of Rockbridge ready, and let them send at once for arms and amunition, if they cannot be supplied at Lexington.[4]

Breckenridge was well-known to the Valley, for he had served as Vice President of the United States from 1856–1860 and had run on the Democratic ticket against Lincoln in 1860. Only forty-three, he was the grandson of John Breckenridge, who had traveled the Wilderness Road from Virginia to Kentucky in 1792, becoming an early leader of the new state.

Like Washington College and other Southern schools, V.M.I. had lost most of its faculty in the war. However, its cadet corps stood at a healthy 300 youths, ranging in age from sixteen to twenty-one.

[253]

Of these, 250 were assigned to go to Breckenridge's aid while the others remained to defend Lexington and the barracks.

Rising at sunup, the youths packed their haversacks, breakfasted, and departed Lexington at seven in the morning, marching over the North River Bridge and onto the Valley Pike toward Staunton. In the far distance they could hear the great guns of North and South, firing a hundred miles away in the battle of Spotsylvania. As one seventeen-year-old cadet, John Sergeant Wise, later recalled:

> We breakfasted by candle-light and filled our haversacks from the mess-hall tables. In the gray morning we wound down the hill to the river, tramped heavily across the bridge, ascended the pike beyond, cheered the fading turrets of the school; and sunrise found us going at a four-mile gait to Staunton, our gallant little battery rumbling behind.[5]

At the head of the cadets marched Captain Frank Preston, a graduate of Washington College and instructor of V.M.I. The son of Colonel J. T. L. Preston, who had left his Institute professorship to serve Stonewall Jackson as chief of staff, young Preston had lost an arm at Winchester earlier in the war. As the cadets approached the battle area the second day, Captain Preston offered a prayer.

"Few were the dry eyes," Cadet Wise wrote, "when he had ceased to speak of home, of father, of mother, of country, of victory and defeat—of life, of death, of eternity."

The cadets cheered when Breckenridge and his staff rode up to them as they approached New Market. There the cadets left the Valley Pike and took positions in reserve, behind the 4,500 other Confederates and facing 6,000 Federal soldiers from Ohio, West Virginia, New York, Pennsylvania, and Massachusetts.

At eleven o'clock the Confederates began to attack Sigel's forces. About three o'clock, the cadets were called into action. Scattered across a wheatfield, they fired as they advanced toward infantrymen from Pennsylvania, West Virginia, and Massachusetts.

A spring storm deluged the battlefield, and men and cannon were splattered with red mud. Suddenly two Federal regiments gave way, and the V.M.I. cadets surged forward. "Big" Evans, their standard-bearer, mounted a caisson and waved the brave boys on. Then the charging students swept forward, capturing more than a hundred prisoners in the ensuing charge.

But the excited young men paid a price for their bravery. Five were killed outright on the field, and five others died in homes at New Market, Harrisonburg, and nearby where the wounded were taken. "A few of us brought up a limber chest," recalled Cadet Wise, "threw our dead across it, and bore their remains to a deserted storehouse in the village. The next day we buried them with honors of war, bowed down with grief at a victory so dearly bought."

Despite the cadets' stand, the Confederates could not long withstand Grant's superior strength in the war's approaching denouement. Replacing the timid Sigel with the bold General David Hunter, the Federal command directed him to sever the upland Virginia railroads and to "make all the valleys south of the Baltimore and Ohio road a desert as high up as possible."

To cut off the flow of Confederate provisions from the Valley, Grant directed Hunter "to eat out Virginia clear and clean as far as they go, so that crows flying over it for the balance of the season will have to carry their provender with them."

So the fury of war mounted in the direful summer of 1864.

It was in June of that year that the 18,000 troops of Hunter swept southward over the Great Road, looting and burning as they had been directed. After assaulting Staunton, they marched thirty-six miles down the pike to ravage the "Rebel stronghold" of Lexington, home of Jackson, Letcher, and the Virginia Military Institute.

Though local defenders burned the covered bridge across North River, Hunter's troops found another entry into town. Once inside, their artillery angrily shelled it and then burned V.M.I. and ex-Governor Letcher's home. General Hunter occupied the quarters of V.M.I.'s superintendent while other Union generals commandeered the homes of the Reverend William White and other worthies.

Climbing the hillside to Washington College, invading soldiers started to set fire to it, but townspeople interceded. Hunter was persuaded to spare the school befriended by George Washington, but not until after soldiers had pelted the wooden figure of the Father of His Country atop the main hall, mistaking it for Jefferson Davis. Hunter's marauders then swept on down the Great Road, shooting home guards, burning mills and bridges, liberating slaves, and looting everywhere.

Colonel Rutherford B. Hayes of Hunter's staff privately prophesied that "General Hunter will be as odious as Butler or Pope to the Rebels and not gain our good opinion either."

Cruel as Grant's destruction was, it fulfilled his prediction and brought the war close to a halt in 1864. The once green Shenandoah hillsides were now a wasteland, their farms pocked with shell craters and grown up in weeds. Roads and railways were impassable, bridges were burned, and inns and houses along the Valley Pike shattered by gunfire. A Union victory in October over Confederate forces in the Valley of Virginia at Cedar Creek drove one more nail into the coffin of the South's hopes. A crow would be hard pressed indeed to find one grain in the ruined Valley!

After peace came at Appomattox next April, the upland South began to rebuild. By the terms of Lee's surrender, the Confederate soldiers were permitted to keep their horses so that they might make their spring plantings. Every resource would be needed to rebuild all that had been destroyed.

Some men left the ruins and went west. Through the passes of the Appalachians, a new generation of emigrants streamed, following the time-worn course of earlier ones into the Ohio Valley and beyond. This time the goal for many was the far west, where gold and silver had been discovered a few years before.

The Great Wagon Road, once the edge of unknown America, was no longer the gateway to a never-ending land of opportunity. The future seemed to belong to the West.

CHAPTER 28

A Road Is Reunited

The bitterness of the Civil War did not die easily. Commerce between North and South was not soon resumed, for the Southern states were bankrupt. Although new waves of Europeans swept into the North, few emigrants chose to follow the Great Road into the desolate Appalachians—now a land of hunger and unemployment.

Few wagoners now drove their teams between Pennsylvania and the Southern states. Travelers were chiefly farmers and freed Negroes, driving their flop-eared mules and homemade wagons to town.

Thousands of ex-slaves and poor whites moved to the mill towns, seeking work. Villages like Augusta, Salisbury, and Charlotte grew rapidly. New towns sprang up along railroads. Big Lick in the Valley of Virginia became Roanoke, and the Moravian village of Salem became part of Winston-Salem.

After the long four years of war, the face of the land was rapidly changed by new roads, canals, and railways. Most of these sliced eastward from the Ohio Valley to the Atlantic, as other coastal states tried to capture some of the phenomenal profits of the Erie Canal and the New York Central Railroad.

Savage competition grew between Philadelphia, Baltimore, and Southern ports, which vied for the profits in exporting the upland's wheat, cattle, and coal. Every eastern city tried to forge rail links to the West.

Westward emigration from the "black belt" coastal cities continued. Slowly but steadily the uncouth Scotch-Irish flavor of the Appalachian corridor was diluted. No longer was Philadelphia the spiritual capital of this upland region.

Typical of the towns growing along the Great Road was Columbia, which had become the rustic capital of South Carolina in 1790. Until then a mere trading post halfway between Charlotte and Augusta, it was chosen by South Carolina's legislature after the Revolution to succeed Charleston because of its central location in the state. Laid out with wide streets and dignified by a handsome capitol, it soon attracted lawyers and merchants. Cotton-growing suddenly began to enrich the region after Eli Whitney invented the cotton gin in 1792.

When the strident voice of John C. Calhoun began to whip the Deep South into a secessionist frenzy in the 1830s, Columbia became the eye of the approaching storm. In some respects it exerted more influence than rich old Charleston, for political power in the South was steadily moving inland with population and prosperity.

The dilemma of the Civil War South was peculiarly exemplified in the tragic history of Columbia and of a remarkable family whose name became synonymous with it. These were the Hamptons—father, son, and grandson—who captured the imagination of South Carolinians as the Lees did in Virginia.

The fifth generation of an English family which had come to Jamestown in its early years, the first of the three Wade Hamptons was born in western Virginia about 1751, the son of a humble flaxbreaker. He survived a Cherokee massacre on the South Carolina frontier which killed his parents and a brother, growing into young manhood just as the Revolution swept southward from Bunker Hill and enflamed the rural provinces of the South.

Along with four of his brothers who had escaped the Cherokees' wrath, the first Wade Hampton joined the back-country militia and fought through the Revolution. By the time victory was won he had risen to be a colonel under South Carolina's Thomas Sumter. Then he bought a farm on the Congaree River in the uplands at Columbia. When cotton came in demand, Hampton bought more Negro farmhands and added acreage. In 1799, his crop of 600 bales yielded $90,000—the beginning of the biggest plantation fortune in the South.

Ambitious and courtly Wade Hampton adopted the style of Charleston's grandees, who had made their fortunes earlier from rice and indigo. When the territories of Mississippi and Louisiana were opened up, he bought vast cotton acreage there. His Thoroughbreds won prizes at the Charleston Jockey Club's four-day meets.

When the War of 1812 came, Wade Hampton served as brigadier general while his son and namesake served on the staff of Andrew Jackson, a family friend. Like his father, young Wade took a quiet but influential part in South Carolina politics. A contemporary called him the "king-maker" of the Palmetto State.

Emulating the rural English gentry whom the South admired, the Hamptons led a vigorous outdoor life at their country estate, Millwood, near Columbia. There a third Wade Hampton was brought up with his brothers at the height of cotton's prosperity, mixing the sports of horse and hounds with the business of planting. To Millwood came the leading grandees of the day, including Jackson, Clay, and George Bancroft, the New England historian.

Each July the family went by carriage to White Sulphur Springs, Virginia, where they bathed and drank medicinal waters to ward off the dread fevers of the Carolina summer. At such upland spas rich planters whiled away the "dog days," a small and privileged aristocracy which controlled much of the slave-ridden South.

Then the cotton boom burst. By the 1830s South Carolina no longer enjoyed the simple prosperity which had enriched the first Wade Hampton. The South was being victimized, cried John C. Calhoun, and the fault lay with Federal tariffs to protect Northern manufactures. The capitol at Columbia shook with indignation when the legislature met in 1832 and asserted its right to declare the new tariff contrary to the Constitution and therefore null and void.

In this age of rising tempers, Wade Hampton III grew to manhood. Though South Carolinians were momentarily conciliated by a compromise tariff in 1833, their concern at the growth of Federal power persisted. Talk of secession was increasingly heard, despite the efforts of cooler heads to dispel it and to prove the advantage of continued Federal union.

In all this, Wade Hampton III remained on the side of moderation. "The South should studiously avoid making any new issue that might avert her from the only true one," he warned fellow state senators in 1859. This was "the union of the South for the preservation of the South." He opposed re-opening the slave trade with Africa, which many cotton and sugar planters in the Deep South openly advocated.

The election of Abraham Lincoln in 1860 provoked an outcry which was heard throughout the South. In South Carolina, the most disaffected of the states, politicians began raising militia companies. When secessionists gathered, they toasted, "The sword! The arbiter of national dispute. The sooner it is unsheathed in maintaining Southern rights, the better!"

When Governor Francis Pickens in 1860 called the South Carolina legislature together to secede, Hampton stayed away. When it decided unanimously to secede, he shook his head in despair.

But the claims of blood and kinship proved stronger than reason. Like Lee and other leading Southerners who had opposed secession, Wade Hampton concluded that he had no choice but to remain with "his people." Like the English squires who enlisted their neighbors in feudal warfare, the tall horseman signed up a thousand upcountrymen and led them north to resist the Federal onslaught against Richmond.

(Many of them, also in medieval tradition, took with them their Negro grooms or stableboys to look after their horses.)

Though he was untrained in warfare, the six-foot Hampton won a reputation in the next four years as a sterling soldier and an inspiring leader of men. He had what Southern romanticists called "the habit of command." And long days on horseback in his cotton- and sugar-fields had made him a superb and durable horseman.

Entering Confederate service at forty-three, Wade Hampton rose through difficult assignments to command the cavalry of Robert E. Lee's Army of Northern Virginia. Described by a contemporary as "broad-shouldered, deep-chested, . . . with legs which, if he chose to close them in a grip, could make a horse groan with pain," he was well fitted to lead the mounted troops which were the Confederacy's special pride.

A realist, Hampton had foreseen the South's defeat unless it followed aggressive and unanticipated strategy. "West Point tactics prevailing," he warned, "we are sure to lose the game. They have every advantage. They can lose pawns *ad infinitum*. . . . We will be throwing away all that we hoped so much from—Southern hot-headed dash, reckless gallantry, spirit of adventure, readiness to lead forlorn hopes . . ."[1]

But by the time Pickett's reckless Confederates had charged the Gettysburg heights—and been mowed down by suicidal Federal fire —even Hampton could see that "Southern hot-headed dash" was no match for the endless arsenals of the North.

Worse was to come. When Hampton's cavalry could no longer find horses to ride, he was sent to protect endangered South Carolina. Having burned Atlanta, General William Tecumseh Sherman was marching northward through Carolina to confront Lee's forces. Blaming South Carolina for starting the war—a "hell-hole of secession"—Sherman was determined to break its spirit. Burning and looting wherever they passed, his advance units marched into Columbia a day after Hampton had arrived to take command of the city's defense.

While Hampton's 2,600 troops guarded a trainload of women and children which had stalled beyond the Congaree River, they were amazed to see the city go up in flames. Sherman's troops then destroyed the Hampton plantations, Millwood and Sand Hills, east of the city, and moved on northward toward Virginia.

Sherman's acts so embittered Hampton that the South Carolinian urged the South to fight to the last ounce of its strength. Rather than surrender, he proposed to Jefferson Davis that they flee across the Mississippi River into the West. "If you will allow me to do so," he advised, "I can bring to your support many strong arms and brave hearts—men who will fight to Texas, & will seek refuge in Mexico, rather than in the Union." However, he was dissuaded from this course.

Once perhaps the wealthiest planter in the South, Hampton returned after Appomattox to find most of his holdings in ruin. Once Columbia had been a proud town of wide streets, shade trees, and handsome buildings. Some called it the finest state capital in the nation. Now, except for its Statehouse, it was in ashes. "A wilderness of ruins," someone wrote, "its heart is but a mass of blackened chimneys and crumbling walls. Two-thirds of the buildings in the place were burned, including, without exception, everything in the business portion."[2]

The most serious problem was the Negroes, many now homeless, who outnumbered the whites of South Carolina by 402,000 to 291,000. Another was famine, which threatened all. In Columbia the populace would have starved but for rations from the Army commissary.

"I can embody it all in a few words," groaned the poet, Henry Timrod: "Beggary, starvation, death, bitter grief, utter want of hope!" In a few months Timrod himself was dead.[3]

To heighten the crisis, Congress in 1867 repudiated President Andrew Johnson's conciliation of the defeated South. In its place it imposed a military occupation which enfranchised all Negroes and denied to Confederate veterans any political office in the re-formed states.

Hampton for eight years devoted himself to rebuilding and replanting his wasted lands. Once, in 1868, he rode northward again to Virginia, where he visited Robert E. Lee in the president's house at Washington College in Lexington. To many Southerners the two were the most respected figures remaining from the prewar South.

"I think it wise not to keep open the sores of war," said Lee. And Hampton wholeheartedly agreed.

Though he was already South Carolina's greatest hero, Hampton faced a more important role. This was to revive orderly government in South Carolina—the despised "hellhole of secession"—when military occupation came to an end. Nominated by the Democrats for governor in 1876, he swallowed his pride and campaigned widely for the office. Freedmen like Beverly Nash, who had been a slave, endorsed him and excoriated "scalawags" and "carpetbaggers" who fattened on war's miseries. To such Negroes, native moderates such as Hampton seemed the best hope against the Ku Klux Klan, which had arisen in reaction against Federal policy in the South.

Between the time of Hampton's election as governor in 1876 and Federal troops' withdrawal in 1877, open rebellion threatened South Carolina. When the seating of Democrats in the South Carolina legislature was contested by Federal officials, a grim crowd of 5,000 gathered outside the capitol.

When Governor Hampton saw the mob, he became the commanding figure of Civil War forays fifteen years earlier. Quietly he asked the men to put away their guns and preserve peace. "One act of violence may precipitate bloodshed and desolation," he warned. "I have been elected your Governor, and, so help me God, I will take my seat."

The magic of the old warhorse worked. In three minutes the capitol grounds were vacated. Five months later the last Federal soldiers marched out of Columbia and left it to Hampton and his Democratic administration. Order had been restored to the burnt-out center of slavery and secession. Carpetbaggers and scalawags were in retreat.

And what of the future? Along the Appalachians, from the Potomac southward to Georgia, disillusioned farmers left their overgrown fields to find work on the railroads or in the mills. You could see them in their mule carts, hauling their pine furniture and leading the family cow. Thus they deserted the once precious land with its hard-won clearings, its weatherbeaten houses, and its family burying-grounds.

The face of rural America was changing, for the Union's triumph was the triumph of the machine. The Lees and Hamptons who had led the South would soon be replaced by tycoons like Cyrus Mc-Cormick and James Buchanan Duke, both Scotch-Irish uplanders. The amiable, indolent South which Jefferson had described in 1787 must become more like prosperous Pennsylvania: an industrious land, "free from the extremes both of vice and virtue."

Slowly the familiar landmarks disappeared: mountain grist mills, plank roads, turnpikes, and blacksmiths who shod the wagoners' horses. Gone, alas, were the Indian villages, post riders, and frontier explorers like Daniel Boone and Davy Crockett.

The Great Road changed, too. No longer did endless wagon trains and stagecoaches pass over it; the railroads were taking their trade. Disappearing, too, were the roadside inns which had poured so many dollops of corn whiskey to revive the weary traveler. New waves of European emigrants no longer came south. Now they headed west. The old hatred between Cohee and Tuckahoe softened, and sectionalism waned as the nation grew. The once rustic "back country" no longer looked to the east for amenities or enlightenment; by the late nineteenth century, it had a strong cultural vitality of its own. The Scotch-Irish especially had established a wealth of colleges and universities. The fame of that tough breed grew with the generations. The whole world knew of Andrew and Stonewall Jackson, Andrew Pickens, Sam Houston, Andrew Johnson, Cyrus McCormick, James K. Polk, James Buchanan, John Caldwell Calhoun, John C. Breckenridge, and their kinsmen.

Though the actors changed, the setting of the Great Road remained much the same. The character of its people still was formed by the rugged lineaments of the Appalachians. There, where prehistoric hunters had slain the mammoth and the bison, the ever hopeful immigrant pursued the vision which was America.

Some found it. Most did not. But the pursuit—the search for something better than they had—in itself produced a new and better way of life for mankind.

The Great Wagon Road was the pathway to opportunity, and opportunity made America grow great.

Epilogue

As railroads spread over the continent after the Civil War, travel over the Great Philadelphia Wagon Road declined. Gradually the locomotive displaced the stagecoach and the wagon train in American life.

But the birth of the automobile gave new importance to the Road. When Henry Ford's "tin Lizzie" ushered in the new era just before World War I, the Road became an early feature of the nation's highway system. Ferries and covered wooden bridges were replaced by concrete spans, and roadbeds of logs and planks disappeared.

Turnpike companies were bought up with money from gasoline taxes, and state highway departments took over the Wagon Road as part of their road systems.

In its overnight modernization, the Wagon Road then lost its character and even its name. Though a few old-timers referred to "the Philadelphia Road," or "the Lancaster Pike," or "the Valley Road," to highway map makers it became merely a number. Turnpike tollgates were torn down, and wayside inns were converted to service stations and roadhouses.

Horse carts and mule wagons slowly disappeared amid exhaust fumes of Model T's. Drovers of cattle and hogs no longer dared enter the dangerous thirty-mile-per-hour traffic.

Old stagecoach stops like the General Paoli Inn grew into townships, and serene villages like Lancaster and York became bustling cities. Mileposts were removed as souvenirs, and roadside shade trees were hacked down for safety's sake. Beauty gave way to utility, and comfort surrendered to speed.

Five towns besides Philadelphia grew lustily in the twentieth century: they were Big Lick, which became Roanoke; Salem, which was incorporated into Winston-Salem; the "hornet's nest" called Charlotte, plus Columbia, South Carolina, and Augusta, Georgia.

Despite the decline of regionalism and of European legacies, a few Great Road towns—Gettysburg, Hagerstown, and Harrisonburg among them—remained Germanic. Though few Americans learned the language after the Hun scares of the First World War, they kept

[265]

memories of the Old Country alive with *Schmierkäse* (cottage cheese), superstitions, love of the land, and simple piety. In their names, architecture, and foods they savored of the Rhine.

Other towns remained as stubbornly Scotch-Irish, especially in upland Carolina and in Virginia's "Irish Tract." There the counties of Rockbridge and Augusta retained the highest percentage of Ulster descendants to be found anywhere in the United States. There one might still see the austerity which struck Cadet John Sergeant Wise when he entered Virginia Military Institute at Lexington in 1862:

> The blue limestone streets looked hard. The red brick houses, with severe stone trimmings and plain white pillars and finishings, were stiff and formal. The grim portals of the Presbyterian church looked cold as a dog's nose. The cedar hedges in the yards, trimmed hard and close along straight brick pathways, were as unsentimental as mathematics . . .[1]

Along much of its early 800 miles, the bed of the Great Philadelphia Wagon Road is now obscured by a modern highway. However, the old path is still visible near such towns as Martinsburg and Winchester, where it crosses and recrosses narrow upland rivers. Paralleling much of the Road is the scenic Blue Ridge Parkway, which was built as a national park in the 1930s along the mountain crest from Virginia into North Carolina. From this lofty drive, one may see the Great Valley as the eagles see it.

Many of the landmarks which the wagoners passed along this road still testify to the glorious past. From Pennsylvania to Georgia the traveler finds a wealth of old churches, colleges, courthouses, farmhouses, and onetime inns. Gettysburg and Hagerstown are full of memories. Pioneer Salem village is beautifully preserved. Salisbury, North Carolina, and Camden, South Carolina, retain links with Andrew Jackson's day. Nearby are preserved the Revolutionary battlefields of Guilford Courthouse, Cowpens, Kings Mountain, and Cheraw.

The twentieth century also preserves its mementoes of the Wilderness Road, which Daniel Boone cut through the Cumberland Mountains in 1775. Along the old route in southwest Virginia are early towns like Abingdon. In this region are the Holston, Clinch, and Watauga river valleys, where the first Tennesseeans settled.

The rockbound Cumberland Gap which led settlers into the fabled riches of Kentucky is now preserved in a national park abutting three Appalachian states.

Thus the highways of yesterday merge into the America of today. Past becomes present, and present becomes future, and none can stop the clock. But in a conformist world, let Americans not lose the healthy individualism of those earlier generations which grew up along the rugged Appalachians in America's infancy.

They worked hard, faced terrible enemies, and usually died young. Let it not be forgot that they left a great, free nation to show for it.

Acknowledgments

I would like to express appreciation to a number of people who have kindly provided help in the preparation of this book.

The late Victor Barringer of Richmond made available his collection of early maps of the southern colonies of North America and assisted me in locating early Indian trails. His knowledge of the fauna and flora of the region was invaluable, and his comments on the completed manuscript were most useful.

Colonel Paul Downing of Staten Island and J. E. Keyser, Jr., of Colonial Williamsburg answered inquiries about horses, wagons, and harness. Joseph W. Watson of Rocky Mount, North Carolina, provided information about the Green Path, which led from southwest Virginia into Edgecombe and Nash counties, North Carolina. Royal Hassrick of Surry County, Virginia, provided sources of Indian lore and read two chapters dealing with the Algonquins and Iroquois.

James S. Brawley provided extensive material on early Salisbury, North Carolina, and Francis Jennings of Quakertown, Pennsylvania, answered many questions and provided copies of his useful accounts of early Pennsylvania. The Hon. Lewis McMurran, Jr., of Newport News read the manuscript and made many helpful suggestions.

I am also indebted to Mrs. Martha Aycock and Mrs. Catherine T. Slay, Union Theological Seminary library, Richmond; Robert P. Turner, York, Pennsylvania; Prentice Price, Richmond; Henry D. Green, St. Simon's Island, Georgia; Hugh B. Jonston, Wilson, North Carolina; A. T. Dill, West Point, Virginia; Tom Wilson, Office of Public Information, U.S. Bureau of Indian Affairs, Washington, D.C.; Lewis Williams, Birmingham, Alabama; James I. Robertson, chairman, department of history, Virginia Polytechnic Institute, Blacksburg, Virginia; Albert W. Coates, Jr., Virginia Department of Highways, Richmond; C. F. W. Coker, North Carolina Department of Archives and History, Raleigh; John F. Rauhauser, Jr., York, Pennsylvania; J. Ambler Johnston, Richmond; James J. Geary, New Market Battlefield Memorial, New Market, Virginia; and Granville B. Liles, superintendent of Blue Ridge Parkway, Roanoke.

Also, the late William J. Van Schreeven, director of research and publications, Virginia Independence Bicentennial Commission, Richmond; Miss Alice Gilmer, Russell County Public Library, Lebanon, Virginia; Dr. Grace L. Tracey, Hampstead, Maryland; Robert Land, Library of Congress, Washington, D.C.; Alexander O. Vietor, Yale University Library, New Haven; Mrs. Roberta Ingles Steele, Radford, Virginia; Fred P. Painter, Woodstock, Virginia; Frank L. Horton and Miss Frances Griffin, Old Salem, Winston-Salem, North Carolina.

Also, William S. Powell, University of North Carolina Library, Chapel Hill; Louis H. Manarin, Virginia State Archivist, and John W. Dudley, Assistant Archivist, Richmond; John C. Frye, Washington County Free Library, Hagerstown, Maryland; Sidney R. Bland, assistant professor of history, Madison College, Harrisonburg, Virginia; Hon. Bentley Hite, Christiansburg, Virginia; Sidney Briggs, Williamsburg, Virginia; Hon. Francis Pickens Miller, Washington, D.C.; John Tyler, William Penn Memorial Museum, Harrisonburg, Pennsylvania; and Clinton Broadwater, Middlesboro, Kentucky.

Also, John W. Heisey, Historical Society of York County, York, Pennsylvania; Josephine L. Harper, State Historical Society of Wisconsin, Madison, Wis.; James Barnette, director, South Carolina Tricentennial Commission, Columbia; William H. Shank, York, Pennsylvania; Judge John W. Tisdale, Clarksville, Virginia; Mrs. India L. Cann, Goode, Virginia; Frank H. Goodyear, Jr., Rhode Island Historical Society, Providence; Misses Lynn Thaxton and Marie Ellis, E. G. Swem Library, the College of William and Mary, Williamsburg; Edward M. Riley, Mrs. Rose Belk, and Miss Patricia Gibbs, Colonial Williamsburg; Mrs. Maria Williams Minor, Williamsburg; and Ben C. McCary, The College of William and Mary.

Finally, I would like to express my continued thanks to Mrs. Jacqueline Taylor for her assistance in compiling information and in preparing the manuscript; and to my wife, for her encouragement and interest.

Parke Rouse, Jr.

Bibliography

Alexander, Archibald. *The Log College.* London: The Banner of Truth Trust, 1968.

American Heritage Editors. *The American Heritage Book of Great Historic Places.* Narrative by Richard M. Ketchum; Introduction by Bruce Catton. New York: American Heritage Publishing Co., in cooperation with Simon and Schuster, Inc., 1957.

Anburey, Thomas. *Travels Through the Interior Parts of America.* 2 vols. Boston and New York: Houghton Mifflin Company, 1923. With a foreword by Major General William Hardin Carter.

Aresty, Esther B. *The Delectable Past.* New York: Simon and Schuster, Inc., 1964.

Arnow, Harriette Simpson. *The Flowering of the Cumberland.* New York: The Macmillan Company, 1963.

Asbury, Herbert. *A Methodist Saint: The Life of Bishop Asbury.* New York: Alfred A. Knopf, 1927.

Babcock, C. Merton. *The American Frontier: A Social and Literary Record.* New York: Holt, Rinehart and Winston, Inc., 1965.

Bean, R. Bennett. *The Peopling of Virginia.* Boston: Chapman & Grimes, Inc., 1938.

Belden, Albert D. *George Whitefield, The Awakener.* New York: The Macmillan Company, 1953.

Benét, William Rose. *The Stairway of Surprise.* New York: Alfred A. Knopf, Inc., 1947.

Beverley, Robert. *The Present State of Virginia.* Edited by Louis B. Wright. Chapel Hill: The University of North Carolina Press, 1947.

Blanchard, Elizabeth Amis Cameron, and Manley Wade Wellman. *The Life and Times of Sir Archie.* Chapel Hill: University of North Carolina Press, 1958.

Boley, Henry. *Lexington in Old Virginia.* Richmond: Garrett & Massie, Inc., 1936.

Bolton, Charles Knowles. *Scotch Irish Pioneers in Ulster and America.* Boston: Bacon and Brown, 1910.

Boyd, Julian, ed. *Indian Treaties Printed by Benjamin Franklin, 1736–1762.* Philadelphia: The Historical Society of Pennsylvania, 1938.

Bridenbaugh, Carl. *Myths and Realities: Societies of The Colonial South.* Baton Rouge: Louisiana State University Press, 1952.

Bruce, H. Addington. *Daniel Boone and the Wilderness Road.* New York: The Macmillan Company, 1922.

Byrdon, G. MacLaren. *Virginia's Mother Church,* 2 vols. Philadelphia: Church Historical Society, 1952.

BIBLIOGRAPHY

Byrd, William, II. *History of the Dividing Line Between Virginia and North Carolina.* Edited by William K. Boyd. Raleigh: The North Carolina Historical Commission, 1929.

Cartmell, T. K. *Shenandoah Valley Pioneers and Their Descendants: A History of Frederick County, Virginia.* Berryville, Va.: Chesapeake Book Company, 1963.

Chambers, Lenoir. *Stonewall Jackson,* 2 vols. New York: William Morrow and Company, 1959.

Clarke, Desmond. *Arthur Dobbs Esquire, 1689–1765.* Chapel Hill: University of North Carolina Press, 1957.

Couper, Colonel William. *One Hundred Years at V.M.I.* With a foreword by General George C. Marshall. Richmond: Garrett and Massie, Inc., 1939.

Crenshaw, Ollinger. *General Lee's College: The Rise and Growth of Washington and Lee University.* New York: Random House, 1969.

Davis, Chester. *Hidden Seed and Harvest: A History of the Moravians.* Winston-Salem. N.C.: Wachovia Historical Society, 1959.

Duren, William Larkin. *The Top Sergeant of the Pioneers.* Emory University, Ga.: Banner Press Publishers, 1930.

Durrenberger, Joseph Austin. *Turnpikes: A study of the Toll Road Movement in the Middle Atlantic States and Maryland.* Valdosta, Georgia: Southern Stationery and Printing Company, 1931. (Submitted in partial fulfillment of the requirements for the degree of Doctor of Philosophy, in the Faculty of Political Science, Department of History, Columbia University.)

Dykeman, Wilma and James Stokely, and the Editors of Time-Life Books. *The Border States: Kentucky, North Carolina, Tennessee, Virginia, West Virginia.* New York: Time-Life Books, 1968.

Dykeman, Wilma. *The French Broad.* New York: Rinehart & Company, Inc., 1955.

Eisenberg, William Edward. *The Lutheran Church in Virginia, 1717–1962.* Roanoke, Va.: The Trustees of the Virginia Synod, Lutheran Church in America, 1967.

Edwards, Gordon. *Introduction to Literature.* Boston: Ginn and Company, 1964.

Executive Journals of the Council of Colonial Virginia, 4 vols. Edited by H. R. McIlwaine. Richmond: Virginia State Library, 1925–1930.

Exiles in Virginia: with observations on the conduct of the Society of Friends during the Revolutionary War, comprising the Official Papers of the Government relating to that period. 1777–1778. Philadelphia: Published for the subscribers, 1848.

"Federal Indian Policies, A Survey of Major Developments from the Pre-Revolutionary Period through the 1960s," Bureau of Indian Affairs, U.S. Department of the Interior, 1969.

Foote, William Henry. *Sketches of Virginia: Historical and Biographical.* First and second series. Richmond: John Knox Press, 1966. New edition with index.

BIBLIOGRAPHY

Ford, Henry Jones. *The Scotch Irish in America.* Princeton: Princeton University Press, 1916.

Foreman, Grant. *Indian Removal: The Emigration of the Five Civilized Tribes of Indians.* Norman, University of Oklahoma Press, 1953 (New edition).

———— *The Last Trek of the Indians.* Chicago: The University of Chicago Press, 1946.

Forty-Second Annual Report of the U.S. Bureau of American Ethnology to the Secretary of the Smithsonian Institution, 1924–1925. Washington: U.S. Government Printing Office, 1928.

Franklin, Benjamin: *The Autobiography of Benjamin Franklin.* Boston and New York: Houghton Mifflin and Company, 1906.

Fries, Adelaide L. *The Road to Salem.* Chapel Hill: The University of North Carolina Press, 1944.

————. *Records of the Moravians in North Carolina,* 2 vols. Raleigh: Edwards and Broughton Printing Co., 1922.

The Fry & Jefferson Map of Virginia and Maryland. With an introduction by Dumas Malone. Princeton: Princeton University Press, 1950. A fascimile of the first edition in the Tracy W. McGregor Library.

Gewehr, Wesley M. *The Great Awakening in Virginia, 1740–1790.* Durham, North Carolina: Duke University Press, 1930.

Gottmann, Jean. *Virginia at Mid-Century.* New York: Henry Holt and Company, 1955.

Hagy, James W. "Castle's Woods: Frontier Virginia Settlement, 1769–1799." Unpublished master's thesis. East Tennessee State University, 1966.

Hanna, Charles Augustus. *The Scotch-Irish.* New York: G. P. Putnam's Sons, 1902.

Hawke, David. *The Colonial Experience.* Indianapolis: The Bobbs-Merrill Company, Inc., 1969.

Hervey, John. *Racing in America, 1665–1865.* 2 vols. New York: Privately printed for The Jockey Club, 1944.

Hooker, Richard J. *The Carolina Backcountry on the Eve of Revolution: The Journal and Other Writings of Charles Woodmason.* Chapel Hill: University of North Carolina Press, 1953.

Howe, Henry. *Historical Collections of Virginia.* Charleston, South Carolina: William R. Babcock, 1856.

Hulbert, Archer Butler. *Boone's Wilderness Road.* Cleveland: The Arthur H. Clark Co., 1903.

The Hymnal of the Protestant Episcopal Church in the United States of America. New York: The Church Mission Fund, 1940.

"Indians of North Carolina." Washington: U.S. Government Printing Office, 1968. No. 0-287-680.

"Indians of The Eastern Seaboard." Washington: U.S. Government Printing Office, 1967. No. 0-276-039.

Ingalls, Fay. *The Valley Road.* Cleveland and New York: The World Publishing Company, 1949.

BIBLIOGRAPHY

Jackson, George Pullen. *Spiritual Folk-Songs of Early America.* New York: Dover Publications, Inc., 1964.

————. *White Spirituals in the Southern Uplands.* New York: Dover Publications, Inc., 1965.

James, Marquis. *The Life of Andrew Jackson.* New York: Garden City Publishing Company, Inc., 1940.

Johnson, Gerald W. *Andrew Jackson: An Epic in Homespun.* New York: Minton, Balch & Company, 1927.

Josephy, Alvin M., Jr., *The Indian Heritage of America.* New York: Alfred A. Knopf, 1968.

Kegley, F. B. *Kegley's Virginia Frontier.* Roanoke: The Southwest Virginia Historical Society, 1938.

Kercheval, Samuel. *A History of the Valley of Virginia.* Fourth edition. Strasburg, Virginia: Shenandoah Publishing House, 1928.

Legislative Journals of the Council of Colonial Virginia, 8 vols., edited by H. R. McIlwaine. Richmond. The Colonial Press, Everett Waddey Co., 1913–1919.

Lewis, Thomas. *The Fairfax Line: Thomas Lewis's Journal of 1746.* With footnotes and index by John W. Wayland, Ph.D. New Market, Virginia: The Henkel Press, 1925.

Leyburn, James G. *The Scotch-Irish: A Social History.* Chapel Hill: The University of North Carolina Press, 1962.

Mackay-Smith, Alexander. *The Thoroughbred in the Lower Shenandoah Valley, 1785–1842.* Winchester, Virginia: Pifer Printing Company, 1948.

Maury, Ann. *Memoirs of a Huguenot Family.* New York: G. P. Putnam's Sons, 1907.

The Methodist Hymnal. Nashville: Publishing House of the Methodist Episcopal Church. South. 1918.

Nead, Daniel Wunderlich. *Pennsylvania Germans in the Settlement of Maryland.* Lancaster, Pennsylvania: Press of the New Era Publishing Co., 1914.

Pattee, Fred Lewis. *Century Readings for a Course in American Literature.* New York: The Century Company, 1921.

The Pennsylvania-German Society. Proceedings and Addresses at Harrisburg, Pa., October 20, 1911. Vols. XXI and XXII. Lancaster, Pennsylvania: Published by The Pennsylvania-German Society, 1914.

Records of the Presbyterian Church in the United States of America. Philadelphia: Presbyterian Board of Publication, 1841.

Roosevelt, Theodore. *The Winning of the West.* 2 vols. New York: G. P. Putnam's Sons, 1889.

Rothrock, Mary U. (ed.) *The French Broad—Holston Country: A History of Knox County, Tennessee.* Knoxville, Tennessee: East Tennessee Historical Society, 1946.

Rouse, Parke S., Jr. *Virginia: The English Heritage in America.* New York: Hastings House, 1966.

————. *Planters and Pioneers: Life in Colonial Virginia.* New York: Hastings House, 1968.

BIBLIOGRAPHY

————. *Below the James Lies Dixie.* Richmond: Dietz Press, 1967.

Sachse, Julius. *The Wayside Inns on the Lancaster Roadside Between Philadelphia and Lancaster.* Lancaster, Penn.: J. P. Sachse, publisher, 1912.

Schlesinger, Arthur M., Jr. *The Age of Jackson.* Boston: Little, Brown and Company, 1945.

Schoepf, Johann David. *Travels in the Confederation, 1783–1784.* 2 vols. Translation by Alfred J. Morrison. Philadelphia: William J. Campbell, 1911.

Searight, Thomas B. *The Old Pike: A History of the National Road.* Uniontown, Pa.: Published by the author, 1894.

Shumway, George, Edward Durell, and Howard C. Frey. *Conestoga Wagon 1750–1850.* York, Pa.: Published jointly by Early American Industries Association, Inc., and George Shumway, 1964.

Smith, Elmer Lewis, John G. Stewart, and M. Ellsworth Kyger. *The Pennsylvania Germans of the Shenandoah Valley.* Allentown: Schlechter's, 1964.

Speed, Thomas. *The Wilderness Road.* Prepared for the Filson Club. Louisville, Ky.: John P. Morton & Co., 1886.

Spruill, Julia Cherry. *Woman's Life and Work in the Southern Colonies.* Chapel Hill: University of North Carolina Press, 1938.

Strickler, Harry M. *Massanutten, Settled by the Pennsylvania Pilgrim 1726: The First White Settlement in the Shenandoah Valley.* Strasburg, Va.: Shenandoah Publishing House, 1924.

Summers, Lewis Preston. *Annals of Southwest Virginia, 1769–1800.* Abingdon, Va.: Lewis Preston Summers, 1929.

Sweet, William Warren. *Virginia Methodism: A History.* Illustrations by Erle Prior. Richmond, Va.: Whittet & Shepperson, 1955.

Thompson, Ernest Trice. *Presbyterians in the South, Volume One: 1607–1871.* Richmond: John Knox Press, 1963.

Vandiver, Frank E. *Mighty Stonewall.* New York: McGraw-Hill Book Company, Inc., 1957.

"Virginia Military Institute and the Battle of New Market." Publication by New Market Battlefield Park, New Market, Virginia, based on an address made by Colonel William Couper to the V.M.I. Corps of Cadets at New Market Day ceremonies, May 15, 1939.

Wayland, John W. *Stonewall Jackson's Way.* 2d ed. revised. Staunton, Va.: The McClure Printing Company, 1956.

————. *The Valley Turnpike, Winchester to Staunton.* Winchester, Va.: Winchester-Frederick County Historical Society, 1967.

————. *The Fairfax Line.* New Market, Va.: The Henkel Press, 1925.

Webster, Richard. *A History of the Presbyterian Church in America.* Philadelphia: Joseph M. Wilson, publisher, 1857.

Wellman, Manly Wade. *Giant in Gray: A Biography of Wade Hampton of South Carolina.* New York: Charles Scribner's Sons, 1949.

Wilson, Howard McKnight, Th.D. *The Tinkling Spring: Headwater of Freedom.*

BIBLIOGRAPHY

A Study of the Church and Her People 1732–1952. Fishersville, Va.: The Tinkling Spring and Hermitage Presbyterian Churches, 1954.

Wise, John Sergeant. *The End of an Era.* Boston and New York: Houghton Mifflin and Company, 1899.

Withers, Alexander Scott. *Chronicles of Border Warfare.* Edited and annotated by Reuben Gold Thwaites. Seventh impression. Cincinnati: Stewart & Kidd Company, Publishers, 1920.

Wright, Louis B. *Everyday Life in Colonial America.* New York: G. P. Putnam's Sons, 1965.

Wust, Klaus. *The Virginia Germans.* Charlottesville: The University Press of Virginia, 1969.

Notes

CHAPTER 1

1. Parke Rouse, Jr., *Virginia: The English Heritage in America* (New York: Hastings House, Publishers, 1966), pp. 92–93.

2. Ben C. McCary, *Indians in Seventeenth-Century Virginia* (Charlottesville: The University Press of Virginia, 1957), p. 26.

CHAPTER 2

1. Ann Maury, ed., *Memoirs of a Huguenot Family* (New York: G. P. Putnam's Sons, 1907), pp. 288–289.

2. H. R. McIlwaine, ed., *Executive Journals of the Council of Colonial Virginia*, 4 vols. (Richmond: Virginia State Library, 1925–1930), 1:552–553.

3. *Ibid.*

CHAPTER 3

1. Daniel Wunderlich Nead, *Pennsylvania Germans in the Settlement of Maryland* (Lancaster, Penn.: Press of the New Era Publishing Company, 1914), p. 32.

2. *Ibid.*

3. *Ibid.*, p. 33.

4. *Ibid.*, p. 35.

5. *Records of the Presbyterian Church in the United States of America* (Philadelphia: Presbyterian Board of Publication, 1841), p. 140.

6. Nead, *Pennsylvania Germans*, p. 63.

7. *Ibid.*, p. 60.

8. *Ibid.*, p. 82.

CHAPTER 4

1. Henry Jones Ford, *The Scotch-Irish in America* (Princeton: Princeton University Press, 1916), pp. 202–204, quoting Arthur Young's account, *A Tour of Ireland*, made in 1776–1779.

2. *New Jersey Archives*, 1st series, XI:185.

3. *Ibid.*

4. Charles Augustus Hanna, *The Scotch-Irish*, 2 vols., (New York: G. P. Putnam's Sons, 1902), 2:68–69.

5. Gabriel Thomas, "Historical and Geographical Account of the Province and Country of Pennsylvania and West Jersey in America," *Pennsylvania Magazine of History and Biography*, vol. 68, pp. 408–409.

6. Hanna, *The Scotch-Irish*, 2:63.

7. *Ibid.*

8. Charles Knowles Bolton, *Scotch Irish Pioneers in Ulster and America* (Boston: Bacon and Brown, 1910), pp. 282–284.

CHAPTER 5

1. "Moravian Diaries of Travels Through Virginia," edited by The Reverend William J. Hinke and Charles E. Kemper, *Virginia Magazine of History and Biography*, XII:375 (1903–1904).

2. *Ibid.*, p. 375.

3. *Ibid.*, p. 383.

4. William Rose Benét, "The Stricken Average" from *The Stairway of Surprise* (New York: Alfred A. Knopf, Inc., 1947), p. 188.

CHAPTER 6

1. Julian Boyd, ed., *Indian Treaties Printed by Benjamin Franklin, 1736–1762* (Philadelphia: Historical Society of Pennsylvania, 1938), p. 57.

2. William Byrd II, *History of the Dividing Line Between Virginia and North Carolina*, with introduction and notes by William K. Boyd (Raleigh: The North Carolina Historical Commission, 1929), p. 10.

3. Boyd, *Indian Treaties*, p. 57.

4. *Ibid.*

5. *Ibid.*

6. *Ibid.*

7. *Ibid.*

8. *Ibid.*

9. *Ibid.*

10. *Ibid.*, p. 75.

CHAPTER 7

1. The Reverend George Gillespie, quoted in Richard Webster, *A History of the Presbyterian Church in America* (Philadelphia: Joseph M. Wilson, Publisher, 1857), p. 75.

2. From the collection of the late Victor Barringer.

3. Charles William Dabney, quoted in Ernest Trice Thompson, *Presbyterians in the South, 1607–1871* (Richmond: John Knox Press, 1963), 1:263.

4. Benjamin Franklin, *The Autobiography of Benjamin Franklin* (Boston and New York: Houghton Mifflin and Company, 1906), p. 111.

5. Parke Rouse, Jr., *Planters and Pioneers: Life in Colonial Virginia* (New York: Hastings House, Publishers, 1968), p. 109.

6. H. R. McIlwaine, ed., *Legislative Journals of the Council of Colonial Virginia* (Richmond: The Colonial Press, Everett Waddey Co., 1918–1819), 2:995–996.

7. Dr. Henry Ruffner, quoted by Henry Howe, *Historical Collections of Virginia* (Charleston, S.C.: William R. Babcock, Publishers, 1856), pp. 454–455.

8. The Reverend John Culbertson in 1751, quoted in Hanna, *The Scotch-Irish*, 2:71.

9. The Reverend David McClure in 1775, quoted in Hanna, *The Scotch-Irish*, 2:82.

CHAPTER 8

1. John W. Wayland, *The Fairfax Line* (New Market, Va.: The Henkel Press, 1925), pp. 29–30.

2. *Ibid.*, p. 44.

3. Desmond Clarke, *Arthur Dobbs Esquire, 1689–1765* (Chapel Hill: University of North Carolina Press, 1957), p. 119.

4. Carl Bridenbaugh, *Myths and Realities: Societies of The Colonial South* (Baton Rouge: Louisiana State University Perss, 1952), p. 30.

CHAPTER 9

1. Adelaide L. Fries, M.A., ed., *Records of the Moravians in North Carolina*, 2 vols., (Raleigh: Edwards and Broughton Printing Co., 1922), 1:51.

2. *Ibid.*

3. Adelaide L. Fries, *The Road to Salem* (Chapel Hill: The University of North Carolina Press, 1944), p. 50.

4. Fries, ed., *Records of the Moravians*, 1:130.

5. *Ibid.*, p. 40.

6. "If In This Darksome Wild I Stray," by Nikolaus Zinzendorf, *The Methodist Hymnal* (Nashville: Publishing House of the Methodist Episcopal Church, South, 1918), Hymn 359.

7. Fries, *The Road to Salem*, p. 44.

8. *Ibid.*, p. 69.

9. *Ibid.*, p. 115.

10. Chester Davis, *Hidden Seed and Harvest: A History of the Moravians* (Winston-Salem: Wachovia Historical Society, 1959), p. 31.

11. "Jesus, Lead the Way," from *The Hymnal of the Protestant Episcopal Church in the United States of America* (New York: The Church Mission Fund, 1940), Hymn 425.

CHAPTER 10

1. George Shumway, Edward Durell, and Howard C. Frey, *Conestoga Wagon, 1750–1850* (York, Penn.: George Shumway, Publisher, 1964), pp. 36–37.

2. Henry Sengmeister, quoted in Klaus Wust, *The Virginia Germans* (Charlottesville: The University Press of Virginia, 1969), p. 57.

3. *William and Mary Quarterly*, 28 series, 5:140 (1925).

4. From Edmund Burke, *An Account of the European Settlements in America* (1761) cited in F. B. Kegley, *Kegley's Virginia Frontier* (Strasburg, Va.: Shenandoah Publishing House, 1925), p. 295.

5. F. B. Kegley, quoting Hewatt's *History of South Carolina*, in *Kegley's Virginia Frontier*, p. 295.

CHAPTER 11

1. Thomas Anburey, *Travels Through the Interior Parts of America,* 2 vols. (Boston and New York: Houghton Mifflin and Company, 1923), 2:281.

2. *Ibid.,* p. 21.

3. Johann David Schoepf, *Travels in the Confederation, 1783–84,* translated by Alfred J. Morrison, 2 vols. (Philadelphia: William J. Campbell, publisher, 1911) 2:35.

4. Kegley, *Kegley's Virginia Frontier,* p. 390.

5. *Virginia Acts of Assembly,* September 1744.

6. Kegley, *Kegley's Virginia Frontier,* p. 142.

7. Johann David Schoepf, *Travels in the Confederation,* 1:147.

8. Ebenezer Cook, "The Sot-Weed Factor," quoted in Parke Rouse, Jr., *Planters and Pioneers: Life in Colonial Virginia,* p. 77.

CHAPTER 12

1. "Moravian Diaries of Travels Through Virginia," edited by Rev. William J. Hinke and Charles E. Kemper, *Virginia Magazine of History and Biography,* XII, 134–153.

2. Theodore Roosevelt, *The Winning of the West,* 4 vols. (New York: G. P. Putnam's, 1889), 1:138. The carved inscription is preserved in the Filson Club, in Louisville.

3. Archer Butler Hulbert, *Boone's Wilderness Road* (Cleveland: The Arthur H. Clark Co., 1903), p. 32.

4. *Ibid.*

5. Roosevelt, *The Winning of the West,* 1:345.

6. Felix Walker, quoted in H. Addington Bruce, *Daniel Boone and the Wilderness Road* (New York: The Macmillan Co., 1922), p. 107.

7. Hulbert, *Boone's Wilderness Road,* p. 29.

8. Collection of the late Victor Barringer.

9. Hulbert, *Boone's Wilderness Road,* pp. 132–133.

10. *Ibid.,* p. 147.

11. *Ibid.,* p. 157.

12. Roosevelt, *The Winning of the West,* 2:86.

13. Hulbert, *Boone's Wilderness Road,* pp. 290–291.

14. *Ibid.,* p. 138.

15. Brude, *Daniel Boone and the Wilderness Road,* pp. 290–291.

16. Hulbert, *Boone's Wilderness Road,* p. 197.

CHAPTER 14

1. Herbert Asbury, *A Methodist Saint: The Life of Bishop Asbury* (New York: Alfred A. Knopf, 1927), p. 14.

2. *Ibid.,* pp. 18–19.

3. *Ibid.,* p. 131.

4. *Ibid.*, p. 148.

5. *Ibid.*, pp. 165–166.

6. *Ibid.*, p. 245.

7. *Ibid.*, p. 253.

8. *Ibid.*, p. 255.

9. George Pullen Jackson, *White Spirituals of the Southern Uplands* (Hatboro, Penn.: Folklore Association, 1964), p. 224.

10. Asbury, *A Methodist Saint*, pp. 269–270.

CHAPTER 15

1. Collection of the late Victor Barringer.

CHAPTER 16

1. Anonymous, *Exiles in Virginia, With Observations on the Conduct of the Society of Friends in the Revolutionary War* (Philadelphia: Published by the Subscribers, 1848), p. 44.

2. *Ibid.*, pp. 133–134.

3. *Ibid.*, p. 155.

4. *Ibid.*, p. 168.

5. *Ibid.*, p. 211.

6. *Ibid.*, p. 233.

7. *Ibid.*, p. 238.

CHAPTER 18

1. Harriette Simpson Arnow, *The Flowering of the Cumberland* (New York: Macmillan, 1963), p. 400.

2. *Ibid.*, p. 394.

3. From the collection of the late Victor Barringer.

4. Arnow, *The Flowering of the Cumberland*, p. 397.

5. "A Mighty Fortress Is Our God," by Martin Luther, from *The Hymnal of the Protestant Episcopal Church in the United States of America* (New York: The Church Pension Fund, 1940), Hymn 551.

6. From the collection of the late Victor Barringer.

7. Mary U. Rothrock, *The French Broad—Holston Country: A History of Knox County, Tennessee* (Knoxville: East Tennessee Historical Society, 1946), pp. 23–24.

8. Joseph Doddridge, "Notes on the Settlement and Indian Wars of the Western Parts of Virginia and Pennsylvania," quoted in Samuel Kercheval, *A History of the Valley of Virginia*, 4th edit., (Strasburg, Va.: Shenandoah Publishing House, 1928), p. 255.

9. Arnow, *The Flowering of the Cumberland*, pp. 375–376.

CHAPTER 19

1. James Newton Matthews, quoted in Thomas B. Searight, *The Old Pike: A History of the National Road* (Uniontown, Pa.: Published by the author, 1894), p. 197.

2. Robert Beverley, *The Present State of Virginia,* edited by Louis B. Wright (Chapel Hill: University of North Carolina Press, 1947), pp. 312–313.

3. Rothrock, *The French Broad—Holston County,* p. 58.

4. *Ibid.,* p. 59.

5. Laws of Pennsylvania, 1763.

6. "Wayside Inns on the Pennsylvania Turnpike," from *Proceedings and Addresses of the Pennsylvania German Society,* XXII:31–32, (1913).

7. André Michaux, *Flora Boreali-Americana,* quoted in "Wayside Inns on the Pennsylvania Turnpike," *Proceedings and Addresses of the Pennsylvania German Society,* XXII:32 (1913).

8. James G. Blaine, quoted in Searight, *The Old Pike.*

9. "Wayside Inns," *Proceedings and Addresses of the Pennsylvania German Society,* XXII:31–32 (1913).

10. *Ibid.,* p. 43.

11. Searight, *The Old Pike.*

CHAPTER 20

1. "A Mighty Fortress Is Our God," by Martin Luther, *The Hymnal of the Protestant Episcopal Church,* Hymn 551.

2. G. MacLaren Brydon, *Virginia's Mother Church,* 2 vols. (Philadelphia: Church Historical Society, 1952), II:76–97.

3. "A Mighty Fortress," *The Hymnal of the Protestant Episcopal Church,* Hymn 551.

4. *Ibid.*

CHAPTER 21

1. From an article by G. P. R. James, titled "Life in Virginia," published in *Knickerbocker Magazine* (New York: John A. Gray, 1858), LII:279.

2. From the collection of the late Victor Barringer.

3. Traditional Appalachian folk song.

4. Rouse, *Planters and Pioneers,* p. 200.

5. "Bonny Barbara Allan," a Scottish ballad, in Gordon Edwards, *Introduction to Literature* (Boston: Ginn and Company, 1964), p. 424.

6. George Pullen Jackson, *White Spirituals from the Southern Uplands* (Hatboro, Penn.: Folklore Association, 1964), p. 255.

7. From the collection of the late Victor Barringer.

8. *Ibid.*

CHAPTER 22

1. Richard J. Hooker, *The Carolina Backcountry on the Eve of Revolution: The Journal and Other Writings of Charles Woodmason* (Chapel Hill: University of North Carolina Press, 1958), p. 198.

2. *Ibid.,* p. 6.

3. *Ibid.,* pp. 16–17.

[282]

4. *Ibid.*, p. 36.

5. *Ibid.*, p. 45.

6. *Ibid.*, p. 25.

7. *Ibid.*, p. 31.

8. *Ibid.*, p. 61.

9. *Ibid.*, p. 39.

10. *Ibid.*, p. 40.

11. *Ibid.*, pp. 51–52.

12. *Ibid.*, p. 212.

CHAPTER 23

1. Charles Dickens, quoted in Thomas B. Searight, *The Old Pike*, p. 220.

2. Collection of the late Victor Barringer.

3. "The Wayside Inns," *Proceedings of the Pennsylvania German Society*, XXI:11.

4. Collection of the late Victor Barringer.

5. "The Wayside Inns," *Proceedings of the Pennsylvania German Society*, XXI:37.

6. From a letter by Harriet Milton Hammond of Clarke County, Virginia, in 1900, quoted in John W. Wayland, *The Valley Turnpike, Winchester to Staunton* (Winchester, Va.: Winchester-Frederick County Historical Society, 1967), pp. 12–13.

7. Collection of the late Victor Barringer.

8. From the journal of John James Audubon, quoted in *Century Readings for a Course in American Literature*, edited by Fred Lewis Pattee (New York: The Century Company, 1921), pp. 67–68.

9. Julius Sachse, *The Wayside Inns on the Lancaster Roadside Between Philadelphia and Lancaster* (Lancaster, Penn.: J. F. Sachse, publisher, 1912), p. 212.

10. "The Wayside Inns," *Proceedings of the Pennsylvania German Society*, XXI:75–76.

11. George C. Shumway, Edward Durell, and Howard C. Frey, *Conestoga Wagon, 1750–1850* (York, Penn.: George Shumway, publisher, 1964), p. 108.

CHAPTER 24

1. J. F. D. Smyth, quoted by Parke Rouse, Jr., in *Planters and Pioneers: Life in Colonial Virginia* (New York: Hastings House, 1968), p. 174.

2. Elizabeth Amis Cameron Blanchard and Manly Wade Wellman, *The Life and Times of Sir Archie* (Chapel Hill: University of North Carolina Press, 1958), p. 155.

3. *Ibid.*, p. 147.

4. Marquis James, *Andrew Jackson, Portrait of a President* (Indianapolis: Bobbs-Merrill, 1937), pp. 32–33.

CHAPTER 25

1. "Federal Indian Policies, A Survey of Major Developments from the Pre-Revolutionary Period Through the 1960s," Bureau of Indian Affairs, United States Department of the Interior, 1969.

2. Grant Foreman, *Indian Removal: The Emigration of the Five Civilized Tribes of Indians* (Norman, Oklahoma: University of Oklahoma Press, 1953), new edition, p. 286.

3. *Ibid.*, p. 254.

4. John Tisdale, quoted by Parke Rouse, Jr., *Below the James Lies Dixie* (Richmond: Dietz Press, 1969), p. 118.

CHAPTER 26

1. Ollinger Crenshaw, *General Lee's College* (New York: Random House, 1969), p. 123.

2. *Ibid.*, p. 121.

3. *Ibid.*, pp. 23–24.

4. Parke Rouse, Jr., *Virginia: The English Heritage in America* (New York: Hastings House Publishers, 1966), p. 187.

5. Thomas Jefferson to the Marquis de Chastellux, 1787, quoted by David Hawke, *The Colonial Experience* (Indianapolis: The Bobbs-Merrill Company, Inc., 1966), p. 486.

6. Crenshaw, *General Lee's College*, p. 122.

7. *Ibid.*, p. 127.

CHAPTER 27

1. Lenoir Chambers, *Stonewall Jackson*, 2 vols. (New York: William Morrow and Company, 1959), 1:392.

2. *Ibid.*, 1:508.

3. *The War of the Rebellion, A Compilation of the Official Records of the Union and Confederate Armies*, 18 vols. (Washington: Government Printing Office, 1895), XI:1:29–30.

4. William Couper, *One Hundred Years of V.M.I.*, 4 vols. (Richmond: Garrett and Massie, Inc., 1939), 2:263.

5. John Sergeant Wise, *The End of an Era* (Boston and New York: Houghton Mifflin and Company, 1899), pp. 288–289.

CHAPTER 28

1. Manly Wade Wellman, *Giant in Gray* (New York: Charles Scribner's Sons, 1949), p. 75.

2. *Ibid.*, pp. 193–194.

3. *Ibid.*, p. 195.

EPILOGUE

1. John Sergeant Wise, *The End of an Era*, p. 240.

Index

INDEX